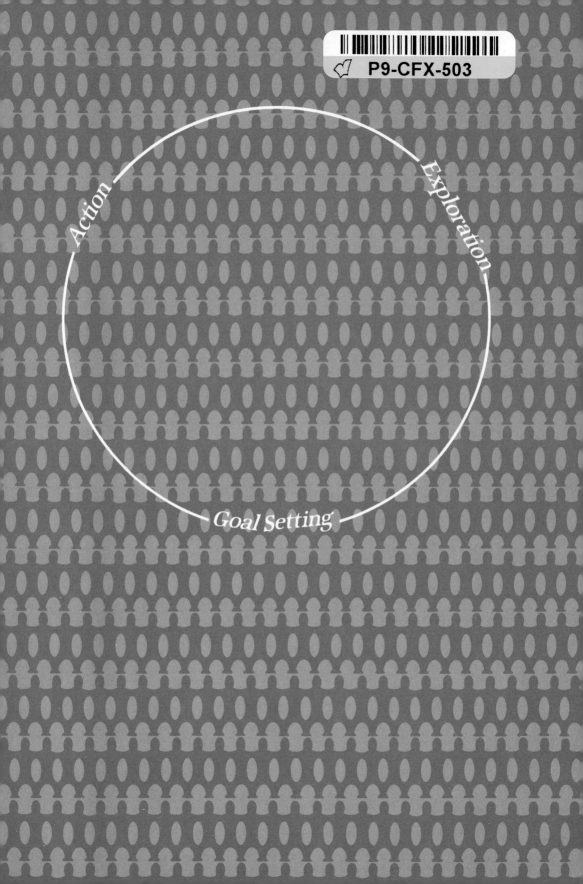

The
Skilled Helper

The
Skilled Helper
SECOND EDITION

Model, Skills, and Methods for Effective Helping

Gerard Egan

Loyola University of Chicago

Brooks/Cole Publishing Company

Monterey, California

Brooks/Cole Publishing Company
A Division of Wadsworth, Inc.

Printed in the United States of America
10   9   8   7   6   5   4   3   2   1

Library of Congress Cataloging in Publication Data:

Egan, Gerard.
    The skilled helper.

    Bibliography: p.
    Includes index.
    1. Counseling.   2. Helping behavior.
I. Title.
BF637.C6E38   1981   158'.3   81-10160
ISBN 0-8185-0479-X   AACR2

Subject Editor: Claire Verduin
Manuscript Editor: Sylvia Stein
Production Editor: Fiorella Ljunggren
Interior and Cover Design: Katherine Minerva
Typesetting: Graphic Typesetting Service, Los Angeles, California

About the Author

Gerard (Gerry) Egan is Professor of Psychology at Loyola University of Chicago and currently coordinator for the program in Community and Organizational Development. His doctorate is in clinical psychology. He does consulting work with a variety of organizations and conducts workshops in counseling, counselor education and training, and organization design, assessment, and consultation. He has taught in England and conducted workshops in Canada, Europe, and Africa.

His other publications—all with Brooks/Cole Publishing Company—include:

- *Exercises in Helping Skills, Second Edition*
- *Encounter: Group Processes for Interpersonal Growth*
- *Face to Face: The Small Group Experience and Interpersonal Growth*
- *Interpersonal Living: A Skills/Contract Approach to Human Relations Training in Groups*
- *You and Me: The Skills of Communicating and Relating to Others*
- *People in Systems: A Model for Development in the Helping Professions and Education (with Michael A. Cowan)*
- *Moving into Adulthood: Knowledge and Skills for Effective Living (with Michael A. Cowan)*

Preface

This second edition of *The Skilled Helper*, like the first, is meant to be a very *practical* introduction to the art of helping and counseling. It builds on the strengths of the first but expands and clarifies the helping model and the skills and methods that make it operative. It is not an introduction to many different theories of counseling, though it draws on and integrates what these theories have in common. Many helper training programs are still overly cognitive, and trainees have difficulty translating theories and research findings into effective helping.

This edition of *The Skilled Helper* presents an expanded and clarified three-stage model of helping. My intent has been to preserve the simplicity of the original model while updating and augmenting it. What is presented here is basically the same model, but it is now identified specifically as what it was in fact—a *problem-management* model or framework for helping. The skills and methods that make the model work are spelled out in detail. Stage I has been updated and the important skill of probing has been added. Stage II has been reworked and clarified and the centrality of goal setting has been emphasized. Stage III, the action stage, has been expanded in terms of both the helping framework and the skills and methods needed to aid clients in pursuing and accomplishing the kind of behavioral goals that allow them to manage the problem situations of their lives more effectively. Throughout the model, client self-responsibility is emphasized and helpers are seen primarily as *consultants* who are effective to the degree that they help their clients manage problems in living a little bit (or a great deal) more effectively.

The problem-management model presented here, although practical, is not atheoretical. It is based on learning theory and the principles underlying the maintenance and change of behavior, social-influence theory, and the rich body of theory and research associated with problem solving. Because the model presented here is systematic and integrative, it stands on the shoulders of many "giants" who have contributed to making the process of helping more reliable. Their names and references to their work are scattered throughout this book.

This edition has benefited greatly from the suggestions offered by people who have used the first edition as a classroom tool. I would like to thank Terry D. Anderson of Fraser Valley College, William D. Burcky of Southern Illinois University, Dennis Haubrich of Ryerson Polytechnic Institute, Philip O. Hwang of the University of San Diego, Marvin Moore of Colorado State University, Ronald L. Partin of Bowling Green State University, and Thomas Skovholt of the University of Minnesota.

I would also like to thank the clinical and counseling psychology students at Loyola and the participants in many workshops conducted both here and abroad. Their enthusiasm and responsiveness to experiential learning and their critical comments have continued to remind me that I am at my best when I am a learner. For this I am very grateful.

Gerard Egan

Contents

Chapter *6*

Stage II: Developing New Perspectives and Setting Goals

PART ONE: THE SKILLS OF SUMMARIZING, INFORMATION GIVING, AND
ADVANCED EMPATHY; THE CONDITIONS FOR EFFECTIVE CHALLENGING

Chapter *7*

Stage II: Developing New Perspectives and Setting Goals

PART TWO: THE SKILLS OF CONFRONTATION, COUNSELOR SELF-SHARING,
AND IMMEDIACY; THE TASK OF SETTING GOALS

Chapter *8*

Stage III: Action

PART ONE: THE DEVELOPMENT AND SEQUENCING OF PROGRAMS

Chapter *9*

Stage III: Action

PART TWO: IMPLEMENTING AND EVALUATING PROGRAMS

Chapter *10*
Epilogue

The
Skilled Helper

Chapter **1**

Introduction

This chapter deals with the following topics:

The skills needed by all people who try to help others
The ongoing crisis in helping: Does helping really help?
Different models of helping
Choosing a helping model: A problem-management model as both systematic and integrative
A skills approach to helping
Client self-responsibility: A guiding value in helping
Helpers as consultants
Principles of behavior and behavioral change and their application to the helping process
The contract between helper and client
Group approaches to training and treatment
Portrait of a helper

The Helping Professions: Who Needs Helping Skills?

Throughout history human beings have felt that, under the proper conditions, some people are capable of helping others come to grips with the problems of living (Frank, 1973). This conviction has become institutionalized in a variety of helping professions. For instance, all the professionals listed here try to help individuals face one kind of human problem or another:

chaplains
child-care workers
church workers
clinical psychologists
community workers
correctional-system workers
counselors
dentists
group leaders
hospital workers
human-relations specialists
interviewers
lawyers
ministers
nurses
orderlies
organizational-development
   consultants
peer counselors
physicians
police
probation officers
psychiatrists
rehabilitation workers
residence-hall directors and
   assistants
social workers
teachers
trainers
tutors
volunteer workers
youth workers

Although these professionals have different kinds of technical expertise, they all often come face to face with people who are in crisis situations. Unfortunately, professionals may be effective in delivering the technical services of their own professions and still be deficient in terms of the human encounters involved. If they are helpers in the sense in which this term is being used in this book and not just good technicians, they deal with their clients from a holistic perspective, helping them face crisis situations resourcefully as full human beings. This means that they also help them manage the kinds of debilitating emotions that often accompany crises. For instance, dentists care for people's teeth and gums, but they can also help patients overcome their fears of being treated and their resistance to oral hygiene programs. Teachers teach English, history, and science; but because their students are growing physically, intellectually, and social-emotionally, and therefore struggling with normative developmental tasks and crises, they can also help them, in direct and indirect ways, explore, understand, and deal with these tasks and crises. Failure to be helpful in the fuller sense of this term is not due to ill will but rather to such factors as time constraints and their not having been trained in the human helping skills I develop in this book. Therefore, although this book focuses specifically on counselors and psychotherapists, the skills discussed and illustrated are seen as skills needed by all the professionals mentioned here.

The Ongoing Crisis in Helping: Does Helping Really Help?

It would be unfair to imply that counselors and psychotherapists are all skilled helpers and that the other professionals or paraprofessionals mentioned are not. Before embarking upon a career in counseling or psychotherapy, you should know that a debate about the usefulness of these professions has been going on for at least thirty years. The disturbing question "Does helping really help?" is still being asked. Some answer this question with a resounding yes. "Results of nearly 400 controlled valuations of psychotherapy were coded and integrated statistically. The findings provide convincing evidence of the efficacy of psychotherapy. On the average, the typical therapy client is better off than 75% of untreated individuals" (Smith & Glass, 1977, p. 752). It would seem, then, that the evidence lies overwhelmingly in the favor of the efficacy of counseling and psychotherapy.

However, there are others who express serious doubts that helping is really helpful (Eysenck, 1952, 1960, 1965, 1978; Gallo, 1978; Mansfield & Busse, 1977; Presby, 1978; Rimland, 1979; Tennov, 1975). Rimland (1979) attacks the Smith and Glass (1977) study directly. To make matters worse, some people even claim that psychotherapy and counseling can be dangerous to the emotional well-being of clients (Lambert, Bergin, & Collins, 1977; Strupp, Hadley, & Gomes-Schwartz, 1977). That is, some contend that a significant number of clients get *worse* from treatment (see Bergin, 1980; Mays & Franks, 1980, for a discussion of this issue).

Although all this may be anxiety arousing to you, it is not meant to discourage you from entering a helping profession. Bergin (1971, 1980; Bergin & Lambert, 1978) and Carkhuff and his associates (Carkhuff, 1969a, 1969b; Carkhuff & Anthony, 1979; Carkhuff & Berenson, 1976) have long claimed that helping is never neutral, that it is always "for better or for worse." Helping is a powerful process that is all too easy to mismanage. Unskilled and mismanaged helping can do a great deal of harm. But skilled and socially intelligent workers can do a great deal of good (Sloane, Staples, Cristol, Yorkston, & Whipple, 1975). Outcome studies in counseling and psychotherapy do not usually make a distinction between high-level and low-level helpers, and the research on deterioration effects in therapy suggests that there are many low-level or inadequate helpers in the world; so the negative results found in such studies are predictable.

Acquaint yourself with the literature dealing with the ongoing debate concerning the efficacy of helping. After reading the research, the discussions, and the summaries, you may well shake your head and repeat what Carl Rogers said in 1958: "[I have] never learned much from controlled studies of therapy" (Rubenstein & Parloff, 1959, p. 313). Research findings are often so tentative and contradictory that it is difficult to formulate a coherent approach to practice based on them. However, I suggest you study this literature not to become discouraged, but to (1) appreciate the complexity of the helping process, (2) acquaint yourself with the issues involved in evaluating the outcome of helping, (3) appreciate that helping can actually harm others, (4) become reasonably cautious as a helper, and (5) find practical guidelines for helping. Because clients' needs are urgent, the practice of helping will always move ahead of its research base. Staying in touch with the best in current theory and research will help you provide the best service for your clients.

In a more positive vein, Norman Kagan (1973, p. 44) has suggested that the basic issue confronting the helping professions is not validity (whether helping helps or not), but *reliability:* "Not, can counseling and psychotherapy work, but does it work *consistently?* Not, can we educate people who are able to help others, but can we develop methods which will increase the likelihood that *most* of our graduates will become as effective mental health workers as only a rare few do?" More effective training programs for helpers are needed. The studies just mentioned suggest that although there are many professionals with the "proper" credentials, many of them do not have essential skills. Carkhuff (1971a) calls helpers "functional" professionals if they have the skills needed for effective helping. There is a great need for functional helpers, whether they are "credentialed" or not. The model presented in this book, together with the skills and techniques that make it operative, is designed to increase both the validity and the reliability of the helping process.

Models of Helping: Richness or Clutter?

The number of models or approaches to helping is staggering. For instance, if you were to read the sections of the *Annual Review of Psychology* that deal with approaches to helping, if you were to leaf through compilations of the different "psychotherapies" (for instance, Binder, Binder, & Rimland, 1976; Corey, 1977;

Corsini, 1979; Harper, 1975; Jurjevich, 1973; Lichtenstein, 1980; Patterson, 1980; Shaffer & Galinsky, 1974, to name but a few), or if you were to keep abreast of the fairly steady stream of "new" approaches, you would soon discover a bewildering number of schools and systems, approaches and techniques, all of which are proposed with equal seriousness and all of which claim a high degree of success. However, is this multiplication of helping models or approaches to be seen as richness or simply as clutter? It can be seen as richness *if* helpers have an integrative model or framework that helps them organize and borrow from all these models. Helpers, especially beginning helpers, need a practical, working model of helping that tells them:

- What to do to help people facing problems in living
- What stages and steps make up the helping process
- What skills they need to help clients move through this process
- How they can acquire these skills
- What clients must do to collaborate in the helping process
- What resources and skills clients need for this kind of collaboration
- How clients can acquire these skills and develop these resources
- How to determine whether helping has worked

Furthermore, the model of choice will help the counselor organize and make sense of the vast helping literature. A flexible, humanistic, broadly based *problem-solving* model or framework meets all these requirements.

Choosing a Helping Model: A Problem-Management Approach

The three-stage model explored in the previous edition of this book was a problem-solving or problem-management model, although it was not so labeled. The social sciences are currently showing a renewed interest in problem solving and decision making (Hill, Bedau, Chechile, Crochetiere, Kellerman, Ounjian, Pauker, Pauker, & Rubin, 1979; Janis & Mann, 1977; Robertshaw, Mecca, & Rerick, 1978). The value of problem-solving approaches to helping is being recognized more and more (Carkhuff & Anthony, 1979; Dixon, Heppner, Petersen, & Ronning, 1979; D'Zurilla & Goldfried, 1971; Goldfried & Davidson, 1976; Heppner, 1978; Jacobson, 1977; Jones, 1976; Mahoney, 1977; Mahoney & Arnkoff, 1978; Scott, 1979; Wagman, 1979, 1980a, 1980b; Wagman & Kerber, 1980).

Among the cognitive learning therapies, it is our opinion that the problem-solving perspectives may ultimately yield the most encouraging clinical results. This is due to the fact that—as a broader clinical endeavor—they encompass both the cognitive restructuring and the coping skills therapies (not to mention a wide range of "noncognitive" perspectives). With the

problem-solving approaches, clients are not only taught specific coping
skills, but also the more general strategies of assessment, problem definition,
and so on [Mahoney & Arnkoff, 1978, p. 709].

Furthermore, problem solving has been a useful approach not only with adults
but also with children, and the technology for training children in problem-
solving skills has been developed (Shure & Spivack, 1978; Spivack, Platt, & Shure,
1976; Spivack & Shure, 1974). Finally, although no approach to counseling or
therapy is valid unless it proves to be useful in individual cases, the use of the
problem-solving model in counseling and therapy is backed up, at least in a
general way, by the extensive research done on human problem solving itself
(Davis, 1966).

When people are presented with the basic steps of a problem-solving model
or process, they tend to say "Oh yes, I know that." Recognizing the logic of
problem solving, however, is a far cry from *using* it.

In ordinary affairs we usually muddle ahead, doing what is habitual and
customary, being slightly puzzled when it sometimes fails to give the intended
outcome, but not stopping to worry much about the failures because there
are still too many other things still to do. Then circumstances conspire against
us and we find ourselves caught failing where we must succeed—where we
cannot withdraw from the field, or lower our self-imposed standards, or ask
for help, or throw a tantrum. Then we may begin to suspect that we face a
problem. . . . *An ordinary person almost never approaches a problem systematically and exhaustively unless he has been specifically educated to do so*
[Miller, Galanter, & Pribram, 1960, pp. 171, 174; emphasis added].

If you examine the curriculum in primary, secondary, and higher education,
you will discover that *explicit* education and training in problem solving appears
nowhere. As important as problem solving is for everyone, it appears nowhere
in our formal educational processes. Problem solving is perhaps one of the most
readily available and, paradoxically, most underused tools of human development.

Using a Problem-Solving Framework

Although many counselors and psychotherapists like to consider themselves
"eclectic" (Garfield & Kurtz, 1974, 1977), there is some confusion among them
as to just what eclecticism means (Swan, 1979; Thorne, 1973a, 1973b). An
effective eclecticism must be more than a random borrowing of ideas and techniques from here and there. Helpers need a conceptual framework (Dimond,

Havens, & Jones, 1978) that enables them to borrow ideas, methods, and techniques *systematically* from all theories, schools, and approaches and *integrate* them into their own theory and practice of helping. The problem-solving framework presented here provides the kind of conceptual framework for such "integrative" (Brammer & Shostrom, 1977) or "systematic" eclecticism. It is a practical, operational rather than a merely theoretical model; and as Thorne (1973a, p. 882) notes, "operational approaches simplify the study of the various schools of psychology and differentiate their respective contributions."

A comprehensive problem-solving model can be used to make sense of the vast literature in counseling and psychotherapy in at least two ways.

1. *Organization.* The principles, methods, and techniques discussed in the literature can be "isolated" in the "geography" of the problem-solving model. That is, any given principle or technique contributes to the work to be done in one or more of the stages of the model. For instance, a number of contemporary therapies have elaborated excellent techniques for helping clients develop new perspectives on the problem situations they face. These techniques can be organized, as we shall see, in Stage II under the "new perspectives" task of the problem-solving model. Using an integrative framework helps reduce the amount of clutter found in the literature.

2. *Mining.* In a more active way, helpers can use the problem-solving model to mine or "dig out" whatever is useful in any given school or approach without having to accept everything else it offers. Helpers can use the problem-solving model as a *tool* to go searching for whatever methods will fit their style and their clients' needs.

A Skills Approach to Helping

A problem-solving approach to helping involves skills in two ways. First it points out the skills counselors need to be helpful—that is, the skills they need to execute each of the tasks at each stage of the model. Second, the model points out the skills clients need, both to collaborate with helpers in the helping relationship and to face problems in living in their day-to-day lives.

Helper Skills

The skills you will need to develop in order to become an effective helper will be discussed in the separate chapters dealing with the stages of the problem-solving process. They include such skills as the ability to establish a relationship, to understand others from their point of view and to communicate this to them (empathy), to help people develop new perspectives on themselves and their problems, to set goals, to develop and implement programs, and to evaluate what is happening in the helping process.

Your skill development will have four interrelated phases:

1. *Conceptual understanding.* Reading this book, reviewing examples, and listening to lectures will give you a conceptual or cognitive understanding of these skills.
2. *Behavioral feeling.* By watching instructors model these skills and by doing the exercises in the manual that accompanies this book, you will develop a behavioral rather than just a conceptual feeling for these skills.
3. *Initial mastery.* You will begin to master these skills by actually practicing them with your fellow trainees under the supervision of a trainer.
4. *Further mastery.* You will deepen your hold on these skills by using them in practicum or internship experiences under the supervision of a skilled and experienced helper.

Skill- or competency-based training in counselor education programs makes a great deal of sense. In fact, Hatcher, Brooks, and associates (1977) reported that of over 400 counselor education programs surveyed in 1977, 76.1% of those responding reported a commitment to competency-based training. That's the good news. The bad news is that they discovered that only about 7% had actually made the shift.

Client Skills

Everyone faces problems in living of one kind or another. As suggested earlier, most people "muddle through." However, at times the problems are so severe or the person's resources are so deficient that he or she needs help. Helpers provide the support and challenge that enable clients to muster their resources and work through their problems. D'Zurilla and Goldfried (1971, p. 107) suggest a deficiency rather than a pathology view of client behavior:

> Much of what we view clinically as "abnormal behavior" or "emotional disturbance" may be viewed as *ineffective* behavior and its consequences, in which the individual is unable to resolve certain situational problems in his life and his inadequate attempts to do so are having undesirable effects, such as anxiety, depression, and the creation of additional problems.

It often happens that people get into trouble or fail to get out of it because they lack the needed *working knowledge* and *skills* and do not know how to mobilize *resources*, both internal and environmental, to cope with problem situations.

Working knowledge refers to information about self, others, and the world that enables individuals to involve themselves with all three resourcefully. It is more than theory and more than raw data. If a person were to give you a lecture on the history of safes and then provide you with the interior and exterior dimensions, the weight, and a rundown on the metallic composition of a safe sitting before you, you still would not be able to open it. However, if this person were to give you the combination, then you would have working knowledge—that is, information you could put to immediate practical use.

One of the definitions of the word *skill* suggested by *Webster's New Collegiate Dictionary* is "a learned power of doing something competently." Skills are physical, intellectual, and social competencies that are necessary for effective living in the areas of learning, self-management, involvement with others, and participation in groups, communities, and organizations. Working knowledge informs and enhances skills, and skills translate working knowledge into effective—that is, accomplishment-producing—behavior.

Anthony (1977, 1979; also see Shaffer, 1978), Carkhuff (1969a, 1969b, 1971b; Carkhuff & Berenson, 1976), Egan and Cowan (1979), and Kanfer and Goldstein (1980) suggest that educating clients in the kinds of working knowledge and training them in the kinds of skills they need to work through problems in living is an extremely important part of the helping process. Part of "giving psychology (and the other social sciences) away" (Miller, 1969, 1980) is giving clients the working knowledge and skills they need to cope. Because, as we have seen, few people receive explicit training in problem solving as part of their formal or informal education and few people systematically approach problems in living, training clients to be more effective problem solvers seems to be the first step.

Let us consider an example.

Jerzy and Zelda fall in love with each other. They marry and enjoy a relatively trouble-free "honeymoon" period of about two years. Eventually, however, the problems that inevitably arise from living together in such intimacy assert themselves. They find, for instance, that they counted too heavily on positive feelings for each other and now, in their absence, cannot "communicate" about finances, sex, and values. They lack certain critical interpersonal communication skills. Jerzy really has little working knowledge of the developmental demands of a 20-year-old woman; Zelda has little working knowledge of the kinds of cultural blueprints that affect her 26-year-old husband. The relationship begins to deteriorate. Because they have few problem-solving skills, they don't know how to handle their situation. Things get worse until they settle down into living miserably, or separate, or divorce, or perhaps take their problems to a helper.

In the case of this young couple, it seems reasonable to assume that helping will necessarily include both education and training as essential elements of treatment. The assumption here is that, first of all, you will be trained systematically in helping skills. Then, as you are being trained, you will also be made aware of the models and strategies used in effective training. Later on you will be asked to train others in helping and human-relations skills under supervision. Finally, you will be prepared to use your own initiative in incorporating training approaches into the helping process.

Client Self-Responsibility: A Guiding Value

One of the primary values fostered by the approach to helping taken in these pages is client self-responsibility. The function of helpers is not to remake their clients' lives but to help them handle problems in living and refashion their lives according to their own values. Knowledge and skills are tools that enable clients to become more self-reliant.

Passivity

Early in the history of modern psychology, William James remarked that few people bring to bear more than about 10% of their human potential on the problems and challenges of human living. Others since James, although changing the percentages somewhat, have said substantially the same thing; and few have challenged their statements (Maslow, 1968). It is probably not an exaggeration to say that unused human potential constitutes a more serious social problem than emotional disorders, for it is more widespread. Maslow (1968, p. 16; emphasis added) suggests that what is usually called "normal" in psychology "is really a *psychopathology of the average*, so undramatic and so widely spread that we don't even notice it ordinarily." Many clients you will see, besides having more or less serious problems in living, will also probably be chronic victims of the psychopathology of the average.

One of the most important ingredients in the generation and perpetuation of the psychopathology of the average is *passivity*, the failure of people to take responsibility for themselves in one or more developmental areas of life or in various life situations that call for action.

> When Zelda and Jerzy first noticed small signs that things were not going right in their relationship, they did nothing. They noticed certain incidents, mused on them for a few moments, and then forgot them. They lacked the interpersonal skills to engage each other immediately and to explore what was happening, but they were also victims of their own learned passivity.

They had both *learned* to remain passive before the little crises of life, not realizing how much their passivity would ultimately contribute to their problems.

Erikson (1964, p. 87) speaks about what may be called the "agency-passivity" (Egan, 1970) dimension of life:

> *Patiens* [being passive, a "patient"], then, would denote a state of being exposed from within or from without to superior forces which cannot be overcome without prolonged patience or energetic redeeming help; while *agens* [being an agent, taking initiative, being assertive] connotes an inner state of being unbroken in initiative and in acting in the service of a cause which sanctions this initiative. You will see immediately that the state of *agens* is what all clients, or patients, in groups or alone, are groping for and need our help to achieve.

Environmental factors can severely limit a person's options and some situations in life may call for prolonged patience, but many call for decisive action. When patience is the outcome of *not* deciding whether to act or not, then it is most likely not a virtue.

"Learned Helplessness"

Seligman's (1975) concept of *learned helplessness* and its relationship to depression has received a great deal of attention (*Journal of Abnormal Psychology*, No. 1, 1978). Clients (and to an extent, all of us) can learn from an early age to believe there is nothing they can do about certain life situations. Obviously, there are degrees in feelings of helplessness. Some clients feel minimally helpless (and minimally depressed) and come to a helper primarily because they believe that getting help will be a more effective or efficient way of facing some problem or difficulty. Other clients feel totally helpless and overwhelmed by the difficulties of life and fall into deep, almost intractable depression.

Disabling Self-Talk

Ellis (1962, 1971, 1973, 1974; Ellis & Harper, 1975) and others have shown that people often talk themselves into passivity:

- "I can't cope."
- "I don't have what it takes to engage in that program; it's too hard."
- "It won't work."

Clients get into the habit of engaging in *disabling self-talk*. These self-defeating conversations with themselves get people into trouble in the first place and then prevent them from getting out.

Self-Efficacy

The opposite of passivity is agency (Egan, 1970), assertiveness (Kelley, 1977), or *self-efficacy* (Bandura, 1977a). Bandura suggests that people's expectations of themselves have a great deal to do with their willingness to put forth effort to cope with difficulties, the amount of effort they will expend, and how long they will persist in the face of obstacles. People tend to take action if two conditions are fulfilled: (1) They see that certain behavior will most likely lead to certain desirable results or accomplishments (outcome expectations). (2) They are reasonably sure they can successfully engage in such behavior (self-efficacy expectations). For instance, Yolanda not only believes that engaging in a job-search program will produce good results—that is, get her a job (an outcome expectation)—but she also believes that she has whatever it takes to engage in the program (a self-efficacy expectation). So she joins the program. Yves is not convinced that a weight-loss program will really help him lose weight (a negative outcome expectation); so he does not participate. Xavier is convinced the program will work but does not feel he has the will power to engage in it (a negative self-efficacy expectation). People's sense of self-efficacy can be strengthened in a variety of ways:

- *Success.* They act and see that their behavior actually produces results. Often success in a small endeavor will give them the courage to try something more difficult.
- *Modeling.* They see others doing what they are trying to do and are encouraged to try it themselves.
- *Encouragement.* Others exhort them to try, challenge them, and support their efforts.
- *Reducing fear and anxiety.* If people are overly fearful that they will fail, they generally do not act. Therefore, procedures that reduce fear and anxiety help heighten a person's sense of self-efficacy.

As a helper, you can do a great deal to help people develop a sense of agency or self-efficacy. First, you can help them challenge self-defeating beliefs and attitudes about themselves and substitute realistic beliefs about self-efficacy. This includes helping them reduce the kinds of fears and anxieties that keep them from mobilizing their resources. Second, you can help them develop the working knowledge, skills, and resources they need to succeed. These resources include other people as models. Third, you can challenge them to take reasonable risks and support them when they do.

Although an overriding aim of helping is to encourage clients to develop more and more responsibility, this does not mean that clients move away from passivity and dependency toward aggressiveness and fierce independence. The goal is reasonable assertiveness and *interdependence.* It is assumed here that the problem-solving model presents a framework for helping clients develop realistic and self-enhancing degrees of agency and self-efficacy. This includes helping clients actively participate in and "own" the helping process itself. It is extremely rewarding to see clients use problem-solving and decision-making skills they have learned in counseling to become change agents (Remer & O'Neill, 1980) in their own lives.

Helpers as Consultants versus Helping as Social Influence

If client self-responsibility and self-efficacy are important values, then helpers can be seen as consultants clients hire to help them face problems in living more effectively. "The therapist serves as a consultant and expert who negotiates with the client in how to go about change and to what end. The interactions are future oriented in that they focus on the development of general repertoires for dealing with problem situations" (Kanfer, 1980, p. 336). Consultants in the business world adopt a variety of roles—they listen, observe, collect data, report observations, teach, train, coach, provide support, challenge, advise, offer suggestions, and even become advocates for certain positions. But the responsibility for running the business remains with those who hire the consultant. Therefore, even though some of the consultant's activities can be seen as directive, the managers still make the decisions. Consulting, then, is a social-influence process, but one that does not rob managers of their responsibilities.

Helping, too, is a social-influence process (Corrigan, Dell, Lewis, & Schmidt, 1980; Frank, 1973; Goldstein, 1980; Rosenthal, Hung, & Kelley, 1977; Strong, 1968, 1978), which, at its best, does not rob clients of their self-responsibility but rather promotes it. Helpers influence their clients to take responsibility for both the helping process and their own lives. Kanfer (1980, p. 334) sees helping at its best as a participative rather than a directive model.

A *participant* model emphasizes the importance of client responsibility in treatment. It represents a shift from the provision of a protective treatment environment toward the offering of rehabilitative experiences in which the client accepts increasing responsibilities for his own behavior, for dealing with the environment, and for planning the future. The therapeutic environment is viewed as a transitory support system that prepares the client to handle common social and personal demands more effectively.

Therefore, helper social influence and client self-responsibility are by no means contradictory terms.

The notion of social influence is seen as central to helping and to the problem-management approach to helping. I will thus consider it at more length once you have had the opportunity to get a better feeling for the helping model itself (see Chapter 5).

Principles of Maintaining and Changing Human Behavior

A revolution in psychology began when Skinner (1953) urged that the principles of learning or behavior be applied to everyday life. These principles refer to the basic ways in which people acquire new behavioral responses to themselves and their environment, maintain other responses, and drop still others. This revolution has affected and is still affecting the development of the helping professions (Bandura, 1977a, 1977b; Kazdin, 1978; Krumboltz, 1966, 1980; Leitenberg, 1976; Marks, 1978), and models of helping solidly based on these principles have become widely used (for instance, Goldfried & Davison, 1976; Hosford & De Visser, 1976; Krumboltz & Thoresen, 1976; Watson & Tharp, 1981). The practical application of these basic principles is central to any approach to helping from beginning to end. Therefore, even though I present a very brief and necessarily oversimplified summary of some of these principles in the next few pages, I urge all who intend to be serious helpers to study these principles at greater length, to make them their own, to learn how to apply them to their own lives, and to integrate them into the helping process to be discussed and illustrated in this book. (There are any number of books at all levels of sophistication that describe these principles in detail and show how to apply them. See Bandura, 1969; Malott, Tillema, & Glenn, 1978; Martin & Pear, 1978; Sherman, 1973.)

The principles of human behavior can work either for you or against you. If you ignore them, they don't go away. They remain operative and you will find yourself stumbling over them. If you learn to appreciate and use them, they can contribute greatly to your work as a helper.

Reinforcement

The principle of reinforcement states that people tend to initiate and repeat behaviors for which they are in some way rewarded. The reward is called a *reinforcement,* and it can be *intrinsic* to the behavior performed. For instance, eating a hot fudge sundae, accomplishing a good day's work, or having an engaging conversation with a close friend can all be intrinsically rewarding. The reinforcement may also be *extrinsic* to the behavior performed (receiving money for cleaning out a sewer, the approval you receive from friends for sticking to a diet). People may receive both intrinsic and extrinsic reinforcement for the same behavior (a nurse finds helping patients rewarding in itself but is further reinforced by the patient's gratitude and the praise he receives from the hospital staff for work well done).

Reinforcement is often *positive*, as in the examples just cited, but it may also be the removal of something unpleasant (giving in to the demands of one's spouse removes his or her nagging) or the prevention of something unpleasant (studying for an exam removes the threat of failing). A reward that takes the form of the removal or prevention of something unpleasant is called *negative* reinforcement. People sometimes misinterpret negative reinforcement to mean punishment. Punishment has the opposite effect on behavior. The precise ways both positive and negative reinforcement work can be complex (Glaser, 1971), but a few simple principles relating to reinforcement will help you understand them.

- *Strengthening behavior.* Both positive and negative reinforcement have the same effect—that is, they tend to maintain and strengthen the behaviors they follow. People tend to repeat behaviors they find rewarding. For instance, a client who finds the first helping session rewarding is likely to return for a second.
- *Individualized rewards.* The reinforcement is not a reward unless it is experienced as such by the person whose behavior is in question. (The promise of a movie is a reward only to those who like movies.) If clients do not react positively to your rewards, for instance, your warmth, it may be that they do not experience what you offer as rewarding. A client might find a high degree of warmth from you threatening.
- *Strength of rewards.* The strength of a reward also depends on how it is experienced by the person receiving it (reading a good novel might be very rewarding for one person but only slightly rewarding for another). Therefore, one person might repeat a behavior many times in order to get a certain reward, but another person might engage in the behavior only once or twice.
- *Undesirable behaviors that are rewarded.* Even undesirable behaviors that are knowingly or unknowingly reinforced will tend to be repeated. For instance, a mother pays attention to a child only when the child throws a tantrum and then wonders why the child persists in tantrum-throwing behavior.
- *Intrinsic versus extrinsic rewards.* In the long run, intrinsic rewards are more effective than extrinsic rewards in maintaining behavior. For

instance, Dell finds staying sober rewarding in itself and no longer needs the extrinsic reinforcement he gets from the encouraging remarks made by the members of his Alcoholics Anonymous group. Celia stays dry because she likes herself better sober and she goes to her AA meetings because of the fellowship she finds there and no longer because she is encouraged to do so by her counselor.

- *Immediacy of reward.* Rewards usually work best when they are not delayed but are given as soon as possible after the behavior is performed (hence the ideal nature of desirable behaviors that are rewarding in themselves). Delayed rewards tend to work better if people receive some symbol or token indicating in a concrete and immediate way that the reward will be conferred. For instance, patients in mental hospitals receive tokens for desirable behaviors. They can save up the tokens and redeem them later on for items at the commissary.
- *The power of intermittent reinforcement.* Behaviors can be reinforced according to different "schedules." For instance, in the beginning every time a new worker reaches her quota, her supervisor tells her that she has done a good job. Once the worker gets the hang of the job and feels some intrinsic reinforcement from simply doing it well, the supervisor no longer reinforces her every time she reaches her quota, but every once in a while she tells her that she is doing well. This is intermittent reinforcement.

You can study the different kinds of schedules of intermittent reinforcement at your leisure. The main point is that such reinforcement can be a very powerful tool in maintaining a behavior. In the previous example, productive working behavior is maintained in part by intermittent reinforcement from the supervisor. However, intermittent reinforcement is also a powerful force in maintaining *unproductive* behaviors.

Sherry nags her husband whenever she wants something. Often it does not work, but every once in a while he gives in. He wonders why she keeps nagging him, since most of the time he does not give in. He does not realize that her unproductive behavior is being maintained, at least in part, by intermittent reinforcement.

Intermittent reinforcement underlies certain kinds of superstitious behavior. For instance, if you spend the night in a graveyard when you want the next day to be sunny, you might continue this behavior if every once in a while the next day is sunny.

In a sense, reinforcement is the central principle of behavior. Most of the other principles involve it in some way. The philosophical principle underlying it is profound. Beings that are not God by their very nature act in order to gain something when they act. There is no such thing as *absolutely* selfless behavior. People who are selfless find some kind of deep satisfaction in altruistic behavior even when altruism means suffering some kind of loss.

Effective helpers are constantly aware not only of the reinforcement dimensions of the helping relationship itself but also of the ways clients can use reinforcement to initiate and maintain desirable behaviors.

Extinction

Lack of reinforcement leads to the *extinction* of even constructive and desirable behaviors. For instance, if a client begins a program with a great deal of enthusiasm but gradually trails off, it may be that he or she is not experiencing any kind of reward, either intrinsic or extrinsic, from it. Extinction of some undesirable behavior seems to work best when some competing, desirable behavior is reinforced at the same time. For instance, a father might help his child reduce her tantrum-throwing behavior by ignoring it (extinction) and by showing attention to the child (reinforcement) when she is engaged in other, more constructive behaviors.

Punishment

Most people understand *punishment* in a general way but don't grasp its many negative implications. If a person does something that is followed by an unpleasant consequence (that is, one the person experiences as unpleasant), then that person is less likely to do the same thing in the same or a similar situation. The unpleasant consequences are called punishers. Punishment is often a powerful, but also a tricky and even dangerous, form of behavior control. Many people fail to appreciate the complexity of punishment (intended or unintended) and are taken aback when it backfires on them. Here are some of the principles related to punishment.

- *Decreasing the strength of behaviors.* Punishment ordinarily reduces the probability, strength, or frequency of the behavior it follows. For instance, if one spouse angrily rejects the other spouse's sexual overtures, then the frequency or the strength of these overtures may be decreased. Furthermore, both undesirable *and* desirable behaviors, if punished, tend to decrease in frequency. A client whose concerns are dealt with lightly by a helper is less likely to reveal his or her concerns to the helper again.
- *Short-term strengthening of behaviors.* Sometimes punishment tends to increase the strength of a behavior for a short time before decreasing it. For instance, one spouse may increase his or her sexual overtures after a

rebuff before reducing them. A client whose concerns are taken lightly by a helper may present them even more forcefully for a while.

- *No new learning.* Although punishment tends to suppress behaviors, it does not, of itself, teach new behaviors. It tends to leave a vacuum that needs to be filled by reinforced alternate behaviors. For instance, if a knife is taken away from a child, a harmless toy can be offered in its place. Clients can be challenged to stop talking about irrelevant or insignificant issues and at the same time encouraged to discuss relevant or significant issues.
- *Negative emotional climate.* Punishment often creates a negative emotional climate between the punisher and the one punished. For instance, a client who feels punished by a helper may harbor resentment that keeps getting in the way of the helping process. Or a helper who experiences a client's resistance as punishing might try to punish the client in return.
- *Unintended generalization.* It sometimes happens that when undesirable behaviors are punished and tend to decrease, desirable behaviors that are somewhat similar to the undesirable ones also decrease. For instance, a teacher yells at Carmen for speaking out of turn, but then Carmen no longer participates in class discussions—that is, she does not speak in class at all.
- *The punisher's needs.* Punishment too easily satisfies the needs of the punisher to vent anger and frustration rather than the needs of the person being punished to grow. For instance, a helper blows up when a client reports that she has not implemented a program they had spent a great deal of time designing.

Punishment is a fact of life and can be put to positive use (Johnston, 1972; Rudestam, 1980). However, as a form of behavior control, it needs to be carefully examined and monitored. Helpers would do well to learn much more about it before trying to incorporate it into the helping process.

Avoidance

People try to *avoid* what they see as harmful, but this means that sometimes they also avoid behavior that, although it involves some unpleasantness, leads ultimately to growth and development. For instance, Sheila would like to be physically fit, but she avoids physical exams and exercise because they are unpleasant. Avoidance behavior is one of the principal mechanisms contributing to the psychopathology of the average.

Avoidance is closely connnected with both reinforcement and punishment. People ordinarily try to escape from situations they find punishing and to avoid situations that might prove to be punishing. The following issues are involved in avoidance situations:

- *Negative reinforcement.* Successful avoidance of some possibly punishing event is experienced as rewarding, and, according to the principle of reinforcement, behavior that is rewarded tends to be repeated. Therefore, avoidance behavior is often repeated even when it does not contribute to the overall good of a person. For instance, Ted and Alice have some negative feelings about each other and their marriage. Each time either thinks of bringing something up, he or she puts it aside and is automatically rewarded by avoiding a potentially painful interchange. Finally, avoidance becomes habitual. This may go on until concealed resentment blows up in their faces or, at an extreme, until their marriage quietly dies.
- *Learning limited.* Because the potentially painful situation is avoided, there is no chance to learn from it, even though what can be learned might prove, in the long run, to be very rewarding. For instance, a person has a bad experience with a dentist. She then avoids going to any dentist and in so doing prevents herself from learning that many dentists are quite careful in how they deal with patients and their fears.
- *Generalization.* Avoidance learning often generalizes to similar situations. For instance, a man who has a bad experience with a minister also begins to avoid people who seem to be interested in religion.
- *"Danger ahead" cues.* People become sensitive to cues that signal "danger, a situation in which you might be punished is at hand—avoid it!" For instance, whenever Chester picks up cues, such as rising discomfort and anxiety, that the members of the group he is with are about to disagree or conflict in some way, he changes the subject, pours oil on the waters, or leaves. As a result, he never learns how to make productive use of conflict.

Because avoidance in one way or another is involved in most problem situations that clients face, helpers need to develop a detailed working knowledge of the mechanisms of avoidance.

Paul was a teenager who was getting into a great deal of trouble in school. He was an only child. His parents refused to talk to the counselor, saying that Paul was the one with problems. They blamed the staff at school for not being able to control him. Convincing themselves that Paul was the only one with problems and putting him forth as such was their way of avoiding dealing with their own problems. Their reward for such avoidance was to keep at bay their fear, guilt, and shame and to put off working on their own developmental issues.

Avoidance behaviors can cause trouble during the helping process because they are sometimes difficult to identify and, once identified, difficult to treat because of the ways avoidance is reinforced.

Shaping

Shaping is a procedure rather than a principle. Technically, shaping can be defined as the development of a new behavior or group of behaviors by the successive reinforcement of closer and closer approximations to that behavior and the gradual extinguishing of behaviors that are incompatible with movement toward the target behavior. As such, shaping is used by people who train animals to perform seemingly impossible feats. In a human context shaping can be described more broadly as a gradual, step-by-step movement toward a desirable goal in which behavior that leads toward the goal is reinforced and behavior that leads away from the goal is extinguished. The problem-solving process described in subsequent chapters makes generous use of shaping in this broader sense. Some of the principles involved in shaping are the following:

- *Take clients where they are.* Don't put demands on clients for which they are not sufficiently prepared. For instance, if change in interpersonal behavior demands certain communication skills, make sure clients have these skills first.
- *Size of steps.* Ordinarily, the steps in a change program can never be too small, but they can be too large. If any step is too large for a client, help him or her break it down into a number of smaller steps.
- *Reinforcement.* Make sure there is sufficient reinforcement or reward for a client to take any given step. Help clients find the kinds of reinforcement or reward that make sense to them.
- *Eliminating undesirable behaviors.* Some behaviors prevent clients from moving toward their goals. To help clients eliminate an undesirable behavior, help them find an alternate desirable behavior that is incompatible with the undesirable behavior. Help them strengthen the desirable behavior through reinforcement procedures. For instance, train married couples to listen carefully to each other and to respond with understanding. Such behaviors are incompatible with name-calling, accusing, and other behaviors that are harmful to the relationship.

Motivation and Will Power

Helpers are too often prone to blame clients for failures in the helping process. If clients do not follow a behavior change program, they are seen as lacking "motivation" or "will power." Very often deficits in motivation and will power can be traced to poor shaping procedures (Watson & Tharp, 1981) and a general failure to help clients apply the principles of behavior to behavior-change programs. Most clients will not be aware of these principles and how they can use them. It is thus important not only that you develop a working knowledge of these principles and the ability to apply them but also that you are able to help clients become aware of them and use them to their advantage.

Ethical Issues

Some people fear that people who understand and use the principles of behavior modification might use their power in some sinister way to control others. It is therefore useful to understand some of the ethical and legal issues involved in the use of these principles (Begelman, 1975; Braun, 1975; Krasner, 1976; London, 1969, 1972). However, in a "giving psychology away" approach to helping in which the client's self-responsibility is encouraged and promoted, there is little need to worry about helpers as "controllers."

> When everyone involved [in a helping situation] correctly understands the motivational elements of the situation in a concrete behavioral way, then and only then are we likely to bring about change. Therefore, increasing knowledge of motivation does not increase the possibility of manipulation, *because that knowledge has to be shared by the person to be influenced*, in order for change to take place. And giving away your technical information makes it possible for the person to refuse to do what you think he or she should do. Precise technical knowledge permits change, prevents manipulation, and therefore promotes human betterment [McClelland, 1978, p. 201; emphasis added].

Helpers are ideally consultants who enter the lives of others with great respect rather than power brokers pursuing their own goals.

This sketchy overview of some of the principles of behavior is not a substitute for systematic study of them and their application. These principles operate in all human situations, including the helping process to be explored in these pages. They are not the only tools needed for effective helping, but they are basic and essential. A counselor trying to help others without a working knowledge of these principles is like a carpenter trying to remodel a house without benefit of hammer, saw, pliers, and screwdriver.

The Contract between Helper and Client

Both implicit and explicit contracts govern the transactions that take place between people in a wide variety of situations, including marriage (where some but by no means all of the contract provisions are explicit) and friendship (where most of the provisions are implicit).

> The observation that human beings relate to one another in an orderly, pat-
> terned way over a period of time is nothing new or startling. This kind of
> observation is readily made by layman or behavioral scientist. . . . I have
> found in my own practice that conceptualizing human relationships in con-
> tract terms has been most helpful to my clients in clarifying expectations and
> negotiations which go on in the interpersonal drama [Shapiro, 1968, p. 171].

One way of helping clients who have difficulties in interpersonal relationships
is to review with them the implicit interpersonal contracts that exist between
them and the significant others in their lives. Often enough these implicit contracts have provisions that are self-defeating. For instance, over the first couple
of years of marriage a couple might enter into an implicit contract one of whose
provisions is that the man makes all the major decisions. This might work for
a while, but it eventually causes friction.

The notion of contract is also relevant to the helping process itself because
"virtually all counseling is governed by implicit contracts that define both the
treatment goals and procedures and the client-counselor relationship" (Goodyear & Bradley, 1980, p. 512). Traditionally, many therapists fail to tell their
clients much about the therapeutic process (Goldstein, Heller, & Sechrest, 1966),
even though "ethical principles assert that therapists should inform clients about
the purpose and nature of therapy and that clients have freedom of choice about
their participation" (Hare-Mustin, Marecek, Kaplan, & Liss-Levinson, 1979, p.
7). In a sense, clients are often expected to buy a pig-in-a-poke without much
assurance that it will turn out to be very succulent pork. In view of the importance
of client self-responsibility, I urge what Coyne and Widiger (1978) call a *participatory model of helping* (see Kanfer, 1980). The helping process needs to be
"owned" by helper *and* client alike, and there needs to be some basic understanding as to the major goals to be pursued and procedures to be used in the
helping process so they both own the same thing. An explicit contract, whether
verbal or written, between helper and client can help achieve these goals.

The contract need not be too detailed or too rigid. It needs to provide structure
for the relationship and the work to be done without frightening or overwhelming the client.

> Written or at least explicit verbal contracts can do much to clarify mutual
> expectations as to goals and methods, but inflexibility and irrevocable com-
> mitment to initial goals need to be avoided. An optimal form of contracting
> would involve making explicit mutual expectations, while allowing for peri-
> odic reassessment and revision [Coyne & Widiger, 1978, p. 707].

Cormier and Cormier (1979, pp. 507–509) outline the basic features of a
contract for helping a client change some behavior, but, by implication, some
of these features apply to the contract between helper and client. For instance:

- The contract should be negotiated, not proclaimed, by the parties involved—that is, helper and client.
- The contract should be clear to all involved parties. They should know what helping is about.
- Some kind of oral or written commitment to the contract should be obtained.
- The contract should be reviewed as the parties progress and revised if necessary.

Establishing the helping contract is important; it is a practical issue that deserves more thorough treatment than can be given to it here. You are encouraged to read the articles cited. Once you become familiar with the helping process, it will be easier for you to begin to determine what you believe should be in a contract between you and your clients.

Group Approaches to Training and Treatment

The assumption here is that you will learn the problem-solving model and its skills experientially in the context of a small group. Small groups present certain advantages in experiential learning.

- *Observing one's own behavior and receiving feedback.* Because groups are composed of members with different backgrounds, interpersonal styles, and concerns, each member has the opportunity to act out characteristic interpersonal behaviors, watch himself or herself "in action," as it were, and receive feedback from group members.
- *Developing observation skills.* Trainees have the opportunity to develop observational skills as they watch the behaviors of their fellow trainees. The helping model presented here provides a structure that enables trainees to categorize and evaluate behavior.
- *Lowering defenses.* If a group becomes a working/learning community with a sense of caring and cohesiveness, the members can experiment with lowering customary, but often self-limiting, defenses. In a climate in which each member values and is valued by others, the lowering and investigating of defenses becomes feasible.
- *Experimenting with "new" behaviors and the release of emotion.* The group provides a controlled environment in which members can responsibly experiment with behavior, including the expression of emotions that are kept under cover in day-to-day living. For instance, trainees who are less assertive than they would like to be can practice assertiveness.
- *Exploring social influence.* We are constantly influencing one another in a

variety of ways. Group members can exert their interpersonal power in different ways, and both personal power and social influence as expressed in the group can be explored.

- *Discovering models.* Trainees can become models for one another. That is, they can see in one another ways of behaving that they like and would like to develop themselves. This can be done, of course, without resorting to any kind of slavish imitation.
- *Giving and receiving help.* The group provides an opportunity for members both to give and to get help with their own problems, concerns, and developmental issues. In my experience, most group members say the personal growth achieved through the counseling psychology program was the dimension they valued most highly.
- *Seeing the principles of learning and behavior in action.* The group provides its own system of reward and punishment. It therefore can become a laboratory in which the principles of behavior outlined earlier can be learned, studied, and practiced.

These advantages apply not only to groups in which prospective helpers are trained but also to group counseling, especially in groups in which the training-as-treatment approach suggested earlier in this chapter is adopted. All that is discussed in the following chapters applies directly to one-to-one and indirectly to group counseling.

Portrait of a Helper

What should helpers be? Ideally, they are first of all committed to their own growth—physical, intellectual, social-emotional, and spiritual—for they realize that helping often involves modeling the behavior they hope others will achieve. They know they can help only if, in the root sense of the term, they are "potent" human beings—that is, people with both the resources and the will to act. Action needs direction; so they work at formulating and reformulating values that provide this direction.

They show respect for their bodies through proper exercise and diet. They make their bodies work for them rather than against them. They realize that if they are to give themselves completely to the helping process, they need a high level of energy. They also know that a poorly tended body results in loss of energy.

Helpers have adequate basic intelligence, are aware of their own intellectual possibilities, and have respect for the world of ideas. Because ideas are important to them, they read. They often read actively and hungrily, for they are eager to expand their view of the world. They respect good literature and the world of myth and metaphor. They respect good theory and good research, but they are practical people, "translators," who make what they read work for them. Because they are good learners, they are good translators. They can turn good theory and good research into practical programs that enable them to help others more effectively, and they have the skills to evaluate these programs.

Even more important, they have common sense and social intelligence. They are at home in the social-emotional world, both their own and that of others. They have developed an extensive repertoire of social-emotional skills that enables them to respond spontaneously and effectively to a wide range of human needs. For instance, they are not afraid of deep human emotions, either their own or others'. They work at making such skills second nature to themselves.

Good helpers know that helping is a great deal of work, but they also know that working smart is just as important as working hard—that is, they are more interested in accomplishments than in behavior. They attend to their clients both physically and psychologically. They know what their own bodies are saying and can read their clients' nonverbal messages. They listen intently to clients. But they know that the fruit of listening lies in effective responding. They see helping as a goal-oriented, an accomplishment-oriented dialogue. And so they respond frequently to clients, for they are working hard at understanding them. They respond from their clients' frame of reference, for they can see the world through their clients' eyes. They respect their clients and express this respect by being available to them, working with them, not judging them, trusting the constructive forces found in them, and ultimately placing the expectation on them that they do whatever is necessary to handle their problems in living more effectively. They genuinely care for those who have come for help. They are nondefensive, spontaneous, and always willing to say what they think and feel, provided it is in their clients' best interests. Good helpers are concrete in their expressions, dealing with actual feelings and actual behavior rather than vague formulations, obscure psychodynamics, or generalities. Their speech, caring and human, is also lean and to the point.

Skilled helpers are integrators. They help clients explore the world of experience, feeling, and behavior; and as clients produce data about themselves, they help them integrate them so clients can understand themselves and their behavior. They also realize that insight and understanding are not to be pursued or prized for themselves but insofar as they help clients set problem-managing goals and move toward constructive behavior change. Counselors in this process are not afraid to share themselves and their experiences if they see this will advance the helping process. They are not afraid to challenge clients with care, to help clients place demands on themselves, provided that these demands arise from the client's experience and not from the helper's needs. They are not afraid to deal openly with their own relationships with their clients to the degree that it helps clients understand their own behavior and interpersonal style and to the degree that it helps them move toward goals and action. But they do all these things with caution and respect, remembering that helping is for the client.

Action is important to good helpers. Because they are agents in their own lives—that is, people who seize life rather than submit to it—they are capable of helping their clients set goals and elaborate action programs that lead to constructive behavioral change. They know that self-understanding is not enough and that the helping process is not complete until the clients act on their understandings. Skilled helpers are pragmatists: they will draw on all possible helping resources that will enable their clients to achieve their goals. Indeed, they realize that the helping process is developmental, that the entire process is leading to the constructive management of the client's problems in living. Because of their wide response repertoire, skilled helpers can approach a problem from many different vantage points and help clients see alternatives. They are not bound to any single course of action. They may use a variety of techniques in the counseling process, but they are the masters of the techniques they use; they own the techniques; the techniques do not own them. They follow a comprehensive helping model, but they are not rigid in its applications. The model is not central; clients are. The model is an instrument of helping clients live more effectively.

Good counselors are at home with people both in one-to-one situations and in groups. They are not afraid to enter someone's world, no matter how distressing it is. The intimacy of the counseling process is not substitutive for them, for they are not people who need people with problems to help. Although they do not help others in order to satisfy their own needs, they know that "when they make it possible for others to choose life, they increase their own possibilities of continuing to choose life" (Carkhuff, 1969a, xii). They can handle crises; they can mobilize their energies and help others do so in order to act forcefully and decisively. They realize it is a privilege to be allowed to enter the life of another person, and they respect this privilege.

Skilled helpers have their own human problems, but they do not retreat from them. They explore their own behavior and know who they are. They know what it means to be helped and have a deep respect for the helping process and its power. Even though they are living effectively, they also know they are in process, that each stage of life has its own developmental tasks and crises.

This, then, is the ideal helper. The following chapters deal with the kinds of models, skills, and methods that can help you work toward that ideal.

Chapter *2*

Overview of
the Helping Model

This chapter deals with the following topics:

What it means to manage problem situations
The goal of helping
A brief look at the three stages of the helping process
Stage I: Helping clients explore and clarify their problem situations
The skills helpers need in Stage I
What the client does in Stage I
An application of Stage I: The case of Bob
Stage II: Setting goals based on new perspectives and dynamic understanding
The skills helpers need in Stage II
What the client does in Stage II
An application of Stage II: The case of Bob
*Stage III: Facilitating action—helping clients formulate and implement goal-
    related programs*
The skills helpers need in Stage III
What the client does in Stage III
An application of Stage III: The case of Bob

Introduction: Managing Problem Situations

In the previous chapter I referred to the helping model to be used as a problem-*solving* model. That is not entirely accurate. It is perhaps better called a problem-*management* model or framework. Obviously, problems in living are different from mathematical or engineering problems. D'Zurilla and Goldfried (1971, pp. 107–108), in discussing problems in living, prefer the term *problem situation.*

> The term *problem* will refer here to a specific *situation* or *set of related situations* to which a person must respond in order to function effectively in his environment. . . . [T]he term *problematic situation* will be used in most instances in place of "problem." In the present context, a situation is considered problematic if *no effective response alternate is immediately available to the individual confronted with the situation.*

Problems in living are much messier than mathematical problems with clear-cut solutions. One of the principal reasons they are messier is that strong human feelings and emotions are often involved. Further complication arises from the fact that problem situations exist between people and between people and the social settings and systems of their lives. Because of this complexity, helpers face a difficult task. On the one hand, they need to understand and appreciate the complexity of any given problem situation. Oversimplification of problems followed by superficial solutions helps no one. On the other hand, they need to avoid being overwhelmed by the complexity of problem situations. Even in the face of chaos, they must be able to help the client do *something.*

People who come to helpers can be said to have a variety of problems in living. They face problem situations with which they are not adequately coping. They are looking for ways to come to terms with, solve, or transcend their problems—that is, they need to *manage* the problem situations of their lives more effectively than they are presently doing. Being intelligent and still failing in school is a problem. Being unemployed because of a faltering economy is a problem. Having to face life after being told that one has cancer is a problem. A failing marriage is a problem. When people feel that they are not handling such problems well or feel overwhelmed by them, they often look for help.

Sometimes individuals do not feel they have problems, but others do. Truant students might not see their truancy as problematic, but their parents and school officials do. People who annoy others are sometimes endured or shunned, but at other times they are pressured either to change their behavior on their own initiative or to see some kind of helper. These people might not feel they have a problem, but they are problems to others.

The Goal of Helping

Helpers are effective if they help their clients to manage the problem situations of their lives a bit (or even a great deal) more effectively. Even the most devastating problem situations can probably be handled a bit more effectively.

> Fred L. was thunderstruck when the doctor told him that he had terminal cancer. He was only 52, so death couldn't be imminent. He felt disbelieving, bitterly angry, and depressed, all at the same time. After a period of angry confrontations with doctors and members of his family, he finally, in his despair, talked to a clergyman. They decided to have some sessions together, but the clergyman also referred him to a counselor who had a great deal of experience with people who were dying. Between these two helpers, Fred gradually learned how to manage the ultimate problem situation of his life. He came to grips with his religious convictions, put his affairs in order, began to learn how to say good-bye to his family and the world he loved so intensely, and set about the process of managing physical decline. There were some outbursts of anger and some brief periods of depression and despair, but generally, with the help of the clergyman and the counselor and with the support of his family, he managed the process of dying much better than he thought he could.

This case demonstrates dramatically that the goal of helping is not to make everything all right. Fred did die. Some problem situations are simply more unmanageable than others. Helping clients discover what kind and degree of problem management is possible is, as we shall see, a central part of the helping process.

Stages of the Problem-Management Process

The helping framework, as outlined here, has three general stages. I consider each from the point of view of what needs to be accomplished in it.

- *Stage I: The problem situation is explored and clarified.* Clients cannot manage problem situations unless they understand them. Initial exploration and clarification of the problem takes place in Stage I.
- *Stage II: Goals based on an action-oriented understanding of the problem situation are set.* This stage has two parts. First, clients must often be challenged to develop new perspectives on their problems. They must move to the kind of dynamic understanding that calls for some kind of action. Second, they need to set goals (that is, ways of responding to the problem situation) based on their new perspectives.
- *Stage III: Ways of accomplishing goals are devised and implemented.* First, because goals can often be met in a variety of ways, clients need to decide just how they are going to accomplish theirs. The different ways are called programs. Second, clients need to implement the programs they choose.

This model can be called *developmental.* That is, it is systematic and cumulative. The success of Stage II depends on the quality of work in Stage I. The success of Stage III depends on the quality of work in both Stages I and II. Just why this is so will become clear as we move through the model.

As we shall see later on, the problem-solving process in practice is not as clean and linear as described here. However, helpers benefit greatly if they approach the helping process with a broad but still concrete map of what needs to be done. The purpose of this section is to provide that map. It is both a map of the helping process and an outline of this book.

Stage I: Problem Clarification

Helpers cannot be of service to clients if the latter are unaware of problems or difficulties in their lives. Most people handle most problems in living, whether successfully or unsuccessfully, by themselves or with the informal help of family and friends. They live without professional help. But people who find they are not coping with their problems and either do not want to share them with family or friends or feel that family and friends are not competent to help them might turn to some kind of helper—minister, teacher, coach, supervisor, doctor, counselor, social worker, nurse, psychologist, psychotherapist, psychiatrist, and the like. They will usually turn to such a person (1) if the problem is serious or disturbing enough and (2) if they believe that the person to whom they are turning can actually help them.

Some clients do not go to helpers voluntarily; they are sent, for a variety of reasons. For instance, they may be unaware that they are harming themselves or others. In this case the first step is to help them become aware of their behavior and its consequences. There are also those who realize they are harming themselves or others but don't seem to care. In this case their not caring becomes the first problem to be faced. Clients who are sent to helpers can be resistant to help. Ways of handling resistance are discussed in Chapter 10.

THE GOAL

The goal or goals in each stage of the helping process is central. Skills and techniques are merely ways of achieving each of these goals. The goal of Stage I is the initial clarification of the problem situation. Unless the problem situation is clear, not just to the helper but especially to the client, the latter cannot make reasonable decisions as to what to do about it. Skills and techniques are, in a sense, tools to be used to help clients achieve certain goals. If helper and client do not keep the goal of each stage in mind, there is a tendency to overemphasize the helper's behavior. Then the skills, techniques, and even the relationship can become goals in themselves.

THE HELPING RELATIONSHIP

Establishing good rapport with the client, although very important, is not the goal of Stage I. Good rapport is one of the principal means used to help clients pursue the goals of each stage of the helping process and ultimately manage their lives more effectively. A good working relationship contributes to getting the work of helping done. Therefore, helpers establish different kinds of relationships with different clients. For example, although all these relationships need to be based on respect, not all will involve the same degree of warmth. Some clients are helped by a closer, more intimate relationship; others are helped by one that is more matter-of-fact. Some clients need a closer relationship as part of a program of social-emotional reeducation. In the helping relationship or the helping group, they relearn how to relate to others and how to prize rather than despise themselves. When you are listening to the client, one of the things you are listening for is the kind of relationship that best suits his or her individual needs.

SKILLS HELPERS NEED

One way of looking at the skills of Stage I is to see them in terms of orientation and response. First, helpers need to *orient* themselves toward their clients. The skills needed to do so effectively are *attending* and *listening.*

Attending. Helpers, by their very posture, must let clients know that they are with them, that during the time they are together they are completely available to them. This means, positively, engaging in such behaviors as good eye contact; it means, negatively, avoiding distracting behaviors such as nervous tapping.

Active Listening. One reason for attending is that helpers by so doing put themselves in a position to listen carefully to their clients. Active listening means listening to both the verbal and nonverbal messages of those who come for help. It means listening attentively to the client's words, however confused they might be (verbal messages). It means listening to the messages that are carried in the client's tone of voice, silences, pauses, gestures, facial expression, posture, and the like (nonverbal messages). Active listening means that helpers keep asking themselves: What is the core of what this person is trying to communicate? What is this person saying about his or her experiences? What is this person saying about his or her behaviors? What is this person saying about his or her feelings?

You will probably find that some clients are easy to attend and listen to, but others, especially perhaps those whom, for one reason or another, you find unattractive, are difficult to attend and listen to. In the latter case, being with a client is more work, but skilled helpers realize that much that takes place in a helping relationship is hard work.

Responding. Effective attending and listening contribute greatly to the quality of a helper's responding. Helping involves a great deal of dialogue, with specific skills required for the kind of dialogue that helps clients explore and clarify their problems in living. Helpers need to respond to clients in a way that shows they have listened carefully and that they *understand*, to the degree this is possible, how their clients feel and what they are saying about themselves. It is not enough to understand; helpers must *communicate* their understanding.

Probes. Probes are ways of helping a client articulate a problem situation in more specific and concrete terms. For instance, if a client indicates that she is having trouble in relating to her husband, a helper might first respond with empathy and follow it with some kind of probe. She might say, "I'm not sure just what kinds of things are bothering you." This probe encourages the client to speak more concretely and specifically.

A judicious mixture of empathy and probes, a mixture that will be different for different clients, can help clients speak more concretely about themselves—that is, talk about specific experiences, behaviors, and feelings related to specific situations. This is what is meant by the clarification of a problem situation.

Foundational Qualities.   There are certain helper qualities upon which the entire helping process rests. They can therefore be called foundational. They are not exactly skills, but rather helper attitudes that need to be expressed in a variety of behavioral ways during the helping process. Helpers need to *respect* their clients, to be basically "for" them and communicate this in a variety of ways: by working hard with their clients, by maintaining confidentiality, by refraining from manipulation, by respecting their clients' values even when they differ from their own, and by prizing the self-responsibility of those they are helping. Respect, to be effective, cannot remain a mere attitude but must be expressed in behavioral ways in the helping encounter. Skilled helpers are genuine. They do not hide behind professional roles. They are spontaneous and open, remaining human beings to the human beings with whom they are working.

WHAT THE CLIENT DOES

Aided by the helper, the client explores specific concerns, difficulties, misgivings, and problem situations as concretely and specifically as possible. It does not help if what is going wrong in the client's life becomes clear to the helper but not to the client. Ideally, helping is not something being done *to* the client but rather *with* the client. As indicated in the previous chapter, client self-responsibility is an important value. This refers to what the client does not just in his or her everyday life but also in the helping encounter itself. Clients should "own" as much of the helping process as possible. Some will need more direction than others; some will need to be challenged more than others. But both direction and challenge can be provided without the client abdicating self-responsibility.

COMMENTS ON STAGE I AND ITS SKILLS

Each of these stages and the skills it requires will be spelled out in much greater detail in subsequent chapters. It is important to remember the developmental nature of the helping process. The skills of Stage I are needed throughout the helping process. A person who fails to develop these skills will not be able to do the work of Stages II or III, even though he or she might have some of the skills of those specific stages. The ways in which empathy, probing, and the foundational qualities of respect and genuineness are expressed may change somewhat as the helper moves deeper into the helping process, but the need for these skills remains.

APPLYING STAGE I: THE CASE OF BOB

We will use the highlights from an extended example to illustrate each stage of the model and just how it can be used to help counselors know where they are in relationship to their clients and to the problem situations they are presenting. For the sake of clarity, the example will be oversimplified, but it does give some idea of the complexity of problems in living.

Bob is a second-year college student who has just returned to school after a visit with his parents at home. He comes to one of the college counselors quite upset. He comes on his own initiative because he is in pain. He has had some previous experience with counselors, one or two visits on a couple of occasions in high school, but at the time he felt that counseling really didn't do him any good. He comes in, sits down with the counselor, and begins to talk about what is troubling him. Stage I has begun. The first problem he brings up is that he is doing poorly in his studies. He realizes he is in no way achieving according to his talents. The counselor helps him explore the problem area, but she also realizes that this could be a safe problem that Bob is pushing out in front to see how she will handle it, or, more importantly, to see how she will relate to him. In the self-exploration stage, because he is attended and listened to, not judged; understood; and generally respected, Bob produces a great deal of data concerning the problem situation relating to school: poor study habits, refusal to do work, boredom, restlessness, periods of depression, poor relationships with a variety of teachers, and so on.

Bob begins to trust the counselor and, because of the empathy and judicious probing she provides, begins to talk about an area that is even more bothersome than his academic situation. Failing in school is an important part of the problem situation, because Bob is wasting his time and that of others in school, but it is not what is bothering him most. A counselor unwilling to explore the problem areas of his life with Bob might have too quickly assumed that failure in school was the focal problem and would have moved too quickly into Stages II and III in an attempt to help Bob develop a better attitude toward school and more productive approaches toward studying. However, the counselor, because she gives Bob ample opportunity to explore his behavior, does not lead him on a wild goose chase. Well into the first session Bob says, "To be frank, I think I'm much more upset about what is happening at home than the mess I've got myself in here at school. I'm sure they're related." The counselor, using the same skills of empathy and probing, now helps him explore the problem situation at home. He tells the counselor that he has just returned from a very painful visit at home, and he begins to relate a history of what he sees as parental indifference and neglect and, paradoxically, a history of parental demands that he achieve socially and scholastically.

Bob says that when he is at home, he seems to have feelings of being "no good"; at least he feels he never lives up to what he thinks his parents expect of him. He has begun to resent making visits home. The counselor helps Bob explore his relationship with his parents and his feelings about himself in terms of specific experiences, behaviors, and feelings related to specific situations. Bob describes the kinds of fights he gets into with them, and the counselor's accurate responses help Bob make his observations more and more concrete.

Bob does not feel particularly close to his counselor, but he does feel that she is competent, that she knows what she is doing. He feels she respects him and he respects her.

In Stage I, it is important to make sure that the problem situation is understood as fully as possible *from the client's point of view.* The client's perspective may need broadening—as we shall see, in most cases it does—but the client's point of view is the essential starting point.

Stage II: Setting Goals Based on Dynamic Understanding

Three things are important in Stage II. First, it is important to help the client piece together the data revealed in Stage I so he or she can see the "bigger picture." Seeing the data in terms of behavioral themes can help the client decide what to do about a problem situation. Second, it almost always happens that a client's perception of the problem situation is too narrow or distorted. So in Stage II the counselor helps the client develop new and perhaps more objective perspectives or points of view on the problem situation, the kinds of perspectives that enable the client to set reasonable goals. Third, the counselor helps the client set goals (that is, ways of managing the problem situation) based on the client's more integrative and dynamic understanding of the problem situation.

SKILLS HELPERS NEED

First, helpers need the skills of Stage I, for in Stage II, clients still need to be understood and helped to see their problem situations as concretely as possible. Second, helpers need three further sets of skills corresponding to the three briefly mentioned goals of Stage II.

Integrating the Data.   Helpers need the ability to integrate the data the client presents and to identify the behavioral themes associated with the client's problem situation.

Challenging Skills. Challenging skills enable the counselor to help clients develop new, more objective, and more useful perspectives on the problem situation. There are at least five vital challenging skills.

The first is *information sharing.* Sometimes clients are mired down in problem situations because they lack certain kinds of information. If this is the case, counselors can help them get the kind of information that enables them to see problem situations in a new light.

The second is *advanced accurate empathy.* Using this skill, helpers communicate to their clients an understanding of what clients say indirectly and what they merely imply, hint at, and say nonverbally. In doing this, helpers do not invent anything; rather, they base their understanding, as always, on cues clients present.

Confrontation is the third skill. Helpers challenge the discrepancies, distortions, games, and smokescreens in clients' lives and in their interactions within the helping relationship itself, to the degree that this form of challenging helps clients develop the kind of self-understanding that leads to constructive behavioral change.

Fourth is *helper self-sharing.* Effective helpers are willing to share their own experience with their clients if this sharing will help clients understand themselves better. Helpers are extremely careful, however, not to distract clients or to lay another burden (the helper's problems) on them.

A fifth skill is *immediacy.* Helpers are willing to explore their own relationships with their clients ("you-me" talk)—that is, to explore the here-and-now of client-helper interactions—to the degree that this helps clients get a better understanding of themselves, their interpersonal style, and the quality of their cooperation in the helping process.

Challenging skills are "stronger medicine"; they ordinarily place greater demands on clients than the skills of Stage I. Therefore, they need to be used with discretion.

Goal-Setting Skills. Goals refer to what clients decide to *do* about their problem situations. Helping clients establish reasonable goals based on the exploration of the problem situation and the development of new perspectives is, as already noted, central to the helping process. The principal skill here is *shaping*—that is, helping clients move from mere declarations of intent ("I've got to do something about that") to concrete, specific, and measurable goals.

WHAT THE CLIENT DOES

In Stage II, clients ideally collaborate with the helping process in a number of ways. They engage in *nondefensive listening.* Helpers can assist clients in developing the skill of listening, not just to what the helper is saying (as he or she points out behavioral themes, shares information, or challenges in different ways), but the skill of listening to themselves and their environments more carefully, more nondefensively, and more accurately. Because it is often painful to listen to oneself and one's environment objectively, clients frequently need support from helpers to do so.

Clients are not helped if they can merely parrot back what helpers are saying to them. They need to "own" the helping process. Nor is it enough for clients to develop some kind of theoretical or abstract understanding of themselves and their problem situations. *Dynamic understanding* is the kind of understanding that sits on the edge of action. It has the flavor of "Now I see what I am doing and how self-destructive it is, and I've got to do something about it."

With the counselor's help, clients need to choose precisely what they are going to do to manage problem situations more effectively. Helpers cannot make these decisions for them. The *decisions on goals* need to be based on the client's, not the helper's, values.

COMMENTS ON STAGE II AND ITS SKILLS

The skills of Stage II will be explored and illustrated much more fully in subsequent chapters. These skills, especially the skills of challenging, can be destructive if not used with care. Confrontation can become a club; helper self-disclosure can become exhibitionistic; immediacy and the offering of alternate frames of reference can lead to a power struggle. Some counselors look upon themselves as experts in the more dramatic challenging skills without even having mastered the Stage I skills.

Because one of the helper's goals is to help clients listen nondefensively, Stage II behaviors need to be introduced tentatively. Helping is for the client, and if a client is put off because the helper pushes too hard too soon, helping becomes merely a way for the helper to satisfy his or her own needs.

The social-influence nature of the helping process, although certainly present in Stage I, can be seen even more clearly in Stage II. In Stage I, helpers establish a power base (though a benevolent one because it stems from good rapport, empathy, respect, and genuineness). In Stage II, helpers use this power to influence clients to develop more accurate and useful perceptions of themselves, their environments, and both self-self and self-environment interactions. If helpers are not skillful or if they fail to base Stage II behaviors on accurate understanding of clients and their needs, Stage II can degenerate into manipulation and control.

The skills and techniques of Stage II are, like the skills and techniques of Stage I, tools to achieve certain goals. Stage II is successful only if it completes the process of problem clarification and definition. In Stage I, data are gathered and the problem situation is clarified, at least from the point of the client. In the first part of Stage II, the kinds of new perspectives the client needs to see the problem situation more clearly and objectively are pursued. If this is done carefully, the client is in a position to set goals.

Ideally, as Stage II progresses, the client sees more and more clearly the necessity of action on his or her part. Clients may well fear change and even doubt that they have the resources for it. These fears and doubts need to be dealt with. However, in certain cases clients must act *first* in order to see that their fears and doubts are groundless.

The dynamic understanding sought in Stage II should not be confused with an eternal search for deeper and deeper insights, insights that are too often divorced from action. Some people believe that if they can only understand themselves fully, everything will be all right. This is magical thinking.

APPLYING STAGE II: THE CASE OF BOB

When Bob begins to explore the experiences, behaviors, and feelings related to his interactions with his parents freely, the helper moves into Stage II. In this stage she calls on what skills she sees as useful for helping Bob achieve the goal of dynamic understanding—piecing the data together into a larger picture, pulling together behavioral themes, self-sharing, immediacy, confrontation, and suggesting alternative frames of reference. She does so tentatively and to the degree that they help Bob achieve the kind of dynamic self-understanding that enables him to set reasonable goals. For instance, she helps him explore the relationship between what is happening at home and what is happening at school. This includes helping him explore his own hunches about the relationship between what is happening in school and what is happening at home. She shares with Bob a hunch of her own based on the behavioral themes he is exploring—that failing in school might have a double payoff: it confirms in Bob's eyes that he is "no good" and it also punishes his indifferent and overly achievement-oriented parents.

She also believes that Bob might benefit from some information on his developmental stage. For instance, she points out to him that struggling with independence from home and ambivalent feelings about one's parents is part of a fairly normal developmental picture. This helps Bob realize that some of his reactions to his parents are not "crazy."

She thinks of other possibilities, such as briefly sharing with Bob some of her experiences with her own parents, but will do so only if such self-sharing is to the point, if it keeps the focus on Bob's problem and helps him understand himself better, and if it does not make Bob feel burdened with someone else's problems. At one time she senses that Bob's distrust of his parents has generalized to other adults and that he is at times having difficulty trusting her. She shares with him her perception of what is happening in their relationship: "You have distrusted adults so long that you might even be wondering whether you can trust me. On my part, I'm asking myself whether I am working with you in such a way as to merit your trust." The skilled counselor is not afraid of such "you-me" talk and engages in it to the degree that it helps clients get a deeper, action-oriented understanding of themselves. In this example, the counselor sees that the difficulties Bob has with adults in his day-to-day life are also asserting themselves in the interaction between him and his counselor. But notice that she does not use immediacy as a way of blaming him. She sees it as an opportunity for evaluating her side of the relationship. The helper does not engage in "you-me" talk in order to fulfill her own needs or for the sake of immediacy; instead she uses it to help Bob understand his feelings and behavior more fully.

The counselor might also offer Bob alternative frames of reference for viewing himself and his behavior. Although Bob experiences himself as worthless, the helper suggests that he has *learned* to consider himself worthless through the interactions he has had over the years with the significant adults in his life. In many respects, his contacts with his parents have been "for the worse." However, learned feelings of worthlessness are different from being worthless. Alternative frames of reference are valid and useful to the degree that they are based on an accurate understanding of Bob.

Finally, in Stage II, the counselor thinks that Bob might benefit from some kind of challenge or confrontation; but she realizes that confrontation, too, is not an end in itself and must be based solidly on an accurate, empathic understanding of Bob. For instance, if Bob is using his past as an excuse for not doing anything now—if, in effect, he is saying "My parents destroyed me in the past, so I'll destroy myself in the present," or "They made me the way I am now and I can't do anything about it"— the counselor challenges this kind of thinking. She says something like "Maybe dwelling excessively on what your parents have done to you robs you of the energy you need to take responsibility for yourself."

In summary, whatever kind of interaction the helper uses with Bob— self-sharing, immediacy, suggesting an alternative frame of reference, confrontation, or any combination of these—she knows precisely what she is doing and what she is trying to achieve. The model lays out both the counseling goals for each stage and the skills needed to achieve these goals. Bob's general response is "Now I'm beginning to see much more clearly what is really bothering me and what underlies this mess in school."

Once Bob has a fairly clear picture of what is going wrong in his life and of how he is contributing to it, the counselor helps him decide what he wants to do about it. As a sign that the first part of the Stage II process is going well, Bob begins to see that, although he cannot control his parents' behavior, he can control his behavior and his responses to his parents. He wants to do something about his relationship with his parents, and he feels

> *freer to act now that he realizes that struggling with independence from home is a normal problem for many people his age. One goal he chooses is to eliminate fighting with his parents. He is not quite sure how to do that, but at least he knows what he wants to do. Another goal relates to life at school. He has let himself become a loner; and having no friends, besides being a problem in itself, makes most other problems look worse. He has no real community life at school; so he decides he is going to do something about his social life. He wants to develop a circle of friends.*

Clear, reasonable, problem-managing goals are the pivotal point in the helping process. In a sense, up to this point everything—exploring and clarifying the problem situation and developing new perspectives—has been done in order to set goals. And everything that happens from this point on is to see to it that the goals are accomplished. The final stage of the helping process relates to the client's acting in his or her own behalf.

Stage III: Facilitating Action

Helping is not just about talking and planning. Clients must ultimately *act* if they are to live more effectively. Intending to act and making decisions as to what to do in order to manage their lives more effectively end Stage II. Determining how to implement goals and then actually going out and initiating goal-achieving programs is the work of Stage III.

SKILLS HELPERS NEED

The skills of Stages I and II continue to be used in this third stage, for clients still need to clarify, to be understood so they might understand, and to be challenged. The skills specific to Stage III can be divided into three parts: program-development skills, facilitating-action skills, and evaluation skills.

Program-Development Skills. Programs are simply the means chosen to implement goals. Full program development calls for two different kinds of skills. The first is *helping clients identify program possibilities.* A goal is an *end,* an accomplishment; a program is a *means,* a step-by-step process for achieving a goal. If there is more than one goal, then each goal will have its own program. Programs can be very simple or they can be long and relatively complicated. In the latter case, a goal is ordinarily divided into a sequence of related subgoals, each with its own program. This process can lead to seemingly amazing and virtually impossible achievements, such as placing a person on the moon. In the first part of Stage III, counselors help their clients develop a census or list of concrete, realistic programs that will lead to the accomplishment of the goals set in Stage II.

One reason people fail to achieve goals is that they do not explore the different ways they can be accomplished. They choose one means or program without a great deal of exploration or reflection, try it, and when it fails, conclude they just can't achieve that particular goal. Coming up with as many ways of achieving a goal as possible raises the probability that one of these ways or a combination of several will suit a particular client's resources. At this stage of the problem-solving process, as many means as possible (within time and other constraints) should be uncovered. Furthermore, time need not be wasted criticizing them. Even seemingly outlandish programs can provide clues for realistic programs. Techniques such as brainstorming and fantasizing are often useful in identifying different ways of achieving goals.

The second skill is *helping clients choose programs.* Once a client and helper have identified a number of different program possibilities, client and helper, in collaboration, review them and try to choose either the best single program or the best combination. "Best" here means the one or the combination that best fits the client's needs and resources and the one that is least likely to be blocked by factors in the client's environment. The program must also be in keeping with the client's values. For instance, even though one of the ways a young woman can afford to stay in college for the coming year is to accept a gift from a close relative, she might reject that option because she considers it more important to develop a healthy independence from her family. In that case, she will either have to forego this year in school or find other ways of financing it. At this stage, programs need to be evaluated in terms of their realism. For instance, one way to stop drinking is to move to a deserted island where there is no liquor. For most people, this is unrealistic, though a person might move to a dry county.

Facilitating-Action Skills. Helpers can be skillful in two ways in this phase of the helping process. The first is in *helping clients in their immediate preparation for action.* Effective counselors help clients foresee difficulties that might arise when they begin to carry out the program. There are two extremes here. One is pretending that no difficulties will arise. The client launches into a program optimistically and then runs headlong into the obstacles that can plague any kind of program. The other is spending too much time anticipating obstacles and figuring out ways of handling them. This can be just another way of delaying the real work of behavior change.

A reasonable consideration of obstacles that might arise during program implementation can be most useful. One way of doing this is to consider the principal "facilitating forces" and the principal "restraining forces" that will most likely operate in the client's environment, including the client's "inner" environment of thoughts, feelings, imaginings, and attitudes. For instance, if a person is trying to stop smoking, one facilitating force is thinking about the amount of money that could be saved and the other things it could buy. Over a year this could mean a nice vacation somewhere. A principal restraining force will probably be the longing that comes from withdrawal from a pleasurable habit. Another will be the envy the person will experience when in the company of his or her friends who are still smoking.

The second skill is in *providing challenge and support during the action phase.* The probability that any given program will succeed is increased if a reasonable amount of planning leads up to it. But planning without goal-directed action is, of course, meaningless. As clients actually implement programs, they need both support and challenge, from themselves and from others. Helpers can be an important source of both. For instance, when a client feels inadequate and discouraged as he or she moves through a program, the counselor can provide empathic understanding. The counselor can also challenge the client to mobilize whatever resources are needed to stick to a program. For example, if a wife unilaterally institutes a program of improved communication with her husband (who refuses to see the counselor either with his wife or alone), she may have a rough time in the beginning. She may find it extremely discouraging when he does not appreciate her attempts at a more caring kind of communication and even makes fun of them while he still plays communication games. But if there is a reasonable probability that her patience will eventually pay off, then she needs support and challenge to stick to the program. This can come from herself, from her friends, and from the counselor. Helpers at this point of the process do not act *for* clients but rather help them mobilize their resources in order to increase the strength of facilitating forces and decrease the strength of restraining forces.

Evaluation Skills. Evaluation is an extremely important part of the helping process. It is being presented at the end, as the final step. In reality, however, evaluation is effective only if it is *ongoing.* Skilled counselors help their clients ask themselves three principal evaluation questions:

1. *Quality of participation.* Is the client actually carrying out the program? What is the client's quality of participation? If clients are not investing themselves in programs or if they are doing so only halfheartedly, this in itself is a problem and needs to be faced like any other problem.
2. *Quality of programs.* If the client is actively invested in the program, is the goal toward which the program is directed being achieved? Wholly? Partially? If the client is carrying out the program as it has been designed and is not achieving the goal, then the program needs to be redesigned.
3. *Quality of goals.* If goals are being achieved, are the problems they were designed to handle actually being handled? Are the client's needs being

met? If the client's problems persist, if the problem situation is not becoming more manageable, then new goals have to be set and new programs elaborated. If the problem situation is becoming more manageable and the quality of the client's life is improving, this is a sign that the helping process can be terminated.

These questions should be asked at the appropriate time during the helping process and not just at the end.

WHAT THE CLIENT DOES

If the helping process is being carried out skillfully, clients will be learning *cooperation* and how to overcome their reluctance and resistance. Elaborating and choosing programs makes sense only if it is a collaborative effort. So clients involve themselves in planning strategy.

By providing both support and challenge, counselors, at least ideally, help their clients *become better risk takers.* In Stage I, clients risk revealing themselves; in Stage II, they risk seeing themselves in new ways and making decisions to act; and in Stage III, clients risk acting in new ways and facing the consequences. Reasonable risk taking is not the same as jumping off into the void. The helping process described in these pages is designed to help clients take reasonable risks.

Clients go out and implement programs and then share the ups and downs with their helpers. They work collaboratively to iron out snags, handle unforeseen problems, and generally *evaluate the entire helping process.*

COMMENTS ON STAGE III AND ITS SKILLS

Some counselors never get to Stage III with their clients on the assumption that Stage III is the clients' sole responsibility. And it is true that some clients, once they know what they want to do to manage problem situations (goals), go out and do whatever is necessary without needing help from the counselor. However, other clients can still profit from the support and challenge of a helper at this stage.

Other helpers try to *start* with Stage III. That is, they listen briefly to their clients' problems, tell them what to do (the advice-giving approach to helping), and then send them out to do it. They blame any failures on "unmotivated" clients.

When goals and programs are chosen, it is extremely important to make sure the client has the kinds of working knowledge and skills needed to carry out the program. If a shy young man is sent out to "date," he may well be courting failure because he doesn't have the kinds of social skills needed in such encounters. Prior training in communication and social skills and practice in using them assertively can increase the probability of his success.

APPLYING STAGE III: THE CASE OF BOB

One of Bob's goals is developing a more effective social life on campus. This is *what* he wants to do, but he is not exactly sure *how* to do it. He has some ideas, but wants to bounce them off the counselor and see whether she has any ideas. Together they brainstorm some possibilities. For instance, Bob thinks of joining one or more clubs on campus, pledging a fraternity, becoming a volunteer in a youth program run by a local church, talking to people he is attracted to before and after class, and getting on an intramural sports team. All these would put him directly in contact with people immediately. The counselor suggests taking an interpersonal skills training course or participating in one of the assertiveness training groups in the student services center.

Bob chooses to take the course in interpersonal communication skills for a number of reasons. He will meet people who are interested in relating to others; he might find a few people with whom he can develop friendships; he will have the opportunity to review and improve his interpersonal competencies; he believes he might find better ways of communicating with his parents; and he will get three credit hours. He also decides to become a volunteer in the church youth program. He believes that he will find others his own age there who have more or less the same values as he does. All in all, he sees the program he is fashioning as a rather conservative one, but he feels that it fits the way he feels right now. The counselor suggests meeting every once in a while. During these meetings she can help him monitor his progress toward his goals and she will be able to give him some hints on how either to avoid conflicts with his parents or handle them more creatively when they do come up.

He takes the interpersonal communication skills course and joins the church group. In the course he gets an opportunity to talk about his poor communication approach to his parents. He learns how to listen to and be empathic toward them. It had never crossed his mind that listening to them was not the same as doing what they wanted all the time. From the counselor he learned techniques for avoiding the escalation of conflicts that do arise. He liked the community feelings he experienced in the church group. He felt immediately accepted by his peers there, and this did a great deal for his self-esteem. He began to develop a closer relationship with a young woman and a male peer.

As he went about implementing these programs, he would "check in" with the counselor every once in a while. She helped him ask the three evaluation questions. First of all, he noted that he was participating fully in the programs he had chosen. Second, he was getting "into community" and *felt much less isolated at school. He also noted that the conflicts with his parents were less both in number and in intensity. Third, he felt he was managing these two problem areas of his life so well that he no longer needed to see the counselor with any frequency. The fact that he was doing much better in school was a sign that he was managing quite well.*

This example of Bob is necessarily sketchy and overly sanguine; that is, it may make the helping process, which takes a great deal of work and certainly has its frustrating moments, seem too pat. The sole purpose of this example, how-ever, is to provide a picture of the model in action, give some idea of how you can use it to stay on top of what is happening in the counseling sessions, and provide direction to the entire process. Box 2–1 summarizes the three stages of the helping model, the skills helpers need to make each stage work, and the kind of cooperation expected of clients.

Final Considerations and Cautions

Sharing the Helping Model with Clients

Up to this point, much has been said about the *counselor's* knowledge and use of the model as a cognitive map to give direction to his or her interactions with the client. How much should the client know about the counseling model being used? Goldstein, Heller, and Sechrest (1966, p. 245) suggest that "giving patients prior information about the nature of psychotherapy, the theories underlying it, and the techniques to be used will facilitate progress in psycho-therapy." Counselors are often reluctant to let the client know what the process is all about. Some counselors seem to "fly by the seat of their pants," and they cannot tell the client what it's all about simply because they don't know what it's all about. Others seem to think that knowledge of helping processes is secret or sacred or dangerous and should not be communicated to the client. Clients should be told as much about the model as they can assimilate. Obviously, highly distressed clients should not be told to contain their anxiety until the counselor gives them a short course in the helping model. But generally speaking, clients should be given some kind of cognitive initiation into the model, either all at once or gradually, so they can participate in it more actively. The theory is that if they know where they are going, they will get there faster. Like helpers, clients can use the model as a cognitive map to give themselves a sense of direction. This helps to assure that helping, even though it remains a social-influence process, is still a collaborative one. I suggested in the previous chapter that you make the contract between you and your clients as explicit as possible before helping begins. Sharing the helping model with the client can be part of the contract.

Systematic Training

The skills-training model proposed in this book is, like the helping model itself, a structured, systematic approach to training. As a trainee, you will move from the simplest skills, such as attending, to the most complex, such as elaborating action programs. It is crucial that you master the simpler skills, for the more complex skills are based on them. Even if you feel that you already possess some of the skills of the model, there are still advantages to your moving systematically through the training program: (1) You can use the training program as an opportunity to take stock of what skills you already possess. (2) You will be learning not just skills but a methodology, which is both a method of training *and* a method of treatment. (3) You can use the practice sessions as an opportunity to examine some of the problem situations of your own life, especially those that might interfere with your being an effective helper.

Awkwardness

As a beginner, you can expect to experience some awkwardness as you learn and use the model and the skills and techniques it calls for. You need both practice and experience to be able to put all the elements of the model together smoothly. Three activities will help you achieve this integration.

1. *Modeling of extended counseling sessions by skilled helpers.* It helps to watch someone who can "put it all together." Live sessions, good films, and videotapes are all useful. You can read a great deal about the helping process; then you need to watch someone actually do it. Modeling gives you the opportunity to have an "ah-hah" experience in training—that is, as you watch someone competent, you say to yourself, "Oh, *that's* how it's done!"

2. *Step-by-step supervised practice.* Watching someone else do it well will give you a behavioral feeling for the model and its skills, but it will not, of itself, dissipate your feelings of awkwardness. The next step is to learn and practice each skill under some kind of supervision. A supervisor, in this instance, is someone who can tell you what you are doing right, so that you can keep doing it and celebrate your success, and what you are doing wrong, so that you can correct it. You can also give yourself feedback and get it from your fellow trainees. Once you learn basic skills, you can begin to practice mini-counseling sessions with your fellow trainees. As you

BOX 2–1   OVERVIEW OF A THREE-STAGE DEVELOPMENTAL AND
PROBLEM-MANAGEMENT HELPING MODEL

STAGE I: INITIAL PROBLEM CLARIFICATION

Helper Behavior: Attending, Listening, Probing, and Understanding. In this phase the helper attends to his or her client both physically and psychologically; works at "being with" the client; listens actively to what the client is saying; facilitates the client's self-exploration through judicious probing; responds with respect and empathy to what the client has to say; and establishes rapport (that is, a collaborative working relationship) by attending, responding, and working with the client.

Client Behavior: Exploring the Problem Situation. Because of the way in which the helper responds, the client is encouraged and helped to explore specifically and concretely the experiences, behaviors, and feelings that relate to the problem situation. In this way the problem situation begins to be clarified and defined.

STAGE II: SETTING GOALS BASED ON DYNAMIC UNDERSTANDING

Helper Behavior: Promoting New Perspectives and Facilitating Goal Setting. The helper assists the client in piecing together the data produced in the self-exploration phase; helps the client develop the kind of new perspectives needed for goal setting; and facilitates the goal-setting process.

Client Behavior: Developing New Perspectives and Setting Goals. The client begins to see the problem situation in new ways; understands the need for action; and chooses goals (that is, behavioral ways of managing problem situations more effectively).

STAGE III: ACTION—DESIGNING AND IMPLEMENTING ACTION PROGRAMS

Helper Behavior: Facilitating Program Design and Action. The helper collaborates with the client in working out a specific action program; explores with the client a variety of ways of achieving the goals that have been set; encourages the client to act; gives support and direction to action programs; and helps the client evaluate action programs.

Client Behavior: Acting, Achieving Problem-Managing Goals. The client explores the best ways of achieving goals, searches for supportive resources within self and environment, chooses action programs, implements programs, manages problem situation more effectively, copes with problems in living, and evaluates the helping process with the counselor.

become more and more self-assured, you can increase the length of these sessions with one another.

3. *Extended practice in individual skills outside the training sessions.* The skills you will be learning are the skills needed for effective living. They include interpersonal, planning, decision-making, and problem-solving skills. Perhaps a violin lesson analogy can be used here. If you were taking violin lessons, the instructor would gradually and systematically introduce the skills of playing during the lesson. There would also be some minimal time for practice during the lesson because the instructor would want to make sure you had the right idea about each technique. However, once you learned the rudiments of the skills and techniques, it would be essential that you then go off and practice a great deal in order to master what you had learned. It would be a waste of time to return for a second lesson without having practiced what you had learned in the first.

The same holds true in learning how to be a helper. In the classroom or training group, you will learn the rudiments of the model and the skills and techniques that make it operative, and you will have time for some practice. However, because the skills you will be learning are important for everyday living and relating, you will, if you so desire, have ample opportunity to practice them outside the training sessions. For instance, you can sincerely and genuinely practice active listening and accurate empathy in your daily interpersonal life—that is, you can do it unobtrusively, without making a pest of yourself as an "amateur psychologist." Most people find it rewarding to talk to someone who sincerely tries to understand them. And because planning and problem solving are part of everyday life, you will have ample opportunity to practice the other skills of the model. With enough practice, these skills can become second nature, and your feelings of awkwardness will lessen.

Open versus Closed Model

Although the developmental problem-management model presented here is an effective introduction to the helping process—both because it gives trainees a sense of direction in helping and because it lets them know clearly the skills they must develop to be effective—the model is only a tool. Trainees need to own the model, not be owned by it. Helpers must eventually call upon all available resources—their own experience, other approaches to helping, research, developing theories—to clarify, modify, refine, and expand the model. Any model is acceptable only to the degree that it produces results.

Learning from Other Approaches

The helping model presented here does not pretend to be all you've ever wanted to know about counseling; it does not exhaust the ways of helping. It does, however, set forth the basic *tasks* and *goals* of the helping process. Therefore, once you learn it, it can become a tool or framework that helps you read the literature on counseling and psychotherapy critically and organize other approaches to helping around the basic tasks and goals of each of the stages of helping presented here and to draw from these other approaches techniques to help you accomplish each of the basic tasks. Although this model presents a way of approaching any human problem, you will also want to acquire specialized information and skills to deal with specialized problems—juvenile delinquency, alcoholism, sexual deviation, psychosis, mental retardation, family problems, and so on.

Avoiding Rigidity

The beginner or even the experienced but unskilled helper can apply this model rigidly. Helping is for the client; the model exists only to aid the helping process. There are several kinds of rigidity to be avoided.

MECHANICAL USE OF THE MODEL

One rigidity is a mechanical progression through the stages of the model. As indicated earlier, counseling does not always happen as neatly as the overview of the model and the example used to illustrate it suggest. The phases of helping are not always as differentiated and sequential as I present them. Because clients do not divulge all their problems at once, it is impossible to work through Stage I completely before moving on to Stages II and III. New problems must be explored and understood whenever they are presented.

MISUNDERSTANDING THE RELATIONSHIP BETWEEN UNDERSTANDING AND ACTING

A second rigidity is the assumption that because understanding in many cases precedes action, it must always precede action. In some cases, clients will not understand their problem until they act. For instance, socially immature clients might think they have no problems in relating to others simply because they have avoided any deeper contact with people. Their world is filled with superficial interactions. However, if they are assigned homework that involves deeper contact with others or participating in a helping or human-relations training group that moves quickly beyond the superficial, they soon come face to face with their social inadequacies. Once confronted with their problem, they might be more amenable to trying to manage it through the logic of the problem-management model.

A third rigidity is to try to predetermine the amount of time to be spent in any given stage. A general rule is that the helper should move as quickly as the client's resources permit. The client should not be penalized for the helper's lack of skills in Stages II and III. Beginning helpers often dally too long in Stage I, not merely because they have a deep respect for the necessity of accurate empathic understanding, but because they either do not know how to move on or fear doing so. High-level clients may be able to move quickly to action programs. The helper should be able to move with them.

What is presented here is the *logic* of the model. The *literature* of the model—that is, the model in actual use—is not as neat and clean. The problem-solving model gives form and direction to the helping process, but it must also respond to the realities of the actual helping situation. This means that helpers will often find themselves moving back and forth in the model.

> But the process is not that simple! We know that we do not follow such a simple linear or one-way procedure—we double back and repeat ourselves many times. Indeed, we cannot truly separate the processes at times. Sometimes we seem to be doing two of the functions simultaneously—they overlay [Robertshaw, Mecca, & Rerick, 1978, p. 3].

For instance, a client might actually try out some program before adequately defining the problem situation and setting some definite goal. If the program is not successful, the counselor helps the client return to the tasks of clarifying the problem situation and setting some realistic goals. Or goal setting and program census go on simultaneously. Or a new and more realistic concern arises while goals are being set, and the process moves back to an earlier exploratory stage.

Effective helpers are like good basketball players who have learned both standard offensive plays and individual moves that tailor plays to the actual situation. They can use the model to define the helping process, but they develop techniques that enable them to individualize each of its steps.

The Problem of Being a "Stage-Specific" Specialist

Some counselors tend to specialize in the skills of a particular stage in the model. Some specialize in primary-level accurate empathy; others claim to be good at immediacy and confrontation; others want to move immediately to action programs. Helpers who so specialize are usually not very effective even in their chosen specialties because the model is organic; it fits together as a whole. Stage I exists for the action programs of Stage III, and Stage II depends on Stage I. Confrontation is poor if it is not based solidly on an accurate empathic understanding of the client's feelings, attitudes, and behavior. The most effective counselors are those who have the widest repertory of responses and who can use them in a socially intelligent way. Such a repertory enables them to respond spontaneously to a wide variety of client needs. Counseling is for the client; it is not a virtuoso performance by the helper.

Let us now take a more detailed look at each of the stages and skills of the helping process.

3

Stage I:
Problem Exploration
and Clarification

Part One:
Attending and Listening— The Bases of Effective Responding

This chapter deals with the following topics:

The importance of attending and listening in human interactions
Attending as orientation toward the client
An experiment involving attending
The microskills of attending
The helper's body as a communication vehicle
The quality of the helper's presence to the client
Active listening
Attending to nonverbal behavior
A practical framework for listening to the client's verbal messages: Experiences, behaviors, and feelings
The relationship between listening and problem clarification
Identifying and handling bias in listening
How to judge the severity of the client's problems

Introduction: The Importance of Attending and Listening in Human Interactions

At some of the more dramatic moments of life, just being with another person is extremely important. If a friend is in the hospital, sometimes just your presence there can make a difference, even if there can't be much conversation. Similarly, your being with someone who has a wife or husband or child or friend who has just died can be very comforting to that person, even if little is said. In other situations, simply listening to what a person has to say can provide support and comfort. You are not expected to respond; it is enough to show that you are listening.

Being with, attending to, and listening to another person can, in certain situations, be potent reinforcers. Similarly, being abandoned, ignored, and not listened to can have devastating effects in human relationships. Erikson (1964, p. 102; emphasis added) speaks of the effects of both inattention and negative attention on the child:

> Hardly has one learned to recognize the familiar face (the original harbor of basic trust) when he becomes also frightfully aware of the unfamiliar, the strange face, the unresponsive, the averted . . . and the frowning face. And here begins . . . that inexplicable tendency on man's part to feel that *he has caused the face to turn away* which happened to turn elsewhere.

Perhaps the averted face is too often a sign of the averted heart. Most of us are sensitive to others' attention (or inattention) to us; thus it is paradoxical how insensitive we can be at times about attending to others.

Before helpers can respond to clients and their concerns, they must pay attention and listen carefully to what they have to say. Effective helpers are, first of all, *perceptive* helpers, and most of the helping skills to be discussed in this book are based on helpers' ability to perceive both themselves and their clients clearly. Therefore, good helpers attend carefully to clients' verbal and nonverbal messages. They are also in touch with their own thoughts and feelings and how these are interacting with those of the client.

Attending and listening seem to be concepts that are so simple to grasp and so easy to do that you may wonder why I am giving them such explicit treatment here. But simple as they seem, it is amazing how often people fail to attend and listen to one another. How many times have you heard the statement "You're not even listening to what I'm saying!" directed toward someone who is caught not attending very well to another? When the person accused of not attending answers, almost predictably, "I am too; I can repeat everything you've said," this reply seems to bring little comfort to the accuser. What people look for in attending and listening is not provided by someone's ability to repeat their words. A tape recorder could do that perfectly. People want more than *physical* presence in human communication; they want the other person to be fully there; they want *psychological* or *social-emotional* presence, too.

Attending: Orienting Yourself to the Client

Helping and other deep interpersonal transactions demand a certain intensity of presence. This presence, this "being with" the client, is what is meant by *attending* in its deepest sense. Collaborative problem solving involves both establishing a working relationship with clients and helping them gather the kind of data needed to clarify and define the problem. Attending, or the way you orient yourself physically and psychologically to clients, contributes to both these goals. Your nonverbal behavior, and the many messages you communicate through it, influences clients for better or worse. For instance, it can invite or encourage them to trust you, open up, and explore the significant dimensions of their problems, or it can promote their distrust and lead to a reluctance to reveal themselves to you. Furthermore, the quality of your attending, both physical and psychological, influences the quality of your perceptiveness. If you attend poorly to clients, you will most likely miss data relevant to clarifying the problem situation. Many now consider attending to be a basic and important helping skill, and research into its meaning and use is continuing (Carkhuff & Anthony, 1979; Claiborn, 1979; Fretz, Corn, Tuemmler, & Bellet, 1979; Genther & Moughan, 1977; Gladstein, 1974; Haase & Tepper, 1972; Ivey & Authier, 1978; LaCrosse, 1975; Smith-Hanen, 1977; Tepper & Haase, 1978).

An Experiment Involving Attending

An engaging example of the impact of attending behavior is given by Ivey and Hinkle (1970; also see Ivey, 1971, pp. 93–94). At a prearranged signal, six students in a psychology seminar switched from the perhaps not too infrequent slouched posture, passive listening, and note-taking behavior of the student to an attentive posture and active eye contact with the instructor. In the nonattending condition, the teacher had been lecturing from his notes in his usual monotone, using no gestures, and paying little attention to the students. However, once the students began to attend, the teacher began to gesture, his verbal rate increased, and a lively classroom session was born.

At another prearranged signal later in the class, the students gradually stopped attending and returned to their more typical passive participation. The teacher, after some painful seeking for continued reinforcement, returned to the unengaging instructor behavior with which he had begun the seminar. In the nonattending condition, the teacher paid no attention to the students, and the students reciprocated in kind. It seems that both students and instructor got what they deserved: mutual boredom. But simple attending was able to change the whole picture.

Effective attending does two things: it lets the client know you are with him or her and therefore helps establish good rapport, and it puts you in the best position to be an effective listener. We can consider attending from three perspectives: (1) the microskills involved, (2) the helper's awareness of nonverbal communication, and (3) the values and the attitudes that underlie the quality of the helper's presence to the client.

Microskills

Consider the following five ways you can make sure you are physically present to the client. These ways of orienting yourself toward the client can be summarized in the acronym SOLER.

First, *face the client Squarely—that is, adopt a posture that indicates involvement.* In North American culture facing another person squarely is often considered a basic posture of involvement. It usually says, "I'm available to you; I choose to be with you." Turning your body away from another person while you talk to him or her can lessen your degree of contact. Even when people are seated in a circle, they usually try in some way to turn toward the individuals to whom they are speaking. By directing your body toward the other person in some way that is meaningful to you, you say "I'm with you right now." *Squarely* here may be taken literally or metaphorically. What is important is that the bodily orientation you adopt conveys the message that you are involved with the client.

Second, *adopt an Open posture.* Crossed arms and crossed legs can be signs of lessened involvement with or availability to others. An open posture can be a sign that you're open to the client and to what he or she has to say. In North American culture an open posture is generally seen as nondefensive. It can say "I'm open to you right now." Again, *open* can be taken literally or metaphorically. If your legs are crossed, this does not mean you are not involved with the client. But it is important to ask yourself to what degree your posture communicates openness and availability to the client.

Third, *remember that it is possible at times to Lean toward the other.* Watch two people who are intimately engaged in conversation. Very often they are both leaning forward as a natural sign of their involvement. The main thing is to remember that the upper part of your body is on a "hinge"; it can move toward a person and back away. In North American culture a slight inclination toward a person is often seen as saying "I'm with you, I'm interested in you and in what you have to say." Leaning back (the severest form of which is a slouch) can be a way of saying "I'm not entirely with you" or "I'm bored." Leaning too far forward or doing so too soon may frighten a client. It can be seen as a way of demanding some kind of closeness or intimacy. Effective helpers are not rigid but can move back and forth naturally according to what is happening in the dialogue. In this sense, *lean* can refer to a kind of bodily flexibility or responsiveness that enhances your communication with a client.

Fourth, *maintain good Eye contact.* In North American culture fairly steady eye contact is not unnatural for people deep in conversation. It is not the same as staring. Maintaining good eye contact with a client is another way of saying "I'm with you; I want to hear what you have to say." Obviously, this principle is not violated if you occasionally look away, but if you catch yourself looking away frequently, it may indicate some kind of reluctance to be with this person or to get involved with him or her. Or it may tell you something about your own discomfort with closeness.

Fifth, *try to be relatively Relaxed while engaged in these behaviors.* This means two things. First, you do not fidget nervously or engage in distracting facial expressions. This can make the client begin to wonder what's making you nervous. Second, you become comfortable with using your body as a vehicle of contact and expression. Once you feel natural in engaging in the behaviors listed here, you will find that they help you focus your attention on the client and "punctuate" your dialogue nonverbally.

These "rules" should be read cautiously. People differ both individually and culturally in how they show attentiveness. The main point here is that an internal "being with" a client might well lose its impact if the client does not see this internal attitude reflected in the helper's nonverbal communication. It is not uncommon for helpers in training to become overly self-conscious and awkward about their attending behavior, especially in the beginning and perhaps even more especially if they are not used to attending carefully to others. However, SOLER is not a set of absolute rules to be applied rigidly in all cases. It is rather a set of guidelines to help you orient yourself physically to the client.

Your Body as a Vehicle of Communication

What is much more important than a mechanical application of the "rules" just listed is to keep in mind that your body is *always* communicating messages to clients, whether you want it to or not and whether you are aware of it or not. Effective helpers are, first of all, mindful of what their bodies are saying at any given moment—that is, they are in touch with and capable of reading their own nonverbal behavior during the interview (a fuller discussion of nonverbal behavior appears later in this chapter). You can use your body as a kind of thermometer, reading in it your reactions to your clients. For instance, you may feel your muscles begin tensing as the client talks to you. You can then say to yourself, "I'm getting anxious here. What is causing my anxiety?" Second, once you read these messages, you can use your body to communicate the messages you see as appropriate. You can even use your body to censor messages you feel are inappropriate. If the client says something that instinctively angers you, you can control your external expression of the anger (for instance, a grimace or frown) to give yourself time to reflect. Perhaps you heard the client wrong or expressing anger toward the client would simply not be helpful at this point.

The Quality of Your Presence to Your Clients

What is most important is the quality of your presence to your clients. You are present through what you say and what you do. If you care about your clients and feel deeply committed to their welfare, it is unfair to yourself to let your nonverbal behavior suggest contradictory messages. On the other hand, if you feel indifferent to them and your nonverbal behavior suggests commitment, then you are not being genuine. Effective helpers stay in touch with how they are present to clients without becoming preoccupied with it. They ask themselves such questions as

- On what values do I base my relationships to my clients?
- What are my attitudes toward this particular client?
- Am I experiencing some kind of conflict in terms of my values or attitudes right now?
- How would I rate the quality of my presence to this client (this group) right now?
- How are my values and attitudes being expressed in my nonverbal behavior?
- How are my values and attitudes being expressed in my verbal behavior?
- How might I be more effectively present to this person (this group)?

Thus far, attending has been considered insofar as it is a relationship-enhancement skill (Goldstein, 1980)—that is, insofar as it is related to and affects rapport between you and your clients. But attending also includes *observing*; so it is related to gathering or helping clients gather the kind of data needed to explore and define problem situations.

Active Listening

As suggested earlier, the counseling relationship is not a goal in itself. What is needed is a *working* relationship, one that enables you and the client to achieve the goals of each step of the helping process. Good attending enables the helper to listen carefully to what clients are saying with their words and expressing through their nonverbal behavior. All this provides both you and the client with data you can use to clarify problem situations.

Total or complete listening involves two things: first, observing and interpreting the client's nonverbal behavior—posture, facial expressions, movement, tone of voice, and the like—and, second, listening to and interpreting the client's verbal messages.

Listening to Nonverbal Behavior

We are only beginning to realize the importance of nonverbal behavior and to make a scientific study of it. The face and body are extremely communicative. We know from experience that even when people are silent with one another, the atmosphere can be filled with messages. Knapp (1978) defines nonverbal behavior as all human communication events that transcend spoken or written words.

The facial expressions, bodily motions, voice quality, and autonomic physiological responses of a client can be extremely communicative. Sometimes the nonverbal messages they provide are more important than the verbal ones. Mehrabian (1971, p. 43) reports on research he and his associates did in the area of nonverbal behavioral and inconsistent messages. The research reported here deals with the way one person expresses his or her liking for another.

One interesting question now arises: Is there a systematic and coherent approach to resolving the general meaning or impact of an inconsistent message? Indeed there is. Our experimental results show:

Total liking equals 7% verbal liking plus 38% vocal liking
plus 55% facial liking

Thus the impact of facial expression is greatest, then the impact of the tone of voice (or vocal expression), and finally that of the words. If the facial expression is inconsistent with the words, the degree of liking conveyed by the facial expression will dominate and determine the impact of the total message.

If you say to a client, "It's hard talking about yourself, isn't it?" and she says "No, I don't mind at all" hesitatingly, while looking away and grimacing a bit, the real answer is probably in her nonverbal behavior.

In Mehrabian's research perhaps the exact percentages are not important, but the clarification of the role of nonverbal behavior in the total communication process is. Effective helpers learn how to listen and "read" (1) such bodily behavior as posture, body movements, and gestures; (2) such facial expressions as smiles, frowns, raised eyebrows, twisted lips, and the like; (3) such voice-related behavior as tone, pitch, level, intensity, inflection, spacing of words, emphases, pauses, silences, and fluency; (4) such observable autonomic physiological responses as quickened breathing, the development of a temporary rash, blushing, paleness, and pupil dilation; (5) such physical characteristics as physique, height, weight, and complexion; and (6) general appearance (grooming, dress, and so forth).

If you notice that a client has developed a temporary rash or reddening of the neck while talking to you, this probably means that he or she feels under some kind of pressure. Taking account of such cues is most important. A person's nonverbal behavior has a way of "leaking" messages to others (Ekman & Friesen, 1969). At times, clients' nonverbal behavior may give more accurate cues to what they are thinking and feeling than what they actually say. "Nonverbal behaviors are generally more spontaneous than verbal behaviors. Words can be selected and monitored before being emitted. . . . Nonverbal behaviors, on the other hand, are not as easily subject to control" (Passons, 1975, p. 102). In this sense, clients' nonverbal expressions can provide access to their inner life.

Besides being a channel of communication in itself, nonverbal behavior in terms of facial expressions, bodily motions, voice quality, and autonomic physiological responses can punctuate verbal messages in much the same way that periods, question marks, exclamation points, and underlinings punctuate written language. Nonverbal behavior can punctuate or modify interpersonal communication in at least four ways (see Knapp, 1978).

1. CONFIRMING OR REPEATING

Nonverbal behavior can *confirm* or *repeat* what is being said verbally. For instance, if you respond to a client with some attempt to understand her and her eyes light up (facial expression) and she leans forward a bit (bodily motion) and says animatedly (voice quality), "Yes, I think you hit it right on the head!" then her nonverbal behavior confirms her verbal message to you.

2. DENYING OR CONFUSING

Nonverbal behavior can *deny* or *confuse* what is being said verbally. If a client tells you he is not upset by the way you have just challenged him and yet he blushes (autonomic physiological response), his voice falters a bit (voice quality), and his upper lip quivers (facial expression) as he says this to you, his nonverbal message seems to deny what he is saying verbally. Or if one member of a counseling group tells another that she is quite angry with him but smiles while doing so, her nonverbal behavior contradicts her verbal message, and this can confuse the person to whom she is talking. Her smile might mean "I'm angry with you, but I don't want to hurt or alienate you" or it might mean "I'm angry, but I'm very uncomfortable trying to tell you about it."

3. STRENGTHENING OR EMPHASIZING

Nonverbal behavior can *strengthen* or *emphasize* what is being said. If a counselor suggests that a client discuss a certain issue with his wife (who is not present) and he responds by saying, "Oh God, I don't think I could do that!" while slouching down and putting his face in his hands, his nonverbal behavior underscores his verbal message. Nonverbal behavior does much to add emotional color or intensity to verbal messages. If a client tells you that she doesn't like to be confronted without first being understood and then stares at you fixedly and silently with a frown on her face, her nonverbal behaviors tell you something about the intensity of her emotion. If she then proceeds to stalk out of the room, her nonverbal behavior further underscores the intensity of her anger and hurt.

4. CONTROLLING OR REGULATING

Nonverbal cues are often used in conversation to *regulate* or *control* what is happening. If, in group counseling, one participant looks at another and gives every indication that she is going to speak to this other person, she may hesitate or change her mind if the person she intends to talk to looks away or frowns. Skilled helpers are aware of how clients send controlling or regulating nonverbal cues.

Interpreting Nonverbal Behavior

There is no simple program available for learning how to read and interpret nonverbal behavior. Once you develop a working knowledge of nonverbal behavior and its possible meanings, you must learn through practice and experience to be sensitive to it and read its meaning in any given situation (Cormier & Cormier, 1979, Chap. 3; Gazda, 1973, p. 89; Gladstein, 1974; Knapp, 1978; Mehrabian, 1971; Passons, 1975; Stone & Morden, 1976; Sue & Sue, 1977). Nonverbal behaviors are usually open to a number of interpretations. How, then, do you know what they mean? The key is *context*. Effective helpers listen to the entire context of the helping interview and do not become fixated on details of behavior. Effective helpers are aware of and use the nonverbal communication system, but they are not seduced or overwhelmed by it. This leads to a general caution that relates to a microskills approach to counseling.

The helping process is presented in these chapters in bits and pieces. Sometimes novice helpers will fasten selectively on this bit or that piece. For example, they will become intrigued with nonverbal behavior and make too much of a half-smile or a frown on a client's face. They will seize the smile or the frown and lose the person. Their failure to keep nonverbal behavior in context distorts their reading of the client and the client's problem situation. Skilled helpers, through practice and experience, learn to integrate all the pieces of the helping process. They do not become victims of their own microskills.

Listening to Verbal Messages

What follows is a simple framework for listening to, organizing, and understanding clients' verbal messages. Clients talk about the following:

- *Experiences* (what happens *to* them). If a client tells you that she was fired from her job, she is talking about her problem situation in terms of an experience.
- *Behaviors* (what they do or fail to do). If a client tells you he has sex with underage boys, he is talking about his problem situation in terms of his behavior.
- *Affect* (the feelings and emotions that arise from or are associated with either experiences or behavior). If the client tells you that he blows up whenever he and his wife get into a discussion about finances, he is talking about the affect associated with his problem situation.

Let's consider an example. A client says to a counselor in the personnel services department of a large company: "I had one of the lousiest days of my life yesterday." The counselor knows that something went wrong and that the client feels bad about it, but she knows relatively little about the specific experiences, behaviors, and feelings that made the day a horror for the client. However, let us say the client continues, "Toward the end of the day my boss yelled at me for not getting my work done [an experience]. I lost my temper [emotion] and yelled right back at him [behavior]. He blew up [emotion] and fired me [an experience]. And now I feel awful [emotion] and am trying to find out if he had the authority to do that [behavior]." Now the problem situation is much clearer because it is spelled out in terms of specific experiences, behaviors, and feelings related to specific situations. This is precisely what is meant by problem clarification. A problem situation is clear if it is seen and understood in terms of specific experiences, specific behaviors, and specific feelings and emotions. Let's take a closer look at each of these three categories.

THE CLIENT'S EXPERIENCES

Most clients spend a fair amount of time talking about what happens *to* them.

- "I get headaches a lot."
- "My ulcers act up when family members argue."

They often talk about what other people do or fail to do, especially when this affects them adversely.

- "She doesn't do anything all day. The house is always a mess when I come home from work."
- "She tells her little jokes, and I'm always the butt of them."

Clients often see themselves, whether rightly or wrongly, as victims of forces not in their control. If these forces are described as being *outside* them, they can be called *external* or *overt* experiences.

- "He treats me like dirt."
- "Company policy discriminates against women."
- "The way the economy is right now, I just can't get a job."
- "There's an unwritten rule here that an innovative teacher is considered suspect."

Or these forces may be described as coming from *within*.

- "These feelings of depression come from nowhere and seem to suffocate me."
- "No matter what I do, I always feel hungry."
- "I just can't stop thinking of her."
- "It's the way I was educated. I was always taught to think of blacks as inferior and now I'm just saddled with those feelings."

Perhaps one of the reasons some clients are clients is that they see themselves as victims. Other people, the immediate social settings of life, society in its larger organizations and institutions, or cultural prescriptions affect them adversely.

They feel they are no longer in control of their lives. Therefore, they talk extensively about these experiences. This kind of talk can include statements about the forces by which they feel victimized.

- "He treats me like dirt. But that's the way it is. He just doesn't care about people and their feelings at all. He needs to be taught a lesson."
- "I just can't get a job. The way the politicians are running the economy they should all be locked up. They talk about the common people in public, but in the back rooms they are all dealing with big business."
- "I can't control my appetite. I've heard that some people are just like that. They have a different sort of metabolism. I must be one of those."
- "I keep hearing voices. They tell me to harm myself. I think they're coming from the devil."

In Stage I, it is critical to understand clients' experiences from their frame of reference because helping best starts from there. This kind of understanding is impossible unless you first listen in as unbiased a way as possible to these experiences.

THE CLIENT'S BEHAVIORS

Some clients talk freely about their experiences but are much less willing to talk about their behaviors—that is, what they do and don't do. The reason for this is rather simple. Although they may not feel accountable for their experiences, what happens *to* them, they realize at some level of their being that they are in some way responsible for their behaviors, or at least the possibility for accountability is much higher when it comes to behavior.

- "When he ignores me, I go off by myself and cry."
- "I haven't even begun to look for a job. I know there are none in this city."
- "When I feel the depression coming on, I take some of the pills the doctor gave me."
- "When I get bored with my studies, I close the books and go and lift a few beers with my friends."

Behaviors, too, can be overt (external) or covert (internal). Overt behavior can be witnessed by others.

- "When he called me a name, I punched him."
- "I haven't told my husband that they found cancer."
- "I find release by going to pornography stores."

Covert behavior refers to the inner life of the person. It cannot be seen directly by others.

- "When he called me a name, I began thinking of the ways I could get back at him. And I told myself that I would."
- "I like to daydream about having a child."
- "I never let myself think bad of another person."

Covert behaviors include thoughts, fantasies, daydreams, attitudes, imagining, decisions, memories, plans, and the like over which people feel they have some control.

- "When she left me, I decided that I would not let myself keep thinking about her."
- "When I'm on business trips, I think about my family a lot."
- "I have every intention of getting a job this month."

If a person feels that he or she has little or no control over what is going on inside, my tendency is to see this as covert *experience* rather than covert behavior.

- "I try to get into my work, but I just can't stop thinking of her and how she played me for a fool."
- "Sexual fantasies seem to keep popping up all the time. I just don't seem to have any control."
- "I know I get depressed and cry when I think of John on his death bed, but I can't help thinking of him."

Part of the counseling process can be to help clients see that they often have more control over their experiences, especially their internal or covert experiences, than they first think.

THE CLIENT'S AFFECT

This means listening to the feelings and emotions that proceed from, accompany, underlie, give color to, or lead to a client's experiences and behaviors.

- "I finished the term paper that I've been putting off for weeks and I feel great!"
- "I've been feeling sorry for myself ever since he left me."
- "I yelled at my mother last night and now I feel pretty ashamed of myself."
- "I've been anxious for the past few weeks, but I don't know why. I wake up feeling scared and then it goes away but comes back again during the day several times."

It is possible to see feelings and emotions, too, as either overt or covert. They are overt if the client both experiences and expresses them.

- "I know I'm dying and I'm very angry and depressed."
- "I told him I'd kill him if I found him messing around with her again."
- "I just feel so listless since I lost my job."

Feelings are covert if the client actually experiences them but does *not* allow them to be expressed.

- "I get angry when she implies that I do little work around the house, but I keep it to myself. It helps keep the peace."
- "When he compliments me, it makes me feel good, but I don't give him the satisfaction of knowing."

Some clients imply that their emotions have a kind of life of their own and that they can do little or nothing to control them. This includes describing others as the causes of their emotions.

- "Whenever I see him with her, I feel hurt."
- "She can get my goat whenever she wants. She's always making me angry."
- "You make me so mad!"
- "The way the economy is going makes me depressed."
- "I can't help crying when I think of what they did to her."

As we shall see later on, people can control their emotions more than they think. Part of the helping process consists of showing people how to get from under the burden of disabling feelings and emotions. This framework for listening to clients is summarized in Box 3–1.

Listening as the First Step toward Problem Clarification

Recall that the goal of Stage I is not attending or listening or even relationship building. All these are important, but they can be meaningless if they do not contribute to helping the client explore and clarify his or her problems in living. But precisely when is a problem situation clear? What constitutes the kind of clarity that helps a client move on to determining what he or she wants to do in order to manage a problem situation more effectively? In view of the model just presented, it can be said that a problem is clear if it is spelled out in terms of specific and relevant experiences, behaviors, and feelings that relate to specific situations. Problem situations are more likely to be managed if they are clearly defined. If they are spelled out very clearly and concretely, then hints of ways to manage the problem begin to emerge more readily. Here is an example.

Client A: My problem is that I'm shy. It bothers me a lot.

Client B: I'm shy. For instance, I don't go to parties and I don't raise my hand in class because I'm afraid that people won't like me or that I'll appear

---

BOX 3–1   FRAMEWORK FOR LISTENING TO CLIENTS

When clients talk about themselves, they do so in terms of *experiences* (the things that happen to them), *behaviors* (what they do or fail to do), and *affect* (the feelings and emotions that accompany and relate to experiences and behaviors).

Experiences: The things that happen to clients.

    Overt: Experiences others can see.

    Examples: "He keeps telling other people that I'm dishonest."

             "I've been fired three times in the last five years."

    Covert: Experiences that take place "inside" the client and are not capable of being seen.

    Examples: "I have high blood pressure and I get headaches a lot."

             "I often hear voices when I'm alone."

Behaviors: The things clients do or refrain from doing.

    Overt: Behaviors others can see.

    Examples: "I beat my child when I get angry with her."

             "When she says I'm not a man, I don't say anything."

    Covert: Behaviors "inside" the client that he or she directs in some way.

    Examples: "Inside my head I rehearse everything I say to him."

             "Every day I think about taking revenge on her."

Affect: The feelings and emotions that precede, accompany, underlie, and give color and intensity to experiences and behaviors.

    Overt: Feelings and emotions the client expresses.

    Examples: "I laugh out loud when he says he loves me."

             "I get depressed when she doesn't call me."

    Covert: Feelings and emotions clients experience but try to keep to themselves.

    Examples: "When he shows off, I fume inside."

             "She hurts me a lot, but I don't let on."

A problem situation is clear when it is spelled out in terms of the client's specific experiences, behaviors, and feelings, whether overt or covert, relevant to the problem situation.

stupid. I don't think I'm unattractive or stupid, but I *feel* that way a lot of the time. When people ask me to do things with them, I make excuses. When I do go and do things with them, for instance, like going to a party or just going out for a few beers, I feel uncomfortable, wondering what others are thinking about me. I get angry with myself for acting in such a stupid way, but I do very little to change it.

Client A describes her problem in terms of a general trait that conveys very little useful information; Client B describes his problems in terms of specific experiences, behaviors, and feelings related to specific situations, for which skilled helpers listen. When clients, for one reason or another, do not come up with them on their own, helpers can encourage them to do so. The kinds of response skills needed to do so are described in the next chapter.

Bias in Listening

FILTERS

Cultural Filters. It is probably impossible to listen to another person in a completely unbiased way. As anthropologist Edwin Hall (1977, p. 85) points out, we all listen to the world around us and the people we meet through cultural "filters" of one kind or another: "One of the functions of culture is to provide a highly selective screen between man and the outside world. In its many forms, culture therefore designates what we pay attention to and what we ignore. This screening provides structure for the world."

As Hall indicates, this process has a positive function: we need filters to provide structure for ourselves as we interact with the world around us. But cultural filters also introduce various kinds of bias into our listening. The stronger the cultural filters, the greater the likelihood of bias. For instance, a white, middle-class helper probably tends to use white, middle-class filters in listening to others. Perhaps this makes little difference if the client is also white and middle class, but if the helper is listening to a well-to-do Asian who has high social status in his or her community, to a black person from an urban ghetto, or to a poor white from a rural area, then the helper's cultural filters might introduce kinds of bias that would impede his or her ability to listen and understand.

Models as Filters. Another possible source of bias is your education and training, for these also provide you with models and frameworks that serve as filters in listening to others. For instance, if you are being trained as a counselor or clinical psychologist, you have likely taken or will take at least one course in psychopathology or abnormal human behavior. Models or frameworks for understanding deviant behavior are presented to you. These models or frame-works add to the filters through which you listen to others, especially to clients. Unless you are careful, psychopathology filters can play too strong a role in your listening—that is, you can begin to interpret too much of what you hear as abnormal human behavior. What you have learned may help you to organize what you hear, but it may also distort your listening.

Counteracting the Influence of Filters. One way to counteract this kind of bias is to become aware of the kinds of filters you have acquired from your culture and your education and training. For instance, if you know that you have too great a tendency to "read" psychopathology in what clients say and do, then you can take measures to counteract it. For me, one of the best ways of doing this is to develop more positive "broad band" models of human behavior that help me listen more fully. For instance, being able to listen to what clients have to say through the filters of a *developmental* model—one that deals with the normative stages, tasks, and crises of the entire life span—can help counter bias introduced by listening through abnormal-behavior models.

> *John, a 41-year-old man, comes to a counselor complaining of a variety of ills. He is having trouble with his marriage; his teenage children seem to be more and more alienated from him; he is bored at work; he is depressed from time to time; and he has begun to steal things, just small things like candy bars and toothpaste, not because he does not have the money, but for the "kick" he gets from it.*

The helper using almost exclusively a psychopathology model to listen to John might well interpret what he is saying more negatively than a helper who is using primarily a developmental model or a combination of a developmental and a psychopathological model. The latter sees a middle-class person in a midlife crisis and listens to and interprets his behavior from that point of view. This helper might well see the client as a person who is not handling this crisis as well as he might, but he or she sees the crisis as predominantly developmental. I am not suggesting that models of psychopathology are useless. I do suggest that narrow-band models for listening to and interpreting human behavior need to be complemented or placed in context by broad-band models.

Egan and Cowan (1979) have developed a broad-band "people-in-systems" model to help counselors do a number of things, including listen to their clients in focused ways with a minimum of bias. The model also urges helpers to become aware of the kinds of bias that affect their interactions with clients. The model deals with three areas: *developmental* stages, tasks, and crises across the life span; the levels of *social systems or settings* in which people live out their lives and in the context of which developmental events take place; and the kinds of *life skills* that people need to pursue the developmental tasks of life and involve themselves in, contribute to, and cope with the various social systems of life. It is not the purpose of this book to spell out in any detail either this or other broad-band models (see Heath, 1980a, 1980b) but rather to sensitize the reader to their existence.

SELF-PREOCCUPATION

Cultural and other kinds of filters are not the only source of bias in listening. Helpers can become preoccupied with themselves and their own needs in such ways that they are kept from listening clearly to their clients. Consider the following possibilities:

- *Attraction.* You find a client either attractive or unattractive. You pay more attention to what you are feeling than to what the client is saying.
- *Physical condition.* You may be tired or sick. Without realizing it, you tune out some of the things the client is saying.
- *Concerns.* You may be preoccupied with your own concerns. For instance, you keep thinking about the argument you've just had with your spouse.
- *Overeagerness.* You may be so eager to respond that you listen to only a part of what the client has to say. You become preoccupied with your responses rather than with the client's revelations.
- *Similarity of problems.* The problems the client is dealing with are similar to your own. As the client talks, your mind wanders to the ways in which what is being said applies to you and your situation.
- *Prejudice.* You may harbor some kind of prejudice toward the client. You pigeonhole him or her because of race, sexual orientation, nationality, social status, religious persuasion, political preferences, lifestyle, or some other characteristic.
- *Differences.* The client and his or her experience are very different from you and your experience. The lack of commonalities is distracting.

You can probably think of other ways in which you might be distracted from full listening.

Becoming Productively Self-Conscious in the Helping Process

To be an effective helper, you need to listen not only to the client but also to yourself when you are with a client. This helps you identify what is standing in the way of your being with and listening to the client. It is a positive form of self-consciousness—that is, a kind of self-awareness that contributes to the quality of your being with the client. For instance, I remember once coming into a room and sitting down with two other instructors who were about to give an oral examination to a student. I didn't think that the student's chances were good. A few moments into the exam I began "reading" my body. The muscles in my neck, shoulders, and back were tight and I was clutching the bottom of my chair with my hands. I was nonverbally communicating my misgivings about his ability to pass to myself and perhaps to both my fellow examiners and the student. This, I thought, was unfair. And so I systematically relaxed and used the microskills described previously to be as effectively present to him as I could. I first "read" my body and realized the strength of my misgivings, and then I tried to use my body to communicate a more positive attitude. (By the way, he passed.)

Another example occurred when a friend of mine who had been in and out of mental hospitals for a few years and whom I had not seen for over six months showed up unannounced one evening at my apartment. He was in a highly excited state. A torrent of ideas, some outlandish, some brilliant, flowed nonstop from him. I sincerely wanted to be with him as best I could. I started by more or less naturally following the "rules" of attending just outlined, but I kept catching myself with my arms and legs crossed, at the other end of the couch on which we both were sitting. I think that I was, almost literally, defending myself from this torrent of ideas. Then I would untwist my arms and legs, only to find them crossed again ten minutes later. It was hard work being with him. I had to admit this to myself and work with it.

Skilled helpers ask themselves from time to time during helping sessions whether there is anything affecting their ability to be with and listen to their clients. They listen to their own verbal and nonverbal behavior for hints of bias, self-preoccupation, and distraction. Once they discover the ways they are being distracted, they do what is necessary to be with and listen to the clients more fully.

> *Tracy was a new counselor at the high school. He was from a white middle-class background. He found himself somewhat disoriented the first time he counseled a black student. After the first session, he spent some time with Art, a black counselor, who helped him identify what was preventing him from being with and listening to the black student. What he discovered is that he was afraid. He was afraid that his own background would keep him from doing a good job. He was also afraid that the black student might resent seeing a white. Once he worked through his fears, he was in a much better position to be with and listen to black students.*

Skilled helpers monitor the quality of their attending and listening. They also realize that probably no one can listen to another in a completely unbiased and undistracted way.

Judging Problem Severity

Skilled helpers listen to clients in such a way as to be able to make some judgment as to how severe the client's problem situation is. Clients come to helpers with problems of every degree of severity, from the objectively inconsequential to the life threatening. But a client can experience even a relatively inconsequential problem as severe. If a client thinks a problem is critical, even though by objective standards it does not seem to be that bad, then for him or her, it is critical. In this case, the client's tendency to "catastrophize," to judge a problem situation to be more severe than it actually is, becomes itself an important part of the problem situation. Then one of the counselor's tasks will be to help the client put the problem in perspective or to teach him or her how to distinguish between degrees of problem severity.

Mehrabian and Reed (1969, p. 328) suggest that the severity of any given problem can be determined by the following formula:

$$\text{Severity} = \text{Distress} \times \text{Uncontrollability} \times \text{Frequency}$$

The $\times$ in the formula indicates that these factors are not just additive. For instance, even low-level anxiety, if it is uncontrollable and/or persistent, can constitute a serious problem—that is, it can severely interfere with the quality of a client's life.

Let's consider an example in which two people react quite differently to the same external situation.

> *Andy and Joan, who work in the same office, are both dissatisfied with their jobs because the work they do is not rewarding in itself, there is little opportunity for social contact with fellow workers, they have a couple of supervisors who are authoritarian and self-centered, and, even though there is some opportunity for advancement, office politics plays a central role in promotions. These two workers experience the problem situation differently, however. The culture from which Andy comes has taught him that a great deal of his identity depends on the kind and quality of work he does. Work for him is a primary value, and to be locked into an unrewarding job with supervisory personnel who see him as just another worker is demeaning. Joan, on the other hand, looks upon work as a necessary evil. She is willing to put up with forty hours of relatively*

meaningless drudgery as long as she gets enough satisfaction from the rest of the hours of the week. She does her work conscientiously enough, but she is not interested in investing time and effort in improving her work situation. Whenever a supervisor gives her negative feedback, she listens to it for what it is worth and then is no longer bothered by it. When Andy gets even mildly negative feedback from a supervisor, he fumes about it for days.

These two people can be compared on the three dimensions of Mehrabian and Reed's formula.

- *Distress*. Andy finds a great deal of distress in his work situation; he experiences a great deal of anxiety. Joan, even though she does not particularly like her work, experiences relatively little distress on the job.
- *Uncontrollability*. Joan finds a great deal of fulfillment in her social life. This is more important to her than work. Because this is the case, she finds that she can control her adverse emotional reactions at work quite easily. On the other hand, almost any kind of problem at work sets Andy on edge.
- *Frequency*. Extremely distressing days at work are relatively infrequent for Joan. For Andy, the opposite is true. In fact, the number of distressful days has come to outnumber the ones of relative calm.

Stress and Distress

When Joan is at work, she experiences what might be called the ordinary stress of everyday life. She can cope quite well with it. As Selye (1974, 1976) notes, the goal is not to rid life of all stress, for a life without any stress would be insipid. However, when increasing amounts of stress turn into *distress*, then trouble is brewing. High levels of stress can begin literally to tear the body apart. For Andy, it is not work that causes stress, but rather his dissatisfaction with his work. His continual intense feelings of frustration and failure add up to a high degree of problem severity.

Reducing Stress and Frequency while Increasing Control

One way of viewing helping is to see it as a process in which clients are helped to control the severity of their problems in living. The severity of any given problem situation will be reduced if the stress can be reduced, if the frequency of the problem situation can be lessened, or if the client's control over the problem situation can be increased. Let us consider an example.

Indira is greatly distressed because she experiences migrainelike headaches sometimes two or three times a week and seems to be able to do little about them. No pain killers seem to work. She has even been tempted to try strong narcotics to control the pain, but she fears she might become an addict. She feels trapped. For her the problem is severe because stress, uncontrollability, and frequency are all high.

She is finally referred to a doctor who specializes in treating headaches. He is an expert in both medicine and human behavior. He helps her see that the headaches are getting worse because of her tendency to "catastrophize" whenever she experiences one. That is, the self-talk she engages in ("God, what a victim I am") and the way she fights the headache simply add to its severity. He helps her control her self-talk and teaches her relaxation techniques.

Neither of these gets rid of the headaches, but they help reduce the stress she feels when she has them. Second, he helps her identify the situations in which the headaches seem to develop. They tend to come at times when she is not managing other forms of stress well—for instance, when she lets herself become overloaded and get behind at work. He helps her see that, although her headaches constitute a very real problem, they are part of a still larger problem situation. Once she begins to control and reduce other forms of stress in her life, the frequency of the headaches begins to lessen. Third, the doctor also helps her spot cues that a headache is beginning to develop. She finds that, although she can do little to control the headache once it is in full swing, there are things she can do during the incipient stage. For instance, she learns that medicine that has no effect when the headache is in full force does help if it is taken soon enough. Relaxation techniques are also helpful if they are used soon enough. Indira's headaches do not disappear completely, but they are no longer the central reality of her life.

The doctor helps the client manage a very severe problem situation much better than she has been doing by helping her reduce stress and frequency while increasing control.

A Behavioral-Analysis Model for Concreteness and Clarity

If a client is involved in a problem situation, this usually means that he or she engages in one or more problematic behaviors. A *problematic behavior* (1) pre-vents an individual from attaining some goal (for instance, having a close relatioship with a person of the other sex), (2) causes the individual significant personal pain or discomfort (for instance, Tess is making it through school but she is always extremely harried and anxious), and/or (3) results in undesirable consequences for others (for instance, Jamie's failure to control his temper causes suffering for his wife and children; Wayne's uncontrolled sexual appetites and penchant for violence make him a menace to women).

Problematic behaviors can involve behavioral excesses or behavioral deficits. The following are examples of excesses:

- Yancy has a good sense of humor; but sometimes he does not know when enough is enough, and he ends up annoying his friends rather than entertaining them.
- Wendy used to let people walk all over her. She always gave in to what others wanted. Now she has gone to the opposite extreme. She is not assertive but aggressive. For instance, she demands that everything at the office be done her way.

An example of a deficit is Sydney, who avoids conflict whenever possible. This means that both at work and at home some of his legitimate needs are not met. For instance, at work he gets more than his share of overtime. Avoiding conflict causes him to settle deeper and deeper into the psychopathology of the average.

Problematic behavior, whether involving self or others, excesses or deficits, can be explored through the A-B-C model. This model is based on the principles of behavior reviewed briefly in Chapter 1. It deals with the antecedents (A) and the consequences (C) of behavior (B). The behavioral sequence is

Antecedents   Behavior-in-a-Situation   Consequences

Let us say that the behavior in question is eating. Alex feels a slight twinge of hunger before going to bed, opens the refrigerator door, and sees the tempting food inside (A). He takes out the makings of a rather large sandwich; assembles it; and eats it (B). He feels immediately rewarded by the enjoyment of eating; but the next day he steps on the scale, notices that he is getting heavier, and feels bad (C).

Alex's 6-year-old son, Toby, sees his father light up and enjoy a cigarette (A). The next day he sees a pack of cigarettes lying on the kitchen table, takes one out, and puts it in his mouth in imitation of his father (B). His mother comes into the kitchen and slaps the cigarette out of his mouth (C).

Both self-enhancing and self-defeating behavior patterns are governed by the principles of behavior. Antecedents include all relevant factors that precede the behavior. Consequences deal with the reinforcement, punishment, or lack of either reward or punishment that follows the behavior. Consequences contribute to the control of behavior through rewards and punishments; antecedents contribute to the control of behavior by acting as stimuli or cues. For instance, opening the refrigerator door and looking at the food (A) cues or signals that eating (B) will lead to an immediate reward (C). Antecedents can signal that a reward or a punishment or neither is likely to follow a possible behavior. Antecedents include the history of the individual insofar as it is present and signaling some possible reward or punishment. For instance, Bridget, who is thinking of having a physical examination, remembers the pain she experienced during the last one. Her present memory of a past event signals the possibility of punishment and she decides to put the examination off. All the present internal dispositions of the individual and the influences of the individual's environment can serve as cues. For example, Brad witnesses the "bad trips" of two of his friends who experiment with hallucinogens. When offered some LSD, he declines because it signals possible punishment.

One way of helping clients explore concretely the behavior involved in a problem situation is to have them examine it in terms of its antecedents and consequences. If a client is engaging in some self-defeating or self-destructive behavior pattern (for instance, alienating others by sarcasm and rude and inconsiderate behavior; overeating and gaining weight even after a heart attack), the following questions can be asked:

- What concretely is the behavior? What exactly does the client do or fail to do that is self-defeating?
- What antecedents within the individual and in the environment cue or stimulate the behavior?
- What consequences reinforce the behavior? Even though the behavior in question seems to be self-defeating in some way, it must in some other way be rewarding. What is the payoff?
- If it is a question of a client's avoiding behavior that seems to be in his or her best interest, is there a lack of reward or a threat of punishment associated with the seemingly desirable behavior?

There are a number of advantages to using this kind of "behavioral diagnosis" (Tryon, 1976) to clarify behaviors involved in problem situations.

First, it is useful for all problems. According to Tryon (1976, p. 495), it can be used not only with "simple unidimensional problems that are thoroughly described from information obtained from the client in an interview setting" but also with problems that are "multidimensional, seemingly vague, and not well articulated by the client." It is a way of articulating such problems.

Second, it is helpful in controlling antecedents. Once the antecedents of self-defeating patterns of behavior are identified and clarified, there is the possibility that they can be changed. This is called *cue control* or *stimulus control*. For instance, one of the reasons Alex overeats is that he keeps the refrigerator full of appetizing food. Stimulus control could begin in the supermarket. He could buy smaller amounts of food and buy less fattening and even less appealing food. This kind of stimulus control is easier than struggling with "will power" in the face of a refrigerator overloaded with high-calorie and tasty food. In the case of Toby, his son, better modeling could be offered him. His parents could refrain from engaging in undesirable behaviors in front of him.

Third, the model helps clients control consequences. Once the consequences of a self-defeating behavior pattern are identified, there is the possibility that they, too, can be changed. For instance, once a wife discovers that her husband actually enjoys the game of "uproar" they get into when they are discussing finances, she can refuse to play the game. Once the reward disappears, the behavior sustained by it will also likely disappear.

Fourth, it is possible to teach clients to analyze their own behavior in terms of its antecedents and consequences and show them how to minimize antecedents that cue self-defeating behavior, maximize antecedents that cue self-enhancing behavior, minimize reinforcement for self-defeating behavior, and maximize reinforcement for self-enhancing behavior.

A couple of cautions are in order. The A-B-C model can be misused in at least two ways. First, it can be used too globally and superficially. A cursory analysis of a complicated problem situation in terms of some antecedents and consequences could well be a useless exercise. If helpers are to use this model, they need an adequate working knowledge of the principles involved (see Malott, Tillema, & Glenn, 1978, Chap. 1–8) and should be able to train clients in the rudiments of their use. Second, this model can be overused. It is possible to spend an excessive amount of time in examining behavioral patterns so thoroughly that the client is lost. If you develop a good working knowledge of the principles of behavior and keep in mind the overall goals of helping and the valued accomplishments of each step, then the A-B-C model can help you and your clients define problems not only clearly and concretely but also in a way that suggests goals and courses of action for handling them.

In this chapter I have considered the ways in which you attend and listen to clients and some of the ways in which you can help them clarify problem situations. In the next chapter I discuss the skills of responding to clients in such a way as to foster a good working relationship and clarify with them problem situations.

Chapter

4

Stage I:
Problem Exploration
and Clarification

Part Two:
Helper Response
and Client Self-Exploration

This chapter deals with the following topics:

The goal of Stage I: Clarification of the problem situation
The three dimensions of helping skills
Accurate empathy in general
Primary-level accurate empathy
The difference between primary-level accurate empathy and advanced empathy
The three elements of the skill of empathy
Hints for improving the quality of empathy
Problems in communicating empathy
The use of probes in problem clarification and definition
Writing approaches to problem clarification
Cautions in the use of probes
The content of the client's self-disclosure
Common problems in Stage I
Whether Stage I is sufficient for some clients

The Primary Goal of Stage I

John Dewey once said that a question well asked is half answered. It can also be said that a problem situation well explored, defined, and clarified is well on its way to being managed. Therefore, the primary work of Stage I is to help the client explore, define, and clarify the problem situation. A problem is clear if it is spelled out in terms of the client's specific experiences, behaviors, and feelings as they relate to specific parts of the problem situation. This is not a question of clarity for the sake of clarity. Rather, the clearer and better defined a problem situation becomes, the clearer it is what needs to be done to manage it more effectively. This model, as we have seen, is developmental. The clarity looked for in Stage I prepares the way for goal setting, which is the primary aim of Stage II.

Attending and listening are preparatory skills. They enable counselors to begin to establish a genuine and respectful working relationship with the client. They also enable counselors to respond effectively to what clients are saying about themselves. *Effectively* here means responding in such a way as to facilitate the client's concrete and specific exploration of the problem situation.

Three Dimensions of Helping Skills

From now on I will be talking a great deal about skills. The kinds of skills discussed here have three components or dimensions. First is *awareness*. Every helping skill has an awareness dimension. Helping skills are based on your perceptions of the client's experiences, feelings, and behaviors; the principal elements of the problem situation; and your own experiences, feelings, and behaviors as you interact with the client. By attending, observing, and listening, you gather the data you need to respond intelligently to clients. If your perceptions are inaccurate, then your skills are flawed at their root.

Jenny is counseling Frank in a community mental health center. Frank is scared to death of what is going to happen to him in the counseling process, but he does not talk about it. Jenny realizes his discomfort but does not identify it as fear. She finally says, "Frank, I'm wondering what's

making you so angry right now." Because Frank does not feel angry, he
says nothing. He's startled by what she says and feels even more insecure.
Jenny takes his silence as a confirmation of his "anger." She tries to get him
to talk about it.

As we have seen, attending and active listening are the bases of the kind of
perceptiveness needed in helping skills. Helpers who fail to attend and to listen
well or who, although they do attend and listen, fail to understand the client
may have the two dimensions to be described below, but because of their lack
of perceptiveness, their responses are marred.

The second component is *know-how*. Once you are aware of what skill is
called for in the helping process, you need to be able to deliver it. For instance,
if you are aware that a client is anxious and confused because this is his first
visit to a helper, it does little good if your understanding remains locked up
inside you.

Frank and Jenny end up arguing about his "anger." Frank finally says that
he would rather see another counselor. Jenny, of course, takes this as a sign
that she was right in the first place. Homer, the second counselor,
interviews Frank. He sees clearly that Frank is scared and confused. But he
does not know what to do with this understanding. As Frank talks, Homer
nods and says "uh-huh" quite a bit. He is fully present to Frank and listens
intently, but he does not know how to respond.

You need to *know how* to communicate your perceptions to clients in such a
way as to facilitate their participation in the helping process. Accurate perceptions are lost without the skill of delivering them to the client in a helpful way.

Third is *assertiveness*. High-level awareness and excellent know-how are
meaningless unless they are actually used when called for. Certainly, to be
assertive in the helping process without awareness and without know-how is to
court disaster. For instance, because Jenny did not understand Frank's behavior
(a lack of the kind of *awareness* needed for effective confrontation) and because
she confronted him in a punitive way (a lack of *know-how* in the area of challenging), her intervention did more harm than good. If you see that a client
needs new perspectives on his or her problem situation, if you know how to
present this new perspective in a responsible way, and if you still fail to do so,
then you are deficient in the third part of the skill.

Edna, a young helper in the office of student development, is in the middle
of the second session with Aurelio, a graduate student. It soon becomes
clear to her that he is making sexual overtures. In her training, she did well
in challenging her fellow trainees. The feedback she got from them and the

> *trainer was that she challenged others directly and caringly. But now she*
> *feels immobilized. She does not want to hurt Aurelio or embarrass herself.*
> *She tries to ignore his seductive behavior, but Aurelio takes silence to mean*
> *consent.*

This lack of assertiveness is a critical issue for many people in training to be helpers.

The principal skills of Stage I are the communication of accurate empathy and the ability to use prompts and probes. Both skills are related to the goal of problem exploration and clarification.

Accurate Empathy

I discuss two levels of empathy in this book. The first, called primary-level accurate empathy (AE I, for short) is a Stage I skill. The second, called advanced accurate empathy (AE II, for short), will be discussed in Stage II. First, an overview of empathy in general.

Helpers are accurately empathic if they can (1) get inside their client's world, get a feeling for what this world is like, and look at the outer world through their client's perspective or frame of reference and can (2) communicate this understanding in a way that shows they have some understanding of their client's feelings and the experiences and behaviors to which these feelings relate. As Mayeroff (1971, pp. 41–42) puts it:

> To care for another person, I must be able to understand him and his world
> as if I were inside it. I must be able to see, as it were, with his eyes what his
> world is like to him and how he sees himself. Instead of merely looking at
> him in a detached way from outside, as if he were a specimen, I must be
> able to be *with* him in his world, "going" into his world in order to sense
> from "inside" what life is like for him, what he is striving to be and what he
> requires to grow.

Huxley (1963, pp. 12–13) notes that it is philosophically impossible to get inside another in such a way as actually to experience reality as the other does: "We live together, we act on, and react to, one another; but always and in all circumstances we are alone. . . . Sensations, feelings, insights, fancies—all these are private and, except through symbols and second hand, incommunicable." And yet he believes that empathy is both possible and necessary: "Most island universes are sufficiently like one another to permit of inferential understanding or even empathy or 'feeling into.' . . . To see ourselves as others see us is a most salutary gift. Hardly less important is the capacity to see others as they see themselves." Accurate empathy at its fullest is more than just a communication or helping skill; it is an attempt to penetrate this metaphysical aloneness of the other.

For instance, if a person comes to you, sits down, looks at the floor, hunches over, and haltingly tells you that he has just failed a test, that his girlfriend has told him she does not want to see him anymore, and that he might lose his part-time job, you might respond to him by saying something like this:

> *Helper:* So it's pretty miserable for you right now—your world has all of a sudden begun to fall apart.

By attending and listening, you see his depression *(affect)* and what underlies this depression *(experiences)*, and then you communicate to him your understanding of his world. This is empathy. If your perceptions are correct, then it can be called *accurate* empathy. Or let us say that a friend tells you he has just finished nurse's training and has been accepted into an M.A. program to become a nurse practitioner, something he's wanted ever since his second year in nursing school. You say something like the following:

> *Friend:* I've never seen you so happy. You've got just what you've wanted.

This, too, is accurate empathy. The thesis of this book is that empathy is useful both in counseling and in the ordinary interpersonal transactions of life (see Rogers, 1951, 1957, 1961, 1967).

Primary-Level Accurate Empathy (AE I)

Primary-level accurate empathy means communicating *initial basic* understanding of what the client is feeling and of the experiences and behaviors underlying these feelings. This is the kind of empathy that ordinarily fits Stage I of the developmental model best because it helps clients explore and clarify their problem situations *from their frames of reference.* In this response, helpers try merely to let their clients know that they understand what they have explicitly said about themselves. Counselors at this stage do not try to dig down into what the client is only half saying, implying, or stating implicitly. That kind of advanced empathy belongs, generally, to a later stage of the helping process, for it is designed to help clients develop new perspectives on themselves and their problem situations. Primary-level empathy is useful throughout the entire helping process. Here are a few examples of primary-level accurate empathy.

> *Client* (talking in an animated way): I really think that things couldn't be going better. I have a new job and my husband is not just putting up with it. He thinks it's great. He and I are getting along better than ever, even sexually,

and I never expected that. I guess I'm just waiting for the bubble to burst.

Helper: Things are going so well between you and your husband that it seems almost too good to be true.

Client: I've been to other counselors and nothing has ever really worked. I don't even know why I'm trying again. But things are so bad that I guess something has to be done; so I'm trying it all over again.

Helper: You're uneasy because you're not sure that our sessions will help you manage better, but you feel you have to try something.

Client: And so here I am. I'm two months pregnant. I don't want to be pregnant. I'm not married, and I don't even love the father. This is something that happens to other people!

Helper: The whole picture seems overwhelming, especially because you've never even thought of it happening to you.

In these interchanges, the helper says what the client could have said. Each stays within the client's immediate frame of reference.

IMMEDIATE IMPACT

In most cases, empathy helps greatly to establish rapport with clients; it helps them to develop the kind of openness and trust that is most useful in Stage I; and it helps them explore themselves and their problem situations. So in a sense, it is both a relationship-establishing skill and a data-gathering or problem-clarification skill. Helpers, therefore, have criteria for judging the quality of their empathic responses. Does the response help develop or maintain a good relationship? Does it help the client explore the problem situation in terms of relevant experiences, behaviors, and feelings more fully? Consider the following interchange between a trainee and her trainer.

Trainee: I don't think I'm going to make a good counselor. The other people in the program seem brighter than I am. They seem to be picking up the hang of empathy faster than I am. I'm still afraid of responding directly to others, even with empathy. I have to reevaluate my participation in the program.

Trainer: You're feeling pretty inadequate and it's getting you down, perhaps even enough to think of quitting.

Trainee: And yet I know that "giving up" is part of the problem, part of my style. I'm not the brightest, but I'm certainly not dumb either. The way I compare myself to others is not very useful. I know that I've been picking up some of these skills. I do attend well and listen. I'm perceptive, even though at times I have a hard time sharing these perceptions with others. I'm like a kid—I want everything right away.

When the trainer "hits the mark," the trainee moves forward and explores her problem a bit more fully. In a sense, there is no such thing as an empathic response that is good in itself. Empathy is instrumental; that is, it is good to the degree that it works.

PRIMARY-LEVEL VERSUS ADVANCED EMPATHY

Primary-level empathy can be seen more clearly by contrasting it with advanced empathy, which is explained in detail in the next chapter. Advanced empathy gets at not only what clients clearly state but also what they *imply* or leave only half stated or half expressed. For instance, Peter has been exploring some developmental issues with one of the college counselors. This is the third interview. He talks about relatively safe topics, such as his studies and his relationship with his parents. He drops hints now and again that some sexual issues are troubling him, but they are just hints tacked onto statements about other issues.

> *Peter:* I find biology really tough. I get through it, but I don't think I'm good enough to be in premed. I'm not going to make it into med school. It's not that I get distracted like some other guys—girls and drink and stuff like that. I frankly don't think I'm smart enough for premed. There's too much competition and it's not the only occupation in the world.

Peter has made a number of other statements in which he refers indirectly to sexual concerns, but he does not bring these concerns up directly. Consider the difference between these two responses to what Peter has just said.

> *Counselor A:* So, if you are fairly convinced that it's a question of talent and not just effort, you're wondering whether it might not be time to change majors.
> *Counselor B:* It sounds like you know the decision you want to make about studies and are ready to accept it. But in the last two sessions you've referred briefly to other concerns, perhaps some concerns with relationships with others or some sexual concerns. I may be hearing things that aren't there, but I thought I'd check it out with you.

Counselor A exhibits primary-level empathy. He does not go beyond what Peter says directly. Counselor B, although she begins with primary-level empathy, moves on to an advanced level. She gets at, tentatively and carefully, what Peter has perhaps been skirting. Counselor B does not accuse him of anything but rather offers him an opportunity to explore what might be more substantial concerns.

These two responses can have very different effects on Peter. For instance, he might follow the first response with

Peter: Well, in fact I did make the change this week. You're right. The time for a change has come. I'm moving into business at the beginning of next semester.

His reaction to Counselor B, however, might be quite different. He might, for instance, deny that he has any other concerns and return to the issue of change of majors. Or he might respond something like this:

Peter (after a pause): I guess I'm more transparent than I thought I was. The studies stuff is important. Being here has helped me confirm a decision I think I made before I came into these sessions to change to business. (Pause) But there are some things about sex that are bothering me, perhaps more than I've been willing to admit (said hesitatingly).
Counselor B: And maybe harder to talk about.
Peter: A *lot* harder to talk about.

Again, the value of the counselor's response lies in its impact on the client. In this case, advanced empathy helps Peter move into new territory. But note, once this new area of concern is identified, the counselor begins to use primary-level empathy to help Peter explore it. If advanced empathy and other forms of challenging are used too early in the counseling process, the client might be frightened off or inhibited in other ways. Clients who are challenged prematurely sometimes deny hunches shared by helpers even though they know they hit the mark. Or the rapport that has been building up suffers a setback. In Stage I, it is inefficient to confuse, scare, or anger clients by premature challenge. This does not mean that challenging skills are never used in Stage I. I will discuss this issue further, after I explore the nature and use of challenging skills.

RESPONDING TO FEELINGS OR CONTENT

In most of the examples given so far, the helper responded to both affect and content—that is, to both feelings *and* the experiences and behaviors underlying the feelings. Although this might ordinarily be the best kind of response, at any given time, responding to or emphasizing one or the other might do just as well. There is no such thing as a good empathic response *in itself.* Responses are good to the degree that they are instrumental in achieving the goals of the helping process. In Stage I, this means helping clients understand themselves and the problem situations with which they are struggling. Consider the following example.

Client: This week I tried to get my wife to see the doctor, but she refused, even though she fainted a couple of times. The kids had no school, so they were underfoot almost constantly. I haven't been able to finish a report my boss expects from me next Monday.

Counselor: It's been a lousy, rushed week.

Here the counselor chooses to emphasize the client's feelings because she believes his feelings of frustration and irritation are uppermost in his consciousness right now. The emphasis with another client might be different:

Client: My dad yelled at me all the time last year about my hair. But just last week I heard him telling someone how nice I looked, hair and all. He yells at my sister about the same things he ignores when my younger brother does them. Sometimes he's really nice with my mother and other times he's just awful—demanding, grouchy, sarcastic.

Counselor: He's just so inconsistent.

In this response the counselor emphasizes the content (the client's experience of his father), for he feels this is the core of the client's message. The point of these two examples is that helpers should use any kind of accurately empathic response that will help clients explore themselves more thoroughly. The principal question is always: What is the *core message* in what the client is saying?

DEALING WITH FEARFUL CLIENTS

If the client is easily threatened by discussion of his or her feelings, Hackney and Cormier (1979) suggest that, in responding, the helper start by emphasizing content and proceed only gradually to a discussion of feelings. They further suggest that one tentative way of getting at such a client's feelings is to have the helper say what he or she might feel in similar circumstances.

Client: My mother is always trying to make a little kid out of me. And I'm in my mid-thirties! Last week, in front of a group of my friends, she brought out my rubber boots and an umbrella and gave me a little talk on how to dress for bad weather.

Counselor: If she had treated me that way, I think I probably would've been pretty angry.

Now the client can choose, if she wishes, to explore her own emotions.

Some clients are fearful of intimacy; that is one of their problems. This means they might well be fearful of the kind of intimacy involved in the helping process. Because empathy is a way for helpers to get close to clients, too much empathy too soon can inhibit rather than facilitate helping. The goal of Stage I is to help clients explore themselves and their problems. Sometimes helpers achieve this goal more quickly if, in the beginning, they move slowly.

Three Elements of Empathy

The communication of accurate empathy requires the three elements of a skill: awareness, know-how, and assertiveness. First of all, awareness: you must be able to get into the world, or at least into the shoes, of the client. If your perceptions of his or her world are flawed, then your empathy will not be accurate. Instead of helping the client clarify his or her problem situations, it could prove distracting. Second, if you do have a feeling for the client's world in terms of the experiences, behaviors, and feelings he or she is discussing, it helps only if you can communicate this understanding. In the case of accurate empathy, this means the ability to communicate an understanding of both the affect and the content of the client's message in a way that makes sense to him or her. Merely nodding your head and saying "uh-huh" and "I understand" occasionally are usually inadequate. Finally, assertiveness: you need to engage the client in dialogue, the kind of dialogue that leads to developing a working relationship and to clarifying the problem situation.

Hints for Improving Empathy

GIVING ONESELF TIME TO THINK

Beginners sometimes jump in too quickly when the client pauses. "Too quickly" means they do not give themselves enough time to reflect on what the client has just said in order to identify the core message being communicated. Carl Rogers (1951, 1957, 1961, 1967), who pioneered the use of accurate empathy in the helping process, has made a couple of training films. In them he uses accurate empathy masterfully. But he always gives himself time to assimilate and reflect on what the client says before responding. Because he attends and listens carefully and then gives himself time, his responses are most thoughtful. He can give himself time, especially if taking time is seen as an indication that he cares about what he is going to say.

Many beginners have to practice waiting when the client pauses. During the pause, they can ask themselves: What feelings has the client just expressed? What is the core message? This does not mean that counselors need to lose their spontaneity. They should speak up any time they think they can help the client, even if this means interrupting. In the films, Rogers gives the client some sign, either verbal or nonverbal, that he would like to respond. For instance, he says, "Let me see if I've got what you're saying." Effective helpers interrupt or pause in non-self-conscious ways. They are so "with" the client that they do not have to ask themselves whether they should speak or remain quiet.

SHORT RESPONSES

The helper's responses should be relatively frequent but also lean and trim. In trying to be accurate, the beginner may become longwinded, sometimes speaking longer than the client in trying to elaborate an adequate response. This often happens when the helper tries to respond too quickly. When the helper begins to see that his or her first few sentences have not hit the mark, he or she keeps on talking in hopes of eventually succeeding.

> *Client:* I have never been very spontaneous in social situations. Because I'm shy, I kind of stand off to the side and wait to see how I can get into the conversation. As a result, the conversation often passes me by by the time I'm ready to say something. Then I'm not even at the same place in the conversation as others. I've been inside myself and don't know what's been going on.
>
> *Counselor* (jumping in right away): You're really shy and that cuts down on your spontaneity. It shows up especially when a group is standing around talking. You are listening all right: you know what people are saying. But then you begin to ask yourself, "What should I say? I shouldn't stand around here dumb." But by the time you think of what to say, it's just too late. No, it's worse than that. Now you've lost the thread of the conversation and it's twice as hard trying to get back in. Your shyness backfires on you in more than one way.

This response might ultimately be accurate, but it probably is not very facilitative. It places the focus on the counselor's attempts to understand rather than on the client's self-exploration. The result is that the client is smothered by all that the helper has to say, becomes lost and confused, and finds it difficult to move forward. Again, the question "What is the core of what this person is saying to me?" can help counselors make their responses short, concrete, and accurate.

EMPATHY OF TONE AND MANNER

If a client speaks animatedly with the helper, telling him of her elation over various successes in her life, and he replies in a flat, dull voice, his response is not fully empathic—even though what he says might well be accurate in identifying her feelings and the experiences underlying these feelings.

> *Client* (speaking animatedly): This week I tried to be more understanding with my son. Instead of yelling at him when he did something wrong, I tried to focus on other kinds of interaction with him. When he talked, I just tried to understand what he was saying and let him know that I did. You know,

it worked! I don't mean that it was technique and that I was phony. I was just with him in a different way!

Counselor (speaking in a rather dull, flat voice): This was a new and very rewarding experience, perhaps for both of you. And all from trying to be with him in a simple, understanding way.

The counselor's response is fine on paper but possibly loses its impact from the way it is delivered. Being fully with a client means participating in some reasonable and genuine way in his or her feelings and emotions.

LANGUAGE

The helper is more empathic when his or her language is in tune with the client's. Consider the following somewhat extreme example.

10-year-old client: My teacher thinks I'm crazy. She starts to do that right from the first day of class. I don't fool around more than anyone else in class, but she gets me any time I do. I think she's picking on me because she doesn't like me. She doesn't yell at Bill Smith, and he acts funnier than I do.

Counselor: You're perplexed. You wonder why she singles you out for so much discipline.

The counselor's response is accurate in a sense, but it is not the kind of language that communicates understanding to a 10-year-old. The following response would have much more meaning for the child:

Counselor: You're mad because she picks on you and doesn't seem to like you much at all.

The helper's choice of words reflects his or her ability to assume the client's frame of reference. There is one caution in the use of language. Helpers should not adopt a language that is not their own just to be on the client's "wavelength." For instance, a middle-class probation officer is talking to a client who is tempted to steal in order to pay off a debt to someone he fears.

Helper: Unless you find some bread, man, that cat's going to get you wasted.

He can use informal language without using adaptations of English that are simply not his own. Language is only one way in which helper might differ from client. This brings up the question of indigenous helpers.

INDIGENOUS HELPERS

Clients are probably better off if they are in a position to choose helpers who are likely to understand them. Counselors who share the clients' socioeconomic, educational, and other background variables are likely to understand the client more thoroughly than helpers who are quite distant from their clients on these variables. Therefore, if clients have a choice of two equally skilled helpers, they would do best, generally, to choose helpers who, because of shared experiences, understand them and their situations best. Someone in the army would do better with a skilled helper familiar with the way the army works. A nun would probably do better with a skilled helper who has the religious background to understand her environment. Helpers who have little in common with the members of certain populations might provide a more useful service were they to train counselors indigenous to these populations rather than try to counsel them themselves. For instance, skilled counselors might train ex-addicts, reformed alcoholics, ex-prisoners, men and women from religious orders, army personnel, and ghetto residents to become counselors to clients in these situations (Mezz & Calia, 1972; Weitz, 1972).

Common Problems in Communicating AE I

Though many of the following problems affect beginning helpers, they are not restricted to them.

POOR SUBSTITUTES FOR EMPATHY

Helpers can reply to what clients say in any number of ways. Some of them, however, are poor substitutes for primary-level empathy. Peter and his problems in living will be used to illustrate some poor responses. Let us say that Peter made the following statement about his concerns:

> *Peter* (speaking in a halting voice as he looks at the floor and clasps his hands tightly between his knees): What seems to be really bothering me is a problem with sex. I don't even know whether I'm a man or not and I'm halfway through college. I don't go out with women my age. I don't even think I want to. I may, well, I may even be gay.

The following are some examples of poor responses.

- *No response.* The counselor might say nothing, as if what the client has said is not worth responding to.
- *A question.* The counselor might ask something like "How long has this been bothering you, Peter?" This response ignores the emotion Peter is experiencing. Because a question elicits further information, it implies that Peter has not said anything worth responding to.
- *A cliché.* The counselor might say, "Many people struggle with sexual iden-

tity throughout their lives." This is a cliché. It misses the client's feelings completely and deals only with the content of his statement, even then only in the vaguest way. The impact of such a response is "You don't really have a problem at all, at least not a serious one."

- *An interpretation.* A counselor might say something like "This sexual thing is probably really just a symptom, Peter. I've got a hunch that you're not really accepting yourself." This is a poor and misplaced attempt to offer advanced accurate empathy. The counselor fails to respond to the client's feelings and also distorts the content of the client's communication. The response implies that what is really important is hidden from the client.
- *Moving to action.* Another counselor might say, "There are a few video-tapes on sexuality in the college years I'd like to have you take a look at." This counselor also ignores Peter's feelings and jumps to a sex-education action program. It well may be that Peter could use some good input on sexual development, but this is neither the time nor the way to do it.

All these are poor substitutes for empathy. A more skilled counselor might have said something like

Counselor: You've got a lot of misgivings about just where you stand with yourself sexually, and so it's very disturbing to talk about it.

This counselor responds with primary-level accurate empathy. He recognizes that the client is disturbed and that concern for his sexuality underlies his anxiety. This is the kind of Stage I response that is likely to strengthen the rapport between client and counselor and stimulate further self-exploration.

COUNTERFEITS OF ACCURATE EMPATHY

Some responses look something like primary-level accurate empathy but are really distortions of it.

Inaccurate Empathy. Sometimes helpers' responses are simply inaccurate because they fail to attend and listen well. Consider the following response to Peter.

Counselor: You're eager to start exploring your sexual preferences and make some decisions.

Peter is not eager and has said nothing about making decisions. All helpers can be somewhat inaccurate at times. If any given response is inaccurate, the client often lets the counselor know in a variety of ways: he or she may stop dead, fumble around, go off on a new tangent, tell the counselor that's not exactly what he or she meant, or even try to provide empathy for the counselor and get him or her back on the track. Sometimes counselors, when they are inaccurate, get involved in a game of "catch-up." Their immediate responses would have been excellent had they been given earlier, but they do not fit what the client is saying right now. Catch-up and goodwill are no substitutes for on-the-spot accuracy. What can counselors do about inaccuracy? They must learn to pick up cues from their clients that indicate they have been inaccurate and then work to get back with the client.

Feigning Understanding. Sometimes helpers find it difficult to understand what their clients are saying, even though they are attending fully and listening intently. Clients are sometimes confused, distracted, and in a highly emotional state; all these conditions affect the clarity of what they are saying about themselves. Counselors might become distracted and fail to follow the client. If this is the case, it is best not to feign understanding. This is phony. Genuineness demands that they admit they are lost and then work to get back on the track again. "I think I've lost you. Could we go over that once more?" If the counselor is confused, it is all right to admit this confusion. "I'm sorry. I don't think I got what you just said. Could we go through it a bit more slowly?" Such statements are signs that the counselor thinks it is important to stay with the client. They indicate respect and caring. Admitting that one is lost is infinitely preferable to such clichés as "uh-huh," "ummmm," and "I understand."

If helpers feel that they do not quite understand what clients are trying to express, they should be tentative in their responses and give their clients room to move. In the following example, the helper is tentative, and so the client, a teacher having trouble in the classroom, feels free to correct her and give her a clearer picture of what he means.

> *Counselor:* You seem to be saying that your students don't trust you because your emotions change so much from day to day. Is it something like that?
>
> *Client:* Well, that's partly it. But I also think that the mood of the class changes from day to day; so there are many days when my emotions and theirs just don't seem to mix.

This client feels he has room to move. The counselor's tentative response helps him clarify what he means. Brammer (1973, p. 86) calls this process of checking with the client whenever you are confused or unsure "perception checking."

Parroting. Accurate empathy is not mere parroting. The mechanical helper corrupts primary-level accurate empathy by simply restating what the client has said.

Client: I feel pretty low because all my children have left home, and now I'm lonely, with nothing to do.

Counselor: You feel low because the children are gone, you're all alone, and you have nothing to do.

The effective counselor is always looking for the *core* of what the client is expressing; he or she becomes expert in ferreting out this core and communicating it to the client. It is as if the counselor were constantly asking himself or herself: "Precisely what does the client *mean?*" Empathy, then, does not become just a paraphrase or a repetition. The effective counselor tries to communicate understanding rather than merely mirror what the client has said. Box 4–1 summarizes some suggestions for the use of primary-level accurate empathy.

The Literature on Empathy

There is a growing literature on empathy. Some see empathy as important for both the helping process and interpersonal transactions generally (Bullmer, 1975; Clark, 1980; Schuster, 1979). Others report on strategies for training both

---

BOX 4–1 SUMMARY OF SUGGESTIONS FOR THE USE OF PRIMARY-LEVEL ACCURATE EMPATHY

1. Attend carefully, both physically and psychologically, to the messages transmitted by the client.
2. Listen especially for basic or core messages.
3. Respond fairly frequently, but briefly, to these core messages, but be flexible and tentative enough so that the client has room to move (to affirm, deny, explain, clarify, or shift emphasis).
4. Be gentle, but don't let the client run from the important issues.
5. Respond to both feeling and content unless there is some reason for emphasizing one or the other.
6. Move gradually toward the exploration of sensitive topics and feelings.
7. After you have responded, attend carefully to cues that either confirm or deny the accuracy of your response. Does the client move forward in a focused way?
8. Note signs of client stress or resistance and try to judge whether these arise because you have lacked accuracy or have been perhaps too accurate.

helpers and clients in this skill (for example, Dalton & Sundblad, 1976; Fridman & Stone, 1978; Guzzetta, 1976; Hodge, Payne, & Wheeler, 1978; Shaffer & Hummel, 1979). However, there is also an ongoing debate about empathy not unlike the debate on the usefulness of counseling and therapy discussed briefly in Chapter 1. This controversy deals with the very existence of accurate empathy and whether it contributes in any substantial way to helping people cope with problem situations (Anthony, 1978; Bellingham, 1978; Chinsky & Rappaport, 1970; Gladstein, 1977; Hackney, 1978; Rappaport & Chinsky, 1972; Truax, 1972). More heat than light seems to be generated by this controversy.

The problem with this debate is that it takes accurate empathy out of context. In the problem-solving model, the valued accomplishments of the entire model and each step are considered important. Skills such as empathy are basically *tools* for achieving these goals. There is no intimation that empathy, almost in and of itself, "cures." I find empathy most useful for the following reasons:

1. It is a tool of civility. For me it is a value to try to see the world as the client (and others) sees it and to share this effort with him or her.
2. I often find empathy a good way of establishing rapport and building a relationship. However, I am also aware that not all clients want any significant degree of closeness in the helping process. The goal of counseling is to help clients handle difficulties and problem situations, not to establish close relationships. I think it is important not to overuse empathy.
3. I find empathy a good unobtrusive tool for gathering data. Not that I have some need for amassing data about clients. I mean rather that it is a good way to help clients generate the kind of data they need to clarify problems and to begin to see useful courses of action. However, empathy is only one way of helping clients probe their experience. I consider others later.
4. I find it important to be able to let clients know at any moment throughout the helping process that I am in touch with their experience as much as I can be. Empathy can provide support for a client who is fearful about coming to a helper in the first place. It can also provide support for clients who are experiencing frustrations as they try to implement programs they find difficult.

I also realize that people who grow close to each other do not often use explicit statements of empathy in their conversations. That, I believe, is not because empathy doesn't exist or is unimportant. It is rather that the relationship itself has grown empathic, and the need for explicit statements of empathy lessens. Even then, empathy can prove to be an extremely useful mode of communication at crisis times.

Using Probes in Problem Exploration and Definition

In most of the examples used up to this point to clarify elements of the helping process, clients have been willing to explore themselves and their behavior rather freely. Obviously, this is not always the case. Although it is essential that helpers respond empathically to their clients when they do reveal themselves, it is also necessary at times to encourage, prompt, and help clients to explore problem situations when they fail to do so spontaneously. Therefore, the ability to use prompts and probes well is another important skill for helpers. Prompts and probes are verbal tactics for helping clients talk about themselves and define their problems more concretely and specifically. They can take different forms.

Statements That Encourage Further Clarification and Definition

Such statements by their very nature make some demand on the client to become more specific. They can relate to the client's experiences, behaviors, feelings, or any combination of the three.

Clients' *experiences* are what they see as happening *to* them.

> *Helper:* I realize now that you often get angry when your mother-in-law stays for more than a day, but I'm still not sure what she does that makes you angry.

Another example:

> *Helper:* You feel trapped in the ghetto and want to get out. Maybe you could tell me what it is about living here that gets to you most.

In these examples, the helper's statements place a demand on the client to clarify the experiences that give rise to certain behaviors and feelings.

Clients' *behaviors* are what they do or refrain from doing.

> *Helper:* The Sundays your husband exercises his visiting rights with the children end in his taking verbal pot shots at you and you get these headaches. I've got a fairly clear picture of what he does when he comes over, but it might help if you could describe what you do.

Another example:

> *Helper:* When the diagnosis of cancer came in two weeks ago, you said that you were both relieved because you knew what you had to face and depressed. Tell me what you've been doing since then.

In these instances, the helper encourages clients to describe their behavior as a way of giving greater clarity to the problem situation.

Affect refers to the feelings and emotions clients experience.

> *Helper:* So *he* got the job you worked your tail off for, and you suspect that your being a woman has a lot to do with it. I could imagine that a number of feelings have been bouncing around inside you this past week.

Another example:

> *Helper:* When you talk about your wife and what she does, you use fairly positive emotions. For instance, you "appreciate" it when she points out what you do wrong. I haven't heard any negative or mixed feelings yet, and it could be because there are none.

The helper provides these clients with an opportunity to discuss the feelings that go with their experiences and behaviors.

Questions That Help Clients Define Problems More Clearly

You may have noticed that the statements in the previous section could have been put in the form of questions. For instance, "I could imagine that a number of feelings have been bouncing around inside you this past week" could have been "What kinds of feelings have been bouncing around inside you this past week?"

The following guidelines can be used with respect to asking questions. First, when clients are asked too many questions, they can feel "grilled." This interferes with the *rapport* between helper and client.

> I feel certain that we ask too many questions, often meaningless ones. We ask questions that confuse the interviewee, that interrupt him. We ask questions the interviewee cannot possibly answer. We even ask questions we don't want the answers to, and, consequently, we do not hear the answers when forthcoming [Benjamin, 1981, p. 71; the author devotes an entire chapter to the question, its uses, and his misgivings about it].

Turning questions into statements such as those in the previous section helps. Statements are gentler forms of probes than questions, but even probing statements should not be overused.

Second, remember the goal of this part of the helping process is *problem definition.* Some helpers use questions to amass information, much of which proves to be irrelevant. The purpose of exploration is to help the *client* see the problem more clearly. Helpers who ask too many questions are often meeting their own needs or working under the assumption that information amassed will lead in and of itself to more effective management of the problem situation.

Third, when you feel that a question is called for, generally ask *open-ended questions*—that is, questions that require more than a simple yes or no or similar one-word answer: not "Now that the cancer diagnosis is in, do you have any plans?" but "Now that the cancer diagnosis is in, what do you plan to do?" Counselors who ask closed questions to which clients respond with one-word answers find themselves asking more and more questions. This is often a problem for beginners. However, if you need a specific piece of information to help define a problem situation, you may use a closed question: "How many jobs have you had in the past two years?" Such a question could provide essential background information in a career-counseling session. The point here is not questions in and of themselves but how they relate to and promote or hinder the overall helping process. One way to use a training strategy as a form of treatment is to train clients to ask relevant questions of themselves.

> *Counselor:* What are some of the questions you need to ask yourself if you are to understand what's happening between you and your husband a little better?
>
> *Client:* Hmmmm. I think I'd have to say to myself: "What do you do that makes him want to drink all the time?" That's a scary question for me.

Of course, as a consultant to the process, you could help clients ask relevant, even "impertinent" questions of themselves.

Hackney and Cormier (1979) suggest two other probe-type helper responses that can contribute to problem definition, the accent and direct requests for clarification.

The Accent

"The accent is a one- or two-word restatement that focuses or brings attention to a preceding client response" (Hackney & Cormier, 1979, p. 52).

> *Client:* My son and I have a fairly good working relationship now, even though I'm not entirely satisfied.
> *Helper:* Not *entirely* satisfied?
> *Client:* Well, I should probably say "dissatisfied" because. . . .

> *Client:* At the end of the day with the kids and all and dinner and cleaning up I'm *bushed*.
> *Helper:* Bushed?
> *Client:* Tired, angry, hurt—he does practically nothing to help me.

Request for Clarification

"If you are simply unable to follow the client's train of thought, it is more important to seek clarification than it is to allow the client to proceed" (Hackney & Cormier, 1979, p. 53).

> *Helper:* I didn't follow the last part. Could you go over it once more?

> *Helper:* Could you describe how you feel once more. I'm not sure that I understand.

Obviously, overuse of such requests is distracting and makes the helper look inept. On the other hand, fear of looking inept can keep helpers from using requests for clarification even when they are called for.

Minimal Prompts

Hackney and Cormier (1979, p. 68) talk about the "minimal verbal activity" of the helper. This includes such things as "uh-huh," "mmm," "yes," "I see," "ah," "oh," and the like. They often serve as reinforcers or prompts and lead the client into further exploration. Part of Carl Rogers's approach to attending and listening, at least in his films (Rogers, Perls, & Ellis, 1965; Rogers, Shostrom, & Lazarus, 1977), is a fairly steady use of such prompts.

> *Client:* There are a lot of things I don't like about this school. (Pause)
> *Helper:* Uh-huh.
> *Client:* For instance, the food in the cafeteria is lousy.

Minimal prompts can also be nonverbal.

> *Client:* He never lets me have my way. We always do what he wants.
> (Pause)
> (Helper nods her head.)
> *Client:* Well, I don't mean "always," but when I want to do something my way, I have to fight for it. I go along with his suggestions most of the time, but when I suggest something to do, it's like I have to prove to him that it's worth doing.

> *Client:* I don't know if I can tell you this. I haven't told it to anyone.
> (Helper maintains good eye contact and leans forward a bit.)
> *Client:* Well, my brother had sexual relations with me a few times a couple of years ago. I think about it all the time.

In the last chapter I suggested that as a helper you become *aware of* the messages your nonverbal behavior communicates. Now I suggest that you *use* nonverbal communication to prompt the client to explore and concretize the problem situation.

Writing Approaches

Sometimes questionnaires, diaries, checklists, logs, time-and-motion studies, tests, and other forms of writing can help clients clarify their concerns. For instance, one client said she was overworked at home and had no idea where her time went. For two weeks she kept a kind of time-and-motion log that she would fill in once sometime in the middle of each day and once at the end. She did not evaluate *how* she spent her time; she merely collected the data needed to give her a clear picture of *what* she did. Once the data were collected, the counselor helped her put them into categories and probe the implications of what she discovered.

Another client was having difficulties in relating to others, but he could not put his finger on what was going wrong. The counselor had him use an "interpersonal checklist" (LaForge, 1977) and then used it to probe specific interpersonal situations at home, at work, and with friends.

There are many tests and checklists you can use informally with clients to help them probe specific areas of their experience. I sometimes have clients keep logs of what is happening in the counseling process itself. Clients keep a written account of what they are doing to reach the goals of each step. This is one simple way to encourage clients to "own" the helping process themselves, and it also contributes to concreteness. For instance, if a client writes a vague behavioral analysis of some difficulty, the counselor can help him or her learn how to move from vagueness to concreteness and specificity. Beyond the use of tests and checklists, writing approaches in counseling seem to be relatively unused by helpers.

Cautions in the Use of Probes

Prompts and probes, verbal, nonverbal, and written, can be overused to the detriment of both rapport and problem definition. As already noted, "self-efficacy" (Bandura, 1977a) or client self-responsibility is an ideal in the helping process. If you extort information from clients by a constant barrage of probes and prompts, they are unlikely to take more and more responsibility for the problem-solving process. They are also likely to see you as a demanding parent rather than a collaborative consultant. Use two general principles: (1) Once you have employed a prompt or probe, if at all possible, let the client take the initiative in exploring the information it yields. (2) After you use a probe, apply primary-level accurate empathy rather than another probe or series of probes as a way of encouraging further exploration.

The Content of the Client's Self-Disclosure

What should clients talk about? They should talk about both their problems in living and the resources or potential resources they have to handle them. The goal of self-exploration is not merely quantity, or even intimacy, of self-exploration. Rather, it is relevancy of self-exploration, which includes (1) problem-related information and (2) solution-oriented resources. Resource exploration provides a positive dimension of the self-exploration process. Consider the following example:

> *Client:* I practically never stand up for my rights. If I disagree with what anyone is saying—especially in a group—I keep my mouth shut. I suppose that when I do speak up, the world doesn't fall in on me. Sometimes others do actually listen to me. But I still don't seem to have any impact on anyone.
> *Counselor A:* It's frustrating to be afraid to speak up and to get lost in the crowd.
> *Counselor B:* The times you do speak up, others actually listen—and so you're annoyed at yourself for getting lost in the crowd so often.

Counselor A misses the resource the client mentioned. Although the client habitually fails to speak up, he does have an impact when he does speak. Others listen sometimes. And this is a resource.

There are certain areas of life that are worth investigating with almost every client. The following areas or topics are so pervasive that they are relevant to almost any problem the client might mention.

Interpersonal Relations

People with problems they cannot seem to manage on their own are often "out of community" in some sense. Their interpersonal relationships are impoverished or disturbed; they are withdrawn; they are not getting along with family, friends, or coworkers. Sometimes the problem is directly an interpersonal one:

> *Client A:* You can't say that my wife and I ever really did get along. Things were smoother in the beginning, but they weren't ever right.

Sometimes other problems are complicated because of interpersonal issues:

> *Client B:* I go into the hospital tomorrow. I'm facing this operation and I'm afraid. But I really have no one to talk to.

You can expect to find interpersonal issues in most of the problem situations your clients explore.

Assumptions and the Decisions Based on Them

Frank (1973) stresses the importance of the client's "assumptive world." Unhealthy assumptions often underlie unhealthy behavior. For instance, Client A might be assuming that all adults are as negative and unaccepting as his parents. This assumption contaminates his interactions with adults. Client B assumes that career is central to life, that it is necessary to choose a career and let the rest of life somehow fall in place around it. She finds her career boring, and, because of her assumption, life is boring. Client C assumes that people involved in religion are hypocritical and/or stupid. Because of this assumption, he cuts himself off, on principle, from people and programs that have anything to do with religion. Client D assumes that she is a boring, unattractive person because she has "just" average intelligence. She acts in accord with her assumption and actually does become a boring person. Counselors should ask themselves, with some frequency, what assumptions clients have made about themselves, their jobs, and others, or the world. Assumptions that are not reflected upon can be extremely destructive. If Jose has one unverbalized set of assumptions about marriage while Andrea has another, fighting will be the order of the day—until these assumptions surface and are dealt with.

Unwarranted assumptions can underlie lifestyle decisions. For instance, Harrison learned early in life that only perfect behavior could satisfy his parents. And so, in a sense, he made a decision to do everything in life as perfectly as possible on the assumption that only perfect behavior was acceptable. This worked while he was at home and at school, but once he got married and started a career, he kept tripping over this need to be perfect. He needed a perfectly neat and clean home all the time, but his wife didn't. He needed to do everything at work perfectly, but this took longer. As a result, he was spending a fair amount of unpaid overtime at work and his supervisor saw him as slow. In his case, a decision to be perfect that worked for him for a while was now getting in his way. (See Greenwald, 1975, for a problem-solving approach to counseling based on helping clients remake decisions.)

Directionality in Life

Disorganized people's lives are filled with unformulated, unrealistic, and unmet goals and aspirations. Client A wants to go to graduate school, but she does not have the intellectual resources required. Client B thinks it is critical to take care of his health, but he is overweight, has poor muscle tone, and cannot kick a smoking habit. Client C knows that her present middle-class lifestyle is unrewarding, but she does not know why or what to substitute for it. Client D sees himself becoming more and more anxious and realizes at some level of his being that he is headed for psychic collapse, a collapse obviously unplanned but seemingly inevitable. Client E feels "dead"; she is not going anywhere and does not want to go anywhere. Effective helpers use their skills to help clients examine the directionality of their lives. For instance, if a client's interpersonal life is bland and sterile and is going nowhere, they help him or her ask and answer the question "Does it have to be this way?"

Values

I find out what my real values are by examining how I invest myself and my resources, such as time, energy, and money. As already noted, values differ from attitudes; values refer to de facto, not hoped for, self-investment. Disorganization can stem from a conflict of values; that is, clients invest themselves in two conflicting behavior patterns. For example, Mark finds himself heavily invested emotionally in both his work and his family. He is uneasy when he spends the amount of time he thinks he should spend to do his work well and when he spends leisure hours with his family. A seesaw battle is going on between these two values. The counselor can help him bring his values to the surface and then establish priorities he can share with both his family and his coworkers. Gale is a social worker. She invests herself emotionally and behaviorally in helping others. Yet self-gratification and pleasure are strong values in her life. She drinks hard at times, has a variety of social-sexual involvements, and itches to get away on short vacations. The quality of her helping suffers. The counselor helps her face the discrepancy between helping others live more effectively while she lives much less effectively than she might. Counselors can help clients learn how to clarify both their own values and those of the people who influence them in one way or another (Simon, 1974; Simon, Howe, & Kirschenbaum, 1972; Smith, 1977) and construct a viable value system for themselves (Bargo, 1980a, 1980b).

These are not the only things that clients need to talk about. They are examples of the kinds of *themes* that are often worth exploring. The goal is problem clarification, and exploration of such themes often helps to do precisely this. Of course, pursuing such a theme when it is not relevant to a client's problem situation makes little sense.

Common Stage I Problems

Moving Too Quickly

Counselors can retard the helping process by getting ahead of themselves, moving on too quickly to Stages II and III before adequately doing Stage I work. For instance, they introduce advanced-level empathy too soon (thus confusing or threatening the client), confront without laying down a base of understanding and support, or give advice. These premature responses sometimes indicate a lack of respect for the client ("I want to move ahead at a pace that pleases me, not one that is good for you").

Moving Too Slowly

Counselors sometimes feel very comfortable in Stage I and tend to remain there. They constantly encourage clients to explore themselves further and further until this self-exploration becomes so rarified as to be meaningless. It no longer contributes to the clarification of the problem situation. In this case, helping can degenerate into a game of "insight hunting." Insights into one's experiences, behaviors, and feelings certainly play an important part in the helping process, but searching for insights should never be allowed to become an end in itself.

Fear of Intensity

If the counselor uses high levels of attending, accurate empathy, respect, concreteness, and genuineness, and if the client cooperates by exploring the feelings, experiences, and behaviors related to the problematic areas of his or her life, the helping process can be an intense one. This can cause both helper and client to back off. Skilled helpers know that counseling is potentially intense. They are prepared for it and know how to support a client who is not used to such intensity.

Client Rambling

One reason helpers may be moving too slowly in Stage I is that they are allowing their clients to ramble. Rambling destroys the concreteness, the focus, and the intensity of the helping experience. If the helper punctuates the client's ramblings with nods, "uh-huhs," and the like, then the client's rambling is merely reinforced. Monologues on the part of either helper or client are ordinarily not helpful. Therefore, the counselor should respond relatively frequently to the client, without interrupting what is important or making the client lose his or her train of thought. Frequent use of accurate empathy gives direction to the counseling process. Although clients should explore those issues that have greatest relevance for them (this is another way of saying that the client's needs determine the direction of counseling), effective helpers, because they attend and listen well, are quickly in touch with what is most relevant to their clients.

Obviously, there are times when the clients will speak at greater length—for instance, in the beginning, they may let their stories pour out because this is the first time they have had the opportunity to do so. If the helper judges it is best to let the client pour everything out at once, then the helper should also be asking himself or herself what seem to be the important themes in what the client is saying. At the end, however, it is impossible for the helper to respond all at once with accurate empathy to everything the client has said. Therefore, the helper needs some way of getting back to the most salient issues and of helping the client explore them further. Some of the following expressions can be used at the end of a long client monologue:

- "This whole thing has really hit you hard. Let's see if we can't get at it bit by bit."
- "There's a lot of pain and confusion in what you've just told me. Let's see if I've understood some of the main points you've made."
- "You've said quite a bit. Let's see if we can see how the pieces fit together."

While the client is speaking, the counselor is listening in terms of core experiences, behaviors, and feelings.

Excessive Time and Energy on Probing the Past and Looking for Causes

In helping clients probe their experiences, behaviors, and feelings, helpers would do best to focus on the who, what, where, when, and how of the problem situation. Trying to find out why things are the way they are is an unfruitful pursuit because it does not lead to the kind of clarification of the problem situation that helps clients act in their own behalf. For instance, a helper asks a client, "Why did you two start fighting?" If the client really does not know exactly why, he or she may make up an answer to satisfy the counselor.

Client: Well, I don't know exactly. I don't think she ever got along well with her father. And her mother and I never really got along either. On the surface things seemed to be all right, but they never were.

Answers to why questions are usually too speculative to be useful. The causes of things, especially the remote causes, are seldom evident. To ask the client to come up with such causes is often to whistle in the wind. Clients can talk endlessly about causes, but such talk usually does not produce the kind of insight that leads to effective action programs.

Insight seeking in counseling is not the same as self-exploration. The former deals with the causes of things and the reasons behind them; the latter deals with experiences, behaviors, and feelings in actual situations. Furthermore, knowing the cause of something (assuming that one can get to the real cause) does not necessarily help a client act.

> *Client:* I think I am the way I am with my husband mainly because of some of the things that happened when I was a child. My husband is a lot like my father was, and I did like my mother better.

Such talk is a bottomless pit. Clients can hypothesize forever on the causes of behavior that leads to ineffective living. Deutsch (1954) notes that it is often almost impossible, even in carefully controlled laboratory situations, to determine whether event B, which followed event A, is actually *caused* by event A. In no way does this mean that a person's past does not influence his or her present behavior.

> This is not to deny the significance of the past in indirectly affecting behavior. However, even though the past can create a certain condition which carries over into the present, it is, nevertheless, the *present* condition which is influential in the present. Strictly considered, linking behavior with a past is an extremely difficult undertaking; it presupposes that one knows sufficiently how the past affected the psychological field at that time, and whether or not in the meantime other events have again modified the field [Deutsch, 1954, p. 186].

Carl Rogers (1951, p. 492) had already applied such thinking to the therapeutic situation:

> It should also be mentioned that in this concept of motivation all the effective elements exist in the present. Behavior is not "caused" by something which occurred in the past. Present tensions and present needs are the only ones which the organism endeavors to reduce or satisfy. While it is true that the past experience has served to modify the meaning which will be perceived in present experiences, yet there is no behavior except to meet a present need.

Certain schools of psychotherapy, such as psychoanalysis, put a great deal of emphasis on in-depth investigations of the past. In the problem-management model, the past need not be avoided if it contributes in some substantial way to clarifying the problem situation and making it more amenable to management. However, it should probably never become the principal focus of the client's self-exploration. When it does, helping often loses the name of action.

Obstacles to Effective Client Self-Exploration

Even when helpers are skillful in Stage I, clients may find self-exploration quite difficult for a number of reasons. Why might clients balk at revealing themselves and exploring their behavior? What can helpers do to deal with such resistance?

CONCERNS WITH CONFIDENTIALITY

Some clients find it very difficult to trust anyone, even a most trustworthy helper. They have irrational fears of being betrayed. In this case, because helpers cannot count on either role or reputation to carry the day, they must work at creating trust through the behavioral manifestations of respect and genuineness outlined in the next chapter.

When counseling is done in a group, however, the question of confidentiality becomes more crucial. Especially if group members know one another, worries about confidentiality will be more pressing. In this case, the question needs to be dealt with directly as one of the factors that affect the trust level of the group. The members need to develop a facilitative level of trust as quickly as possible. They can do this as the helper does it—that is, by being genuine, respectful, and understanding in the behavioral ways described in this and the next chapter. These behaviors, in conjunction with a willingness to take reasonable risks in self-disclosure, can do much to raise the trust level of a group.

FEAR OF DISORGANIZATION

Some people fear self-disclosure because they feel they cannot face what they might find out about themselves. This is a critical issue. Clients feel the facades they have constructed, no matter how much energy they must expend to keep them propped up, are still less burdensome than exploring the unknown. Such clients often begin well, but once they begin to be overwhelmed by the data produced in the self-exploration process, they retreat. Digging into one's inadequacies, which is essential to social-influence processes (Mehrabian, 1970; Strong, 1968, 1978), can lead to a certain amount of disequilibrium, disorganization, and crisis (Carkhuff, 1969a, 1969b; Piaget, 1954). But, as Piaget suggests, disequilibrium is a price a child must pay to assimilate new stimuli into an existing schema: it is the price of growth. In a similar way, Carkhuff suggests that growth takes place at crisis points. Skilled counselors realize that the self-exploration process might well be ineffective if it produces either very high or very low levels of disorganization. High disorganization immobilizes the client, but very low disorganization often indicates a failure to get at the central issues of the problem situation.

SHAME

Shame, a much overlooked experiential variable in human living (Egan, 1970; Lynd, 1958), is an important part of disorganization and crisis. The root meaning of the verb "to shame" is "to uncover, to expose, to wound," and therefore it is related to the process of self-exploration. Shame is not just being painfully exposed to another; it is primarily an exposure of self to oneself. In shame experiences, particularly sensitive and vulnerable aspects of the self are exposed, especially to one's own eyes. Shame often has the quality of suddenness: in a flash one sees one's heretofore unrecognized inadequacies without being ready for such a revelation. Shame is sometimes touched off by external incidents, such as a casual remark someone makes, but it could not be touched off by such insignificant incidents unless, deep down, one was already ashamed. A shame experience might be defined as an acute emotional awareness of a failure *to be* in some way.

In a study by Talland and Clark (1954), clients judged the therapeutic value of fifteen topics discussed during counseling. There was general agreement on the relative value of topics. Ratings showed a high correlation between the perceived helpfulness of a topic and its disturbing qualities. The topic of shame and guilt was experienced as extremely upsetting, but the discussion of this area was considered most helpful. A group of psychologists also rated the same fifteen topics for their intimacy. There was a high correlation between what the psychologists deemed intimate and what the clients judged helpful. Self-exploration must eventually deal with intimate areas that are relevant to the client's problem situation. If this exploration entails disequilibrium, disorganization, shame, and crisis, these are the price that must be paid for growth. Effective helpers both provide support for such clients and help them mobilize supportive resources in their environments.

FEAR OF CHANGE

Some people are afraid of taking stock of themselves because they know, however subconsciously, that if they do, they will have to change—that is, surrender comfortable (but unproductive) patterns of living, work more diligently, suffer the pain of loss, acquire skills needed to live more effectively, and so on. For instance, a husband and wife may realize at some level that if they see a counselor, they will have to reveal themselves and that, once the cards are on the table, they will have to go through the agony of changing their style of relating to each other.

In a counseling group, I once dealt with a man in his sixties whose presenting complaint was a very high level of anxiety. It was making his life quite painful. He told the story of how he had been treated brutally by his father until he finally ran away from home. But over the years he had developed a peculiar logic. It went something like this: "No one who grows up with scars like mine can be expected to take charge of his life and live responsibly." He had been using his mistreatment as a youth as an excuse to act irresponsibly at work (he had an extremely poor job record), in his life with himself (he drank excessively), and in his marriage (he had been uncooperative and unfaithful and yet expected his wife to support him). The idea that he could change, that he could take responsibility for himself, even at his age, frightened him, and he wanted to run away from the group. But because his anxiety was so painful, he stayed. He had to learn that a change in his style of living was absolutely necessary if he wanted to break out of the vicious circle in which he was caught.

The Temptation to Stop

Some counselors seem to have the skills needed to be effective in Stage I of the developmental model; yet they do not seem to help the client move on to Stage II and, especially, Stage III. In these cases, self-exploration becomes an end in itself and ceases to be useful. Unless helpers realize that what is happening in Stage I is meaningful only to the degree that it is ultimately related to constructive behavior change, they are in danger of failing. They will probably not even be effective in the skills they think they do possess, for when these skills lose their relationship to the total helping process, they can lose their effectiveness, even in Stage I. These skills are going nowhere because the process is going nowhere. One sign of this problem is what can be called "circular" counseling: counselors, and often their clients, too, begin to realize that they are going over and over the same territory. This kind of "going 'round the mulberry bush" is, unfortunately, all too common.

Rigidity

Skilled helpers, because they have a wide repertory of skills and responses from which they can draw naturally and spontaneously, do whatever is most useful for their clients at any given moment of the helping process, whether it follows the linear nature of the model or not. Beginners and unskilled counselors tend to apply the model too rigidly. For instance, sometimes beginners try to deal with problems sequentially. They want to take care of problem A entirely, then problem B, then C, and so on because this is less confusing for them. Although I present counseling here as a logical, clear-cut, discrete process in order to give trainees a cognitive map and to demonstrate as clearly as possible the repertory of skills and responses that need to be developed, the actual helping process is much messier. In some cases, the counseling process proceeds more or less according to the model. In other cases, it does not take a simple linear path. The final criterion for what is to be done at any given moment in the helping process, however, must be what is helpful *for the client.* Perhaps an application of Horace's principle of the golden mean might be useful here: don't underestimate the value of an integrative model in learning how to be an effective helper, but don't overestimate the value of such a model in the helping process itself.

Sufficiency of Stage I

It would seem at first glance that some clients are "cured" in Stage I. That is, they spend only a relatively limited amount of time with a helper and then seem to go off and manage quite well on their own. This brings up a most important point: *some clients seem to need more of the helper's services than others.* There are at least three ways in which clients seem to need only Stage I.

Declaring Intent and Mobilizing Resources

For some clients, the very fact that they approach someone for help seems to help them begin to pull together the resources needed to manage their problem situations more effectively. Going to a helper cues or stimulates a variety of behaviors. They begin to change their attitudes (covert behaviors)—for instance, they begin to think more positively about themselves. They also begin to interact with others in less self-defeating ways (overt behavior)—for instance, they stop trying to change others' behavior rather than their own. Going to a helper is a declaration on the part of such clients not of helplessness, but of intent: "I'm going to do something about this problem situation." Once they begin to mobilize their resources, they begin to manage their lives quite well and no longer need the services of a helper.

Escaping Self-Defeating Emotions

Some clients come to helpers because they are incapacitated, to a greater or lesser degree, by feelings and emotions. It happens often enough when such clients are shown respect, listened to, and understood in a nonjudgmental way that their self-defeating feelings and emotions subside. Once this happens, they are able to call on their own inner and environmental resources and begin to manage the problem situation that precipitated the incapacitating feelings and emotions in the first place. These clients, too, seem to be "cured" in Stage I. Once they get out from under the emotions that have been burdening them, they once more assume a course of self-responsibility.

Clarifying the Problem

A third class of clients also seems to be "cured" in Stage I. These are clients who come in feeling confused about their problems in living. However, once they understand the critical dimensions of their problem situations in terms of specific experiences, behaviors, and feelings related to specific situations—that is, once they see the problem situation clearly—they know what they need to do and go out and do it. They need the services of a helper to help them clarify their problems.

Clients with a mix of the three needs—a forum where they can declare their intent to manage their lives better, a place where they can deal with incapacitating emotion, an opportunity to find out precisely what is going wrong—may take care of all these needs in Stage I. However, not all clients fall into these categories. Helpers can make two mistakes in this regard. They can assume that all clients need all the services they can provide in terms of the stages of the problem-management model or they can assume that once clients get a fairly good understanding of their problem situations in Stage I, that is *all* they need. Skilled helpers, in collaboration with their clients, are able to help them discover precisely what kind of services they need. They try to provide neither too much nor too little.

Training as Treatment in Stage I

Just as you, as trainee, master the skills of Stage I through practice in a training group, it is possible for you, as helper/trainer, to train an individual or a group of clients in the skills of Stage I, especially attending, listening, accurate empathy, and concreteness of self-disclosure. These skills serve two functions for clients: (1) they help them focus on and explore their own problems and (2) they give them skills that are extremely useful in human relationships. I have already noted that difficulties in interpersonal relationships are often at least part of a client's problem situation. I am not suggesting that clients, by learning communication skills, will automatically solve their problems. However, after a training program, they will have some of the tools they need to deal with human relationships more effectively.

You can use the following general training methodology, which will be used in your training, to train clients.

1. *Presenting the concept.* Explain the skill (for example, accurate empathy or concreteness) cognitively. Answer questions. Be sure the trainees grasp the *concept.*

2. *Clarifying the concept.* Give trainees an opportunity to clarify for themselves just what the skill is. This can be done through questions and discussion.

3. *Modeling.* Model the skill for them. You can use films or videotapes or do a live presentation. One way of modeling is to use the method of contrasts—that is, first show how it should *not* be done and then show how it *should* be done. For instance, show them what nonattending looks like and then what attending looks like.

4. *Demonstrating.* Take the client's part and have the trainees take turns trying the skill out with you. If any trainee is having trouble, give some help—that is, "walk" him or her through the skill.

5. *Practicing.* Break the group into threes (or whatever number is practical for the skill being taught). There will then be three roles: client, helper, and observer. Have the trainees practice the skill in these subgroups.

6. *Providing feedback.* Supervise the groups—that is, encourage the trainees, correct what is not being done well, and reinforce what is being done well. Give the observer a chance to give feedback first. Make sure that feedback is respectful, brief, and concrete.

7. *Taking care of maintenance needs.* Toward the end of the training session, call the whole group together for processing: find out what learning did or did not take place. Celebrate successes. Give the trainees a chance to air their feelings about being trainees and going through the sometimes frustrating work of learning helping skills.

This, then, is the *form* that training takes. The *content*—that is, what trainees talk about—centers on their problems in living.

Skills training as part of the helping process can take place in one-to-one counseling as well as in groups. The counselor can weave into the helping process training in accurate empathy, concreteness, and assertiveness as they are called for. Because self-exploration is an important part of helping, the client can be trained in it. Such training can decrease resistance to self-exploration.

Now that we know a little bit more about the work of helping, let's consider the foundational qualities of respect and genuineness and take a longer look at helping as a process of social influence.

Chapter **5**

Stage I:
Problem Exploration
and Clarification

Part Three:
The Foundations of Helping—
Respect, Genuineness,
and Social Influence

This chapter deals with the following topics:

A behavioral approach to respect
A definition of respect
Respectful orientations toward the client
Working with the client
A behavioral approach to genuineness
A definition of genuineness
The behaviors that constitute genuineness
Helping as a social-influence process
*Social influence: The client's experience of helping in terms of helper
    attractiveness, trustworthiness, and competence*
An overview of client self-disclosure and self-exploration
Client motivation
The ways clients influence helpers

Respect and genuineness are not skills; they are values or attitudes that, when they make their way into overt behavioral expression, become *values* in the helping process. Different people have different values. I see the expression of respect and genuineness in the helping relationship as an important value.

Respect: A Behavioral Approach

Harré (1980), in a book on the social nature of human beings, contends that the deepest human need is the need for respect. Respect can be considered an attitude or moral quality, a way of looking at and prizing people. As such, respect is an inner quality, a form of *covert* behavior. However, when it comes to helping, the kinds of overt behaviors this inner attitude generates are extremely important. As Mayeroff (1971, p. 69) put it, "caring is more than good intentions and warm regards." When someone is interacting with you, how do you know he or she respects you? What overt behaviors indicate respect? How is respect expressed in the counseling situation? These are some of the questions addressed in this chapter. Respect is expressed differently at different stages of the helping model. In this chapter we are interested in both a general overview of respect and the behavioral ways in which it can be expressed in Stage I of the model.

Toward a Definition of Respect

The word *respect* comes from a Latin root that includes the notion of "seeing" or "viewing." Indeed, respect is a particular way of viewing other people. It means prizing others simply because they are human beings. It implies that being human has value in itself. Choosing to prize others simply because of their humanity is also a *value*. It is perhaps difficult to see how people could commit themselves to helping others unless this is a value for them. But a value is a value only to the degree that it is translated into some kind of *action*. Let's say I ask you, "Is reading a value for you?" and you say, "Yes." Then I ask, "How much time do you read and what kind of books?" and you say, "Well, I don't find much time to read. I'm too busy at work and at home. In fact, I haven't read a book this year." If this is the case, then reading is *not* a value for you.

Rather, seeing-reading-as-valuable is an attitude of yours. You have a favorable opinion of reading. You believe that you (and perhaps others) should read if they get the opportunity. Reading *is* a value for persons who actually read. They find or make the time because reading is one of their priorities. Raths, Harmin, and Simon (1960) describe a value as something a particular person prizes and cherishes, is committed to publicly, chooses freely from alternatives after considering the consequences, and *acts* upon (see the *Personnel and Guidance Journal*, May 1980, which deals with values and the counselor).

The same is true of respect. If it is to make a difference, it cannot remain an attitude, just a way of viewing human beings. Respect makes a difference only when it becomes a value—that is, an attitude expressed behaviorally. Some values lead people to act; others induce them to refrain from acting. That is, values can be active or passive. For instance, suppose that social justice is a value for me. If it is a *passive* value, I do nothing to cause injustice to others. If it is an *active* value, I do things to see to it that social justice is promoted—for instance, I might become active in various civil-rights movements, fight for more equitable tax laws, and so on. Some values, then, merely set limits on our behavior; others galvanize us into action. Respect, I assume, is an active value for helpers. Even better, it is both active and passive: it sets certain limits for helpers in their interactions with clients, and it also stimulates them to act toward the client in certain ways.

Verbal Expression of Respect

Respect is not often communicated directly in words in helping situations. Actions speak louder than words. For instance, the helper seldom if ever says, "I respect you because you are a human being," "I prize you," or "I respect you for engaging in self-exploration. You are doing a good thing." Respect is communicated principally by the ways helpers *orient* themselves *toward* and *work with* clients. Orientation toward and working with tend to merge in practice, but we will examine them separately in order to get a better look at the anatomy of respect.

ORIENTATION TOWARD THE CLIENT

"Orientation toward" refers to the attitudes that, once they are translated into concrete behaviors, comprise respect.

Being "for" the Client. The counselor's manner indicates that he or she is "for" the client simply because the client is human. This is not a tender or sentimental attitude. The helper is a caring person in a down-to-earth, nonsentimental sense. As a sign of this, respect ultimately involves placing demands on clients or helping them place demands on themselves. This being for, then, refers to clients' basic humanity and to their potential to be more than they are right now. Respect is both gracious and tough-minded.

Willingness to Work with the Client. Respectful helpers are available to their clients. They feel they can commit themselves to their clients. This willingness is meaningless, of course, unless they have the resources necessary to help the client. For the respectful counselor, helping is a value and not just a job. He or she can say, "Working with this client is worth the investment of my time and energy." Because counseling is a great deal of work, done by someone with a great deal of skill, such a statement is hardly sentimental.

Regard for the Client as Unique. Respect is translated into a regard for clients' individuality. This means that helpers are committed to supporting each client in his or her uniqueness and to helping each develop the resources that make him or her unique. Although effective helpers are committed to helping the client change, this does not mean that they are determined to make clients over in their own image.

Regard for the Client's Self-Determination. The helper's basic attitude is that clients have the resources to help them live more effectively. These resources may be blocked in a variety of ways, or they may be just lying fallow. The counselor's job is to help clients free and cultivate their own resources. Helpers expect clients to be self-determining, but in ways that enhance their humanity. Such a helper can also help clients assess their resources realistically so that aspirations do not outstrip resources. Ultimately, if clients choose to live less effectively than they can, the counselor, after challenging such choices, must respect them.

Assuming the Client's Goodwill. Respectful helpers assume that clients want to work at living more effectively—that is, that they want to manage their lives more effectively. They work on this assumption until it is demonstrated false (until they find, for example, that the client is merely playing at counseling, is not committed to change at all, or stays with the counselor only because he or she is under pressure from others). Even in such cases, respectful helpers do not readily conclude that their clients are choosing not to grow. They first ask themselves whether *they* have contributed in any way to the failure of the counseling relationship. Too many counselors abandon clients because they are not "motivated." This judgment may help the counselor's ego, but it is not necessarily a valid picture of the client's attitude.

WORKING WITH THE CLIENT

The attitudes described previously must be translated into action in order to be useful in the counseling process. There are many ways to manifest these attitudes behaviorally.

Attending. Attending is itself a way of showing respect. It says, behaviorally, "I am with you. I am committed to your interests. I am available to help you live more effectively. It is worth my time and effort to help you." Failure to attend can in itself indicate a lack of respect for the client. It can say, "You are not worth my time. What you say is not worth listening to. I am not really committed to working for your interests."

Suspending Critical Judgment. In Stage I, respect takes the form of suspending critical judgment of the client. Rogers (1961, 1967), following Standal (1954), calls this kind of respect "unconditional positive regard," meaning that "the therapist communicates to his client a deep and genuine caring for him as a person with potentialities, a caring uncontaminated by evaluations of his thoughts, feelings, or behaviors" (Rogers, 1967, p. 102). Consider the differences in the following counselors' remarks.

Client: I am really sexually promiscuous. I give in to sexual tendencies whenever they arise and whenever I can find a partner. This has been the story for the past three years at least.
Counselor A: Immature sex hasn't been the answer, has it? Ultimately, it is just another way of making yourself miserable.
Counselor B: So, letting yourself go sexually is part of the picture also.

Counselor B neither judges nor condones. She merely tries to communicate understanding to the client (understanding is obviously not synonymous with approval) so that both counselor and client can begin to see the context of the client's behavior; she believes that the client's approach to life needs to be understood. But she is not naive. She also realizes that some of the client's experiences must be transcended and that some of his behaviors must change, but she still respects the client as the subject of these experiences. She gives the client room to move, room to explore himself. She sees her function in Stage I as helping the client explore both his behavior and the values from which this behavior springs, and she realizes that judgmental behavior on her part would most likely cut such exploration short.

Respect, even at Stage I, is not completely unconditional. It includes regard for the client's resources. At Stage I, it means regard for clients' ability to commit themselves initially to the helping process and to engage in self-exploration.

Clients might well find this process painful, but counselors show respect by helping them through their pain, not by letting them avoid it. That is, respect includes an assumption on the part of the counselor that the client, even at Stage I, will pay the price necessary in order to begin to live more effectively. Respect, then, places a demand on the client at the same time that it offers him or her help to fulfill the demand. For instance, let's assume that a client has been manifesting a great deal of resistance. He talks about superfluous issues or issues that are serious but unrelated to the real problem situation; he changes the subject when the helper's responses bring him face to face with more crucial issues. Finally, the helper says something like the following:

> *Counselor:* I'd like to share with you my perception of what's happening between you and me and get your reaction. The way I see it, you come close to discussing problems that are quite important for you, but then you draw back. It's almost as if you were saying, "I'm not sure whether I can share this part of my life here and now." My bet is that exploring yourself and putting all the cards on the table can be extremely painful. It's like writing a blank check; you don't know how high a figure is going to be written in.

This counselor is both understanding and gently demanding. Helping is *for* the client, but the effective helper still provides direction.

Communicating Accurate Empathy. In Stage I, one of the best ways of showing respect is by working to understand clients—their experiences, their behavior, their feelings. The communication of accurate empathy is in most instances one of the best ways of showing clients respect. People generally believe that people respect them if they spend time and effort in trying to understand them. All the behaviors associated with the communication of accurate empathy, therefore, are behaviors indicating respect.

Helping Clients Cultivate Their Own Resources. Helping clients cultivate their own resources follows from the helper's attitude toward the uniqueness, the individuality, of the client. Skilled counselors help clients search for resources. For instance, they provide some form of structure clients can use to explore their own problem situations (see Egan, forthcoming, for ways of helping clients [or those in training to be helpers] to explore themselves more concretely). Effective helpers do not act for the client unless it is absolutely necessary, and then only as a step toward helping the client act on his or her own. Consider the following example:

> *Client:* There are a lot of things I find really hard to talk about. I would rather have you ask questions. That would be easier for me.

Counselor A: Okay. You mentioned that you got in trouble in school. What kind of trouble was it? How did it all start?

Counselor B: Well, let's talk about that for the moment. I feel that if I ask a lot of questions, I'll get a lot of information that *I* might think important, but I'm not convinced that it would be important for you. Putting yourself on the line like this is really new to you, and it seems you're finding it quite painful.

Counselor B assumes that the client does have, somewhere, the resources necessary to engage in self-exploration. She expresses her own feelings and tries to understand the client's blocking. She is willing to help the client work through his pain in order to get the work of Stage I done in a way that promotes his self-efficacy. Of course, she has the option of using some of the self-exploration exercises mentioned earlier, an option that would still call for client initiative.

Expressing Reasonable Warmth. Gazda (1973) sees warmth as the physical expression of understanding and caring that is ordinarily communicated through such nonverbal media as gestures, posture, tone of voice, touch, and facial expression. Warmth is only one way of showing respect. It is not necessarily the best way and can easily be misused. The helper can express initial warmth through friendliness, which is not the same as either "role" warmth (standard counselor warmth) or the warmth he or she would accord a good friend. The client is simply not a good friend. Counselors can become "warmth machines," cranking out unconditional positive regard continuously. Such warmth degenerates quickly into an "oh-that's-all-right" kind of response that is both phony and unhelpful.

Client: I'm too easy with myself. As you can see, I've let myself go physically. I'm soft and fat. I don't read any more. And now I find myself fighting with people at work.

Counselor A: First of all, Bill, most men your age let themselves go a little. And you don't look so bad to me. Don't be harder on yourself than you should be.

Counselor B: Things aren't right physically, intellectually, or interpersonally—and you don't like it.

Counselor A translates warmth into not being too hard on the client; he even goes so far as to suggest that the client lower his standards. Counselor B expresses her accurate empathy in an appropriately warm way through tone of voice and posture.

Using Reinforcement Appropriately. As Cormier and Cormier (1979, p. 54) point out, client-helper dialogue constitutes a chain, "with each counselor expression and each client expression representing a link." Clients can experience counselor responses as reinforcing, neutral, punishing, or prompting (cueing). Punitive and neutral responses, as we have seen in Chapter 1, tend to inhibit client self-exploration. They are not ways of respecting clients' attempts to explore problem situations. However, helpers can use reinforcement both appropriately and inappropriately. Consider the following examples:

> *Client:* I have some bad news to report. I talked about being hooked on speed. Well, I took it a couple of times this week.
> *Counselor A:* Don't feel so bad. You can't expect to change your way of living all at once.
> *Counselor B:* You feel you let yourself down a little. And perhaps you also learned that you're not going to kick the habit just by admitting to it.

Counselor A might well have reinforced the client's self-defeating behavior. Counselor B tries to pick up on the client's feelings; she is not judgmental, but neither does she condone (reinforce) the client's self-defeating behavior in any way. The client does not condone his own behavior; so why should the counselor? Consider another example:

> *Client:* I didn't take any drugs all week. This is the first time this has happened since I can remember.
> *Counselor A:* Okay. Let's see if you can repeat that this coming week.
> *Counselor B:* Hey, this is something new, and it makes you feel good about yourself!

The client might take Counselor A's response as punitive in that it does not recognize the client's accomplishment. Instead of recognition, there is a demand for more. Counselor B communicates understanding in a way that reinforces what the client has done. Helpers show respect when they reinforce all constructive action on the part of the client—for instance, when clients work at self-exploration or when they take even tentative steps in the direction of constructive behavioral change. Respect is also shown by refusing to reinforce the client's self-destructive behavior.

Being Genuine. Being genuine in one's relationship with another is a way of showing the other respect. Therefore, the behaviors listed in the next section also constitute ways of showing respect.

Genuineness: A Behavioral Approach

Genuineness, as it is discussed here, refers, like respect, not just to a moral or metaphysical property, quality, or attitude, but also to a set of counselor behaviors. Accordingly, a trainee can learn both what helper genuineness is and how to express it. The moral quality of being genuine is important—I assume it is a human value that should be pursued—but these pages deal more with genuineness behaviorally as a part of a communication process. In helping relationships, it does little good to *be* genuine if the client does not perceive this genuineness.

Toward a Definition of Genuineness

Rogers and Truax (1967, p. 101) describe genuineness under the rubric "congruence" and relate it to therapy:

> In relation to therapy, [congruence] means that the therapist is what he *is*, during the encounter with the client. He is without front or facade, openly being the feelings and attitudes which at the moment are flowing in him. It involves the element of self-awareness, meaning that the feelings the therapist is experiencing are available to him, available to his awareness, and also that he is able to live these feelings, to be them in the relationship, and able to communicate them if appropriate. It means that he comes into a direct personal encounter with his client, meeting him on a person-to-person basis. It means that he is *being* himself, not denying himself.

Genuine people are at home with themselves and therefore can comfortably be themselves in all their interactions. This means that they do not have to change when they are with different people—that is, they do not constantly have to adopt new roles in order to be acceptable to others.

The Behaviors That Constitute Genuineness

Being genuine has both positive and negative implications; it means doing some things and not doing others.

REFUSING TO OVEREMPHASIZE ROLE

Genuine helpers do not take refuge in the role of counselor. Relating deeply to others and helping are part of their lifestyle, not roles they put on or take off at will. Gibb (1968, 1978) suggests that helping at its best is role-free. He says that those in training for a career in helping should learn how to do the following:

- Express directly to another whatever they are presently experiencing
- Communicate without distorting their messages
- Listen to others without distorting their messages

- Reveal their true motivation in the process of communicating their messages
- Be spontaneous and free in their communications with others rather than use habitual and planned strategies
- Respond immediately to another's need or state instead of waiting for the "right" time or giving themselves enough time to come up with the "right" response
- Manifest their vulnerabilities and, in general, the "stuff" of their inner lives
- Live in and communicate about the here-and-now
- Strive for interdependence rather than dependence or counterdependence in their relationships with their clients
- Learn how to enjoy psychological closeness
- Be concrete in their communications
- Be willing to commit themselves to others

What Gibb espouses in no way makes counselors "free spirits" who inflict themselves on others. Indeed "free spirit" helpers can even be dangerous to their clients (see Lieberman, Yalom, & Miles, 1973, pp. 226–267). Being role-free is not license; freedom from role means that counselors should not use the role or facade of counselor to protect themselves, to substitute for effectiveness, or to fool the client.

And yet we talk about helpers, counselors, and psychotherapists as professionals. Doesn't "profession" imply "role"? As we have seen, Carkhuff (1971a) distinguishes between "credentialed" and "functional" professionals. Credentialed professionals are those who have degrees and certificates indicating that they have successfully completed a variety of training programs and on whom the sponsoring agency, often a university, is willing to put some kind of stamp of approval—often a degree. Functional professionals possess the skills discussed in this book, including the ability to express both respect and genuineness in the behavioral ways outlined here. Functional professionals may or may not be credentialed; conversely, credentialed professionals may or may not be functional. Gross (1978) and Koocher (1979) point out that current credentialing procedures in the helping professions provide little assurance of competence.

> In the final analysis it seems that whatever existing credentials in psychology do measure, they are clearly not highly valid measures of professional competence. . . . [W]e must recognize that there are many skilled and competent mental health professionals who will not have the usual credentials, and we must seek to reduce unnecessarily rigid barriers to preclude members of the public from access to their services [Koocher, 1979, p. 702].

Gibb suggests that credentialed professionals who are at the same time functional do not overemphasize their credentials. Being professional and being role-free in Gibb's sense are not contradictory.

BEING SPONTANEOUS

Genuine people are spontaneous. Many of the behaviors Gibb suggests are ways of being spontaneous. Effective helpers, while being tactful (as part of their respect for others), do not constantly weigh what they say to clients. They do not put a number of filters between their inner lives and what they express to others. Rogers (1957) notes that being genuine does not mean verbalizing every thought to the client. For instance, he suggests that helpers express negative feelings to clients only if these feelings persist or if they are interfering with their ability to move with the client through the helping process.

> *Client:* I want to know what you really think of me.
> *Counselor A:* Well, I think you're lazy and that you might like things to get better if that could happen by magic.
> *Counselor B:* Frankly, I am not sure how that would help you grapple with your problems better. But if you mean that it's time for the two of us to take a closer look at how we're relating in these sessions, I think it's a good idea.

Counselor A is literal minded and blunt. Counselor B sees the client's petition as a desire for greater immediacy. He knows that direct, solid feedback is important, but he prefers that it take place in a human way. Unskilled counselors go to extremes; they are blunt or timid. Both behaviors are usually rationalized: the former as "frankness," the latter as "tact." Tact springs from strength, not weakness. Effective helpers know when they are tempted to hold something back as a form of self-protection (for example, because they fear the client's reaction) and when they are doing it for the client's sake (the client is not yet ready to hear it, although he or she will have to hear it eventually).

Genuine counselors are assertive in the helping process without being aggressive. One of the cardinal problems with many trainees in the helping professions is their fear of asserting themselves. Some want to settle for a caricature of "nondirective counseling" as a helping model because this is what they are most comfortable with. Because they do not move out and meet others spontaneously in their day-to-day lives, to do so in counseling seems foreign to them. Many trainees, therefore, need a kind of counselor training program that will teach them experientially that it is all right to be active, spontaneous, free, and assertive.

AVOIDING DEFENSIVENESS

Genuine helpers are nondefensive. They know their own strengths and deficits and are presumably trying to live mature, meaningful lives. When clients express negative attitudes toward them, they try to understand what their clients are thinking and feeling, and they continue to work with them. Consider the following example:

> *Client:* I don't think I'm really getting anything out of these sessions at all. Things are going just as poorly at school. Why should I waste my time coming here?
>
> *Counselor A:* I think *you* are the one wasting time. You just don't want to do anything.
>
> *Counselor B:* Well, that's your decision.
>
> *Counselor C:* There's been no payoff for you here. It seems like a lot of dreary work with nothing to show for it.

Counselors A and B are both defensive. Counselor C tries to understand and gives the client the opportunity to get at the issue of responsibility in the helping process. Because genuine helpers are at home with themselves (though not in a smug way), they can allow themselves to examine negative criticism honestly. Counselor C would be the most likely of the three to ask himself whether he is contributing to the stalemate that seems to exist. Helpers who need to defend themselves constantly lest they be hurt cannot help others effectively. Trainees who feel this way would do best to work out their fears and misgivings before trying to help others.

BEING CONSISTENT

Genuine people do not experience significant discrepancies in their lives. For instance, they do not have one set of "notional" values (such as caring, justice, love, and peace) different from their "real" values (such as influence, money, and comfort). They do not think or feel one thing and say another. Or at least they are able to identify the discrepancies in their lives, especially those affecting their ability to help others, and are willing to deal with them.

> *Client:* Frankly, I don't think you like me. I think you're working hard with me, but I still don't think you like me.
>
> *Counselor A:* I'm not sure that liking or not liking relates to what we're doing here.
>
> *Counselor B:* I'm not sure that that makes any difference. . . . (Pause) Wait a minute. Last time we talked about your being more assertive in our relationship. I think that right now you're being reasonably assertive, and I'm

brushing you aside. You seem to be saying that it's time we take a look at how we're relating to each other here. I think it's a good idea.

Counselor A brushes aside the client's challenge as irrelevant. Counselor B catches herself in a discrepancy. She wants the client to be more assertive toward her and now realizes that she has to take the client's demands seriously.

BEING OPEN

Genuine helpers are capable of deep self-disclosure. To be certain, self-disclosure is not an end in itself for them, but they feel free to reveal themselves intimately when it is appropriate. Because genuineness in the form of helper self-disclosure or self-sharing is part of Stage II, it will be dealt with in greater detail in Chapter 7. As can be seen from a couple of the examples used in this section, genuineness also expresses itself in two other Stage II behaviors: immediacy and confrontation. These, too, will be treated in Chapter 7. Box 5–1 summarizes some of the attitudes and behaviors that are involved in the communication of respect and genuineness.

Helping as a Social-Influence Process

History provides a great deal of evidence that people suffering from a variety of emotional disturbances and physical ailments of psychogenic origin have been "cured" by their belief in a helper's curing powers (Frank, 1973). Very often such cures have taken place in religious contexts, but they have not been limited to such contexts. People may have come to see a certain person as a healer with great powers. People hear that such healers have cured others with ailments similar to theirs. They generally see these healers as acting not in their own interest but in the interest of the afflicted who come to them. This belief enables the afflicted person to place a great deal of trust in the healer. Finally, in a ceremony that is often public and highly emotional, the healer in some way touches the afflicted person and the person is "healed." The afflicted person's tremendous need, the healer's reputation, and the afflicted person's trusting belief in the healer all heighten the person's belief that he or she will be cured. In fact, if such afflicted persons are not cured, it is often laid to their lack of belief or to some evil within them (for instance, possession by a demon or poor motivation), and they not only remain with their afflictions but also lose face in the community (an outcast, a "crazy"). This second state is worse than the first: the afflicted person is not only ill but also an object of opprobrium.

The dynamics of such "cures" are hard to explain empirically. It is obvious that elements of the healing process help marshal afflicted persons' emotional

---

BOX 5–1   SUMMARY OF RESPECT AND GENUINENESS

RESPECT

The value of respect is manifested in both your attitudes toward (covert behavior) and the ways in which you work with (overt behavior) clients. Your attitude toward clients is respectful if you

- Care about their welfare
- See each client as a unique human being rather than a case
- See them as capable of determining their own fate
- Assume the goodwill of clients until this assumption is demonstrated to be wrong

Your attitude becomes respectful behavior when you

- Attend and listen actively to clients
- Suspend critical judgment
- Communicate accurate empathic understanding
- Express reasonable warmth or friendliness
- Help clients identify and cultivate their own resources
- Provide encouragement and support (social reinforcement)
- Help clients get the work of each stage of the helping process done

GENUINENESS

You are genuine in your relationship with your clients when you

- Do not overemphasize your professional role and avoid stereotyped role behaviors
- Are spontaneous but not uncontrolled or haphazard in your relationships
- Remain open and nondefensive even when you feel threatened
- Are consistent and avoid discrepancies between your values and your behavior and between what you think and feel and what you say while remaining reasonably tactful
- Are willing to share yourself and your experience with clients if this is seen as helpful

---

energies and other resources. For instance, they experience hope and other positive emotions, which they perhaps have not experienced for years. The whole situation both mobilizes their resources and places a demand on them to be cured. It presents the afflicted person with a *kairos*, an opportune, acceptable, favorable, legitimate time to leave his or her old way of life behind and take up a new one. The power of suggestion in such cases can be great, even overwhelming. Skilled helpers are aware of and have a deep respect for the "nonrational" factors operative in the helping process.

I have already suggested that social influence is a fact of everyday life—we are constantly influencing one another in many different ways, though not always in the dramatic ways Frank (1973) suggests. He describes mainly a *unilateral* process. Goldstein (1980, p. 2) talks about the unilateral nature of the helping process.

> The *unilateral* aspect of the helping relationship reflects the fact that the participants agree that one person is defined as the helper and the other as the client. It is also agreed, explicitly or implicitly, that the focus of the relationship and all its activities is on solving the problems of the client. In this respect, the change process is unlike most other interpersonal interactions. The personal problems, the private affairs, the worries, and the wishes of one person, the helper, are intentionally not focused upon. Treatment, therapy, or whatever the helping relationship may be called, is one-sided and concentrates exclusively on the client.

Although this is true, it does not mean that clients do not influence helpers in significant ways. Social influence goes on constantly in the helping relationship—helpers influence their clients and clients influence their helpers. Helping is a fully human process only if helpers influence their clients in ways that are consonant with the interpersonal values alluded to earlier.

The Nature of Social Influence in the Helping Relationship

In 1968, Stanley Strong wrote what proved to be a landmark article on counseling as an interpersonal-influence process. It stimulated a great deal of writing and research, which Corrigan et al. (1980) have summarized. They outline the main points of Strong's argument:

> Based on cognitive dissonance theory (Festinger, 1957), Strong hypothesized that counselor's attempts to change clients' behavior or opinions would precipitate dissonance in clients. Clients could reduce dissonance by one of five means: (a) change in the direction advocated by the counselor, (b) discredit the counselor ["she doesn't know what she's talking about"], (c) discredit the

issue ["drinking is really not that important in my life"], (d) change the counselor's opinion, or (e) seek others who agree with the client ["my friends don't see me that way"]. Strong suggested that counselors could increase the likelihood that the first alternative [client change] would occur by reducing the likelihood of the second and third [discrediting the counselor and/or the issue]. . . . Strong postulated that the extent to which counselors are perceived as expert, attractive, and trustworthy would reduce the likelihood of their being discredited. By increasing clients' involvement in counseling, the likelihood of discrediting the issue would be reduced. From these hypotheses, Strong suggested a two-stage model of counseling. In the first stage, counselors *enhance* their perceived expertness, attractiveness, trustworthiness, and clients' involvement in counseling. In the second stage, counselors *use* their influence to precipitate opinion and/or behavior change in clients [p. 396].

Support for Strong's position comes from research in social psychology (Goldstein, 1966, 1971; Goldstein, Heller, & Sechrest, 1966; Krumboltz, Becker-Haven, & Burnett, 1979; McGuire, 1969; Simons, Berkowitz, & Moyer, 1970; Strong, 1978).

Goldstein (1980) describes the social-influence process in helping in a way that is complementary to Strong's. First, he calls behaviors by which helpers establish an interpersonal power base with their clients "relationship enhancers." He suggests that there are various ways of doing this: by providing clients with the kind of structure that enables them to give themselves more easily to the helping process (for instance, by setting up a clear client-counselor contract), by modeling the kinds of behaviors expected of clients so they can imitate them (for instance, the kinds of behaviors associated with respect and genuineness), by attending, by expressing appropriate warmth, by communicating accurate empathy, by sharing their own experiences, and the like. Second, these behaviors, if carried out skillfully, lead to mutual liking, respect, and trust. Third, this kind of relationship helps clients become more willing to engage in dialogues with helpers, reveal themselves more deeply, and open themselves to the different kinds of direction helpers may provide throughout the helping process. Finally, because of all of this, the probability that clients will change their behavior in self-enhancing ways is increased. Constructive behavioral change on the part of the client is always the "bottom line."

Applying Social-Influence Theory to the Problem-Management Model of Helping: The Client's Experience of Helping

Let's take a closer look at social influence as it takes place in the helping relationship in terms of attractiveness, trustworthiness, and competence. We are especially interested in the client's experience or perceptions—that is, the client's *experience* of the helper and his or her behavior both before and during the helping process. Before beginning, however, it is important to note that different clients will experience the same helper in different ways. A complex web of factors goes into any person's perception of another. Therefore, although by engaging in the behaviors outlined below there is *some probability* that you will appear attractive, trustworthy, and competent to clients, outcomes will vary from client to client. It should also be noted that attractiveness, trustworthiness, and competence, even though presented separately here, are often interrelated in the client's perception. For instance, if you are experienced as competent, you well might be experienced as trustworthy.

ATTRACTION

Meaning of Attractiveness. Strong (1968, p. 216) suggested that clients' perceptions of counselor attractiveness are based on "perceived similarity to, compatibility with, and liking for" the helper. For instance, if the client is young and the helper is also at least relatively young, this perceived similarity might help the client to be attracted to the helper. If the client is an addict and the helper is a reformed addict who talks about his or her own experiences of addiction, this self-sharing might help the client see the counselor as similar to and compatible with himself or herself. It may also happen that a client is spontaneously attracted to a helper because of a "package" of such things as friendliness and accepting behavior. When asked to identify the reasons, the client might say, "I don't know; I just like her."

Sources of Perceived Attractiveness. You may appear attractive to clients because of physical characteristics and general appearance (you are good looking or well groomed), because of your particular helping role (counselor, psychologist, doctor, nurse, or minister), because of your reputation (for instance, others have told a prospective client that you are a friendly, understanding person), and/or because of your behavior. I emphasize behavior because there is usually little that can be done about the other categories, even though you know they are affecting a client. For instance, some clients might find ministers more attractive helpers than psychologists, but if you are a psychologist, you would hardly become a minister for that reason.

Increasing Perceived Attractiveness. There are obviously some things you cannot do to make yourself more attractive to clients. For instance, there are a limited number of things you can do to make yourself more physically attractive. This makes little difference, it would seem, because physical attractiveness tends to bias only the client's *initial* perceptions and expectations, and the bias seems to be the result of the negative effect of low attractiveness rather than the positive effect of high attractiveness.

Common sense and some research shows that sometimes the following behaviors on the part of helpers increase their attractiveness to clients:

- Attending to the client in the ways outlined in Chapter 3
- Being friendly and warm
- Being empathic in the ways outlined in Chapter 4
- Not engaging in judgmental behavior
- Being active rather than passive in the helping session
- Letting clients know that you hold attitudes similar to theirs
- Being a female when clients are female
- Talking about yourself in moderate amounts, especially when your self-disclosure shows that you and the client are similar in certain ways

TRUSTWORTHINESS

Meaning of Trustworthiness. Strong (1968, p. 217) suggests that a helper's perceived trustworthiness is based on his or her "(a) reputation for honesty, (b) social role, such as physician, (c) sincerity and openness, and (d) lack of motivation for personal gain." It can mean a number of things:

- *Confidentiality.* The client can say, "If I tell this person about myself, she will not tell others."
- *Credibility.* "Interpersonal trust is defined . . . as an expectancy held by an individual or group that the word, promise, verbal or written statement of another individual or group can be relied on" (Rotter, 1971, p. 444). The client can say, "I can believe what he tells me."
- *Consideration in the use of power.* The assumption here is that the helper is perceived as having power and as being the kind of person who will not misuse it. The client can say, "If I entrust myself to this person, she will act with care toward me."
- *Understanding.* The client can say, "If I tell this person about myself, he will make an effort to understand me."

Rotter (1971, p. 447) suggests that trusting another can be a strength rather than a weakness: "The high truster does not trust out of a need to have someone else take care of him, and apparently he is not regarded (by others) as someone who is easily fooled, tricked, or is naive."

Sources of Perceived Trustworthiness. Trustworthiness has the same general sources as attractiveness. Someone might see you as trustworthy (or untrustworthy) because of your physical appearance ("I just don't trust him; he reminds me of a used car salesman who once did me in"), because of your reputation ("Ira says that she doesn't talk about any of her clients, even in general terms"), because of role ("I can trust him because he's a priest"), and/ or because of behavior. Again, I shall emphasize helper behaviors.

Increasing Perceived Trustworthiness. You may increase your trustworthiness in the eyes of your clients if you do the following:

- Strike a contract with the client and live up to its provisions
- Maintain confidentiality
- Manifest respect in the ways outlined earlier in this chapter
- Are sensitive to their needs and feelings
- Demonstrate genuineness, sincerity, and openness in the ways outlined earlier in this chapter
- Are realistic but optimistic about clients' abilities to come to grips with their problems in living
- Are willing to give them information or feedback that might benefit them
- Use whatever social-influence power you have carefully and in clients' interests
- Are open to clients' feedback and reasonable social-influence attempts
- Avoid behavior that might indicate the presence of such ulterior motives as voyeurism, selfishness, superficial curiosity, personal gain, or deviousness

COMPETENCE

In the literature on social influence, this is usually called "expertness," but I prefer the term *competence*, a term that, at least for me, has a broader meaning. It does not take much experience in life to realize that people who are called "experts" are not always competent. And a person can draw this inference without being cynical. Strong (1968) suggested that competence, from the client's point of view, refers to his or her belief that the helper is, in Hovland, Janis, and Kelley's (1953, p. 21) terms, "a source of valid assertions." It is the client's belief that the counselor has some information, skill, or ability to help him or her. It refers to clients' assumptions that the counselor possesses "answers" to their problems or information that will enable them to come up with their own answers. In any case, clients believe that this information will enable them to live less painfully or more effectively.

Strong (1968, p. 216) goes on to say that this belief is influenced by "(a) objective evidence of specialized training such as diplomas, certificates, and titles, (b) behavioral evidence of expertness such as rational and knowledgeable arguments and confidence in presentation, and (c) reputation as an expert." That is, like attractiveness and trustworthiness, there are three general sources of perceived competence: role, reputation, and behavior. Let's take a closer look at each of these and add one more.

Role Competence. Role competence refers to the fact that helpers belong to some profession (they are counselors, psychotherapists, ministers, social workers, and the like) and that they have a variety of credentials (degrees or certificates) attesting to the fact that they are experts. Other role-related factors that can suggest competence are such things as offices, name plates, and titles. In terms discussed earlier, clients see helpers as "credentialed" professionals.

Reputation Competence. This means that clients are aware of some direct or indirect testimony that the helper is an expert or is competent. This testimony may come from those who have actually been helped by the counselor, or it may come from other helpers who consider their colleague a good helper. Helpers' reputations may also come from the fact that they are associated with a prestigious institution. Evidently, helpers' reputations may or may not be deserved: a reputation is not an absolute indication that any given helper is actually competent. But a reputation for expertness does have at least an initial impact on the client.

Behavior Competence. Some people let themselves be influenced by helpers because the behaviors in which these helpers engage have at least the aura of competence. Helpers are seen as competent because they are active, listen intently, talk intelligently, exude a quiet confidence as they give directives to their clients, and are understanding, genuine, and respectful. However, just because it appears that the helper is acting competently does not mean he or she is actually competent. Clients can be beguiled by a set of behaviors that seems to indicate competence and trust helpers who engage in these behaviors. I suggest a more radical kind of expertness or competence, something that can be called *accomplishment competence.*

Accomplishment Competence. Accomplishment competence represents the "bottom line" of social influence. If helpers are perceived as attractive, trustworthy, and/or competent (in the sense that they engage in behaviors that *seem* competent to the client) and then, in the long run, *do not actually help*, this second state is worse than the first. Clients' reasonable expectations are not met and they lose faith in the helping process itself.

> *Client:* It's just no use. I went to this guy. He was actually a nice guy. I trusted him. He was a doctor and everything. But we got no place. It seems that we went round and round and nothing got any better.

Of course, there is no automatic assumption that most of the fault lay with the helper. But being perceived by the client as attractive, trustworthy, and competent, even though it might have opened the client up to influence, did not accomplish anything.

Therefore, helpers need to be able to *deliver* what is promised by the helping contract, whether that contract is explicit or implicit. According to Gilbert (1978), competence does not lie principally in behaviors but in the *accomplishments* toward which these behaviors are directed. If Brenda comes to a helper with persistently high levels of free-floating anxiety, then "anxiety *reduced*" is one of the hoped-for accomplishments of the helping process. If a year later she is still as anxious as ever, despite weekly visits to a professional helper, then that helper's role-, reputation-, and behavioral-attractiveness, trustworthiness, and competence go for naught. Trust in a helper can evaporate quickly if little or nothing is accomplished through the helping sessions. And yet, too often, it would seem, clients persist in trusting helpers even though they fail to demonstrate competence through verifiable accomplishments. Role, reputation, and behavior still beguile them even in the face of problem situations that remain unchanged.

The problem-solving approach to helping does much to avoid this impasse. Problem situations are translated into solution-related goals; programs are devised and implemented to achieve these goals; and the entire process is shared with the client to the degree that this is possible and continually scrutinized and evaluated. Because accomplishments are identified, it is possible to see whether or not they are achieved.

When I use the word *competence* in subsequent pages, it refers not to role, reputation, or behavior. It does not even refer principally to the helper's working knowledge and skills. Rather, it refers to the helper-consultant's ability to help clients actually achieve their goals.

The Helper's Confidence in the Helping Model. Strong (1968) suggests a possible fifth way in which clients are influenced to see their helpers as competent. It is the confidence the helper displays in the model he or she is using. This confidence means much more than blind faith in a particular system. Counselors who work hard to make any particular theory or model their own manifest their investment in their attitudes and behavior. They speak and act enthusiastically and confidently. More than that, they work hard with their clients.

I have already suggested that counselors share with their clients the model they are using so that clients, too, may have a map to guide them through the helping process. As Strong (1968) suggests, this sharing is in itself a behavioral way of demonstrating competence to the client.

Self-Exploration

Because what clients are being influenced to do in Stage I is to talk about themselves and explore themselves and their problem situations in terms of concrete and specific experiences, behaviors, and feelings, it is useful to take a closer look at self-disclosure as a human process. Psychologists have only begun to study self-disclosing behavior scientifically (Chelune, 1979; Cozby, 1973). It is difficult, then, to situate the kind of self-disclosure that is associated with training groups (Egan, 1976) and the helping process (Doster & Nesbitt, 1979) in a wider context of "normal" self-disclosing behavior.

Jourard (1971a, 1971b), among others, claims that responsible self-sharing is a part of the normal behavior of the healthy actualized person. According to him, persons who cannot share themselves deeply are ultimately incapable of love. Some theoreticians, taking a commonsense approach to self-disclosure, have hypothesized that there is a curvilinear relationship between self-disclosure and mental health: very high and very low levels of self-disclosing behavior are signs of maladjustment; moderate (and appropriate) self-disclosure is optimal. Overdisclosers can be exhibitionistic or, at least, preoccupied with themselves. Underdisclosers may be fearful of intimacy or feel that they have a great deal to hide. Underdisclosers can pour a great deal of energy into building and maintaining facades so that their real selves will not be discovered (see Mowrer, 1968a, 1968b, 1973a, 1973b, for an interesting approach to underdisclosing behavior in counseling and psychotherapy). The overddiscloser discloses a great deal even when the situation does not call for it; the underdiscloser remains closed even when the situation calls for self-disclosing behavior.

Self-disclosure, either within the helping relationship or outside it, is never an end in itself. I assume here that self-disclosure, to promote growth, must be *appropriate* to the setting. Derlega and Grzelak (1979, p. 153) outline seven aspects of self-disclosure that we can use to explore appropriate self-disclosure in a helping context.

- *Informativeness.* This refers to both the quantity (breadth) and quality (depth or intimacy) of the information provided. In counseling this refers, as we have seen, to the experiences, behaviors, and feelings that need to be explored to define the problem situation adequately. This will, of course, differ from client to client.
- *Accessibility.* This refers to the ease with which information can be obtained from the client. Some clients need more help than others in

getting at relevant experiences, behaviors, and feelings. As we have seen, empathy and probing are important skills in this regard.

- *Voluntariness.* This refers to the client's willingness to provide relevant information. Clients who are fearful about revealing themselves need support and encouragement to do so.
- *Reward value.* This refers to the extent that revealing information provides positive (reinforcing) or negative (punishing) outcomes for the client. If you fail to listen to what a client is saying or you respond in a way that the client finds punitive, the client's self-disclosing behavior will most likely diminish. On the other hand, if you attend and listen well and if you deal carefully with his or her revelations, then self-disclosing behavior is likely to be maintained.
- *Truthfulness.* This refers to the extent to which the client's messages provide information about his or her actual psychological state. If you discover that the client is not telling you the truth, it may be that he or she is afraid of telling you or fears other punishing consequences. If this is the case, accusations of being a liar will not help. What is needed are both support and reasonable challenge.
- *Social norms.* This refers to the extent to which what is disclosed conforms with or deviates from cultural expectations about appropriate disclosing behavior. Some clients are very low disclosers in their everyday lives (in fact, this may be part of the problem situation). It is sometimes hard for them to realize that the "rules" are different in the counseling setting. This is especially true of group counseling. Providing such clients with some kind of facilitative structure for self-disclosure can help (see Egan, forthcoming).
- *Effectiveness.* This refers to the extent to which the messages revealed contribute to the client's goals. It makes little difference if clients talk intimately and at length about themselves if such disclosures do not contribute ultimately to the management of the problem situation. Through empathy, probing, and summaries, you can help clients make their disclosures focused and goal-directed.

No claims are made here that self-disclosure in itself "cures," for it is a stage in a developmental helping process. But as Mowrer (1968a, 1968b, 1973a) demonstrates, self-disclosure can in some cases release a great deal of "healing" forces or resources in the client. For instance, it helps a client get out from under a burden of guilt. Therefore, adequate self-disclosing behavior predicts therapeutic outcome (Truax & Carkhuff, 1965).

If we can find a way to expand the statement of a problem to a concrete list of specific behaviors which constitute it, one major obstacle to the solution of the problem will have been overcome. In other words, the initial ambiguity with which most people analyze their interpersonal problems tends to contribute to their feeling of helplessness in coping with them. Knowing which specific behaviors are involved, and thereby what changes in those behaviors will solve the problem, provides a definite goal for action—and having that goal can lend a great sense of relief [Mehrabian, 1970, p. 7].

Self-disclosure does not "cure," but it does contribute significantly to the overall process. Let's look at the difference between the self-disclosing behavior of two different clients.

Client A: Things just don't seem to be going right. My personal life is at a low ebb. I'm overloaded with work. And a lot of other things intervene to clog up the works. I tend to give up.

This client expresses his feelings in a vague way; he does not delineate or own his experiences clearly; and he fails to indicate his concrete behaviors.

Client B: I'm depressed, really down, and this is unusual for me. I find it hard to get out of bed in the morning and I feel groggy most of the day. I try to read but keep putting the book down and wandering around the house. I think I should go to a movie or visit a friend, but I don't do it; I don't even want to. I have even lost my appetite. This has been the pattern for a couple of weeks now. I think I know what's going on. Two weeks ago I received my dissertation back from my committee. They turned it down for the second time. And I really thought I had made the corrections they wanted before. Now I'm beginning to think I'll have to get an entirely new topic, collect new data—the whole bit. But I don't think I have the energy, the drive, the motivation to do so. Yet I don't want my graduate education to go down the drain. Maybe what bothers me even more is that when I began working on the dissertation, I began to withdraw from my friends. I didn't invite anyone over to my place and I turned down their invitations to dinners and parties. I didn't even hang around after class to talk to anyone. I left as soon as class was over to get to my typewriter. Now nobody calls me up anymore or comes over. I don't blame them. Why should they? I put the dissertation before them for months. So, on top of everything else, I'm lonely. I just want to pack up and go back to New York.

This client's statement is filled with specific feelings, experiences, and behaviors. The difference in self-disclosure ability between Client A and Client B is obviously vast. Because many clients will not have the ability to reveal themselves as Client B does here, your probing and empathy skills are needed to help them bridge the gap.

Client Motivation

Attitude and behavior change are facilitated when the client is highly involved in the influence process. The active, highly involved client is seen as a motivated client. Motivation deals with the principles of behavior discussed briefly in Chapter 1. As Gilbert (1978) notes, people tend to do things when there are enough *incentives* to do them. They tend not to do things when there are no incentives or when the incentives are not strong enough. People also tend to avoid behaviors for which they are punished. How does this apply to client motivation?

1. *Reducing psychological pain.* Clients are often highly motivated if they are in psychological pain. The very disorganization in their lives makes them susceptible to helpers' influence. They see in helpers potential sources of relief and are even willing to pay the price for relief, which is self-exploration and behavioral change. The promise of pain reduction can be highly reinforcing. Sometimes, however, clients see the pain of being helped as worse than the pain of their disorganization and therefore refuse to go for help or resist it if they do go. At other times, they do seek help but break off the relationship after getting enough help to make the pain of their day-to-day lives tolerable.

2. *Client-centered helping.* Clients will involve themselves in the helping process more fully if they are dealing with issues of intrinsic importance to them. This fact underscores the importance of the skill of accurate empathic understanding on the part of helpers. The more in tune they are with the client's world, the more probable it is that they will deal with issues that have importance for the client.

3. *Pacing.* The amount of physical and psychological effort demanded of clients by the helping process affects their motivation. If too many demands are made too soon, they might well stop coming for help. If little is demanded of them and they see no progress, they are also likely to discontinue. Watson and Tharp (1981) describe helping as at least in part a "shaping" process in which the helper guides the client step by *gradual*

step toward more constructive patterns of behavior. They see the loss of "willpower" (motivation) at any stage of this process as due to inadequate shaping. The helper or the client becomes too demanding.

How Clients Influence Helpers

Helping is often described as a one-way process. However, the unilateral nature of helping mentioned earlier (Goldstein, 1980) does not mean that clients do not influence their helpers. Even a cursory examination of the helping process reveals that clients can affect helpers in many different ways. I shall discuss four of them.

Dialogue

The helping relationship involves a great deal of dialogue. Each statement the client makes has some impact on the helper. For instance, in the following example, the client, a woman in her forties, is discussing her relationship to her younger brother.

> *Client* (looking at the floor and speaking in a flat voice): I've always been good to him, helped him out when he was at school. Things like that. But now that my husband's gone, I don't hear much from him. He's always been busy.
>
> *Helper:* You're disappointed that he's not around now that you could use a little help.
>
> *Client* (after a short pause): One of the things I liked best about my husband was his sense of humor.

In this interchange, the client influences the helper in two ways. First, her self-disclosure about her relationship to her brother draws from him a statement of primary-level empathy. That is, what she says, as in all dialogue, influences what he says in return. Second, because the client changes the subject abruptly, the helper is puzzled. The dialogue has taken a turn he did not expect. He now has to make a decision to find out what's behind the client's change (for instance, he may have been inaccurate or she might have found the subject too painful) or to follow her new lead.

Norman Kagan (1975) has devised a very useful system called Interpersonal Process Recall, in which helpers are systematically trained to "listen to" themselves as they interact with their clients. This includes listening for the ways they react to what the client is saying. Sometimes helpers react to clients after only half listening to what they have said. One of the goals of the recall process is to help counselors deal with the ways they are being affected by clients at the time it happens. This can increase the efficiency of helping. For instance, Joanne finds herself becoming defensive as she talks to Ian but merely limps through the session without seeing clearly what is happening. Afterwards, in talking to another counselor, she realizes that she was being affected by the sexism in a number of Ian's remarks. This does not mean that at the time she would have necessarily confronted him on this. It does mean that she should have known how he was affecting her. This would have allowed her to make a decision as to the best course to follow. Interpersonal Process Recall can assist helpers in dealing with the kinds of influence involved in the categories that follow also.

Attraction

Helpers are affected by both physical and other forms of attractiveness in their clients. Once they are aware that they see any given client as attractive, unattractive, or somewhere in between, they are in a position to monitor their reactions to the client. For instance, they may realize they will tend to be less demanding of attractive clients and more prone not to listen well to unattractive clients.

Reacting to Clients' Distortions of Helpers

Some clients trip over their own distorted views of their helpers. For instance, a young woman who has had serious problems in her relationship with her mother might begin to act toward her female counselor in unproductive ways similar to those in which she acts or reacts toward her mother. Skilled helpers realize that this might take place and therefore are better prepared for it when it does happen. Unskilled helpers can get caught up in the game. They follow clients' leads instead of understanding and, in due time, challenging the client's distorted views.

Problem Similarity

Clients may bring up problem situations similar to those their helpers are currently experiencing. For instance, Ingrid might discuss her impending divorce with Elsa, who sees herself headed for a divorce. If this so affects Elsa that she cannot work effectively with Ingrid, then a referral to another therapist is in order. Ideally, helpers are striving to become "effective" (Carkhuff, 1969a, 1969b), "intentional" (Ivey, 1980), "transparent" (Jourard, 1971b), "self-actualized" (Maslow, 1968, 1971), and capable of "I-Thou" relationships (Buber,

---

BOX 5–2   A SUMMARY OF THE WORK OF STAGE I

If the problem situation is complex, then help the client choose some part of the problem that, if handled, will probably lead to some significant improvement in the quality of his or her life.

Help the client explore the issues involved in terms of

- Relevant experiences, behaviors, and feelings
- Relevant environmental influences
- Relevant principles of behavior—such as reinforcement, avoidance, and the like

Help the client explore the area as concretely as possible—that is, in terms specific to situations.

Help clients explore not just their deficits but also their resources.

Help clients explore the past only to the degree that it helps them get out from under self-defeating emotions and contributes to the goal of clarifying and defining the present problem situation.

Use the skills of attending and listening to gather data related to the problem area. Observe how the client's here-and-now behavior expresses his or her problems in living.

Use the skill of empathy to help clients gather and clarify data and to develop a working relationship with them.

Use probing techniques to stimulate the client to recall and review data needed to make the problem area as clear as possible.

Encourage the client to participate in and "own" the entire helping process.

Help clients acquire whatever working knowledge of the helping process and self-disclosure skills they need to participate in this problem-clarification stage.

Do not spend more time and energy than the problem is worth—that is, make sure there is a reasonable return for the energy expended.

1937/1970). This means, in part, that they are capable of applying the problem-solving model I am discussing to the management of their own lives. They might do this on their own or take counsel with others. If they are successful, then the problem situations they are facing will not interfere with their ability to help others face similar problems. However, if problem similarity does interfere with their ability to help, then they know that a referral is in order.

Box 5–2 summarizes how you foster a good working relationship between yourself and your clients and achieve the goal of Stage I—that is, initial problem clarification and definition. As we have seen, for some clients this is enough. Given this start, they move on through the rest of the problem-management process on their own or by using resources available to them in their environment. Many clients, however, need further help. This leads us to Stage II.

Chapter 6

Stage II:
Developing New Perspectives
and Setting Goals

Part One:
The Skills of Summarizing, Information Giving, and Advanced Empathy; the Conditions for Effective Challenging

This chapter discusses the following topics:

I shall develop the material on challenging and goal setting in two chapters. In this chapter, the function of challenging; the skills of summarizing, information giving, and advanced empathy; and the conditions for effective challenging of clients will be considered. In Chapter 7, the challenging skills of confrontation, helper self-sharing, and immediacy will be discussed, together with goal setting.

When Stage I Is Not Enough

Some clients seem to do well in Stage I—that is, they seem to explore their problem situations fairly concretely—but then they stagnate. They examine and reexamine certain problems *but don't seem to move on to determining what they want to do about them.* In Stage I, the counselor helps the client explore problem situations from the client's point of view. However, very often the client's point of view or perspective is not enough. These perspectives are too self-limiting or self-defeating. Clients need to move beyond their own frames of reference to new perspectives on themselves and the problem situation. Old ways of thinking are not working; they are not leading to goal setting, program development, and action. Let's consider the case of Delia.

> *Delia, a single, quite verbal woman in her late thirties, has spent several sessions with a counselor in a center associated with her church. She came with a variety of rather vague complaints, among them persistent bodily aches and pains (though a physical examination showed nothing wrong) and complaints about working conditions. She had been a member of the typing pool of a rather large firm for about eight years. She talked about her dissatisfaction with her supervisor and with some of her coworkers. In the counseling sessions she would go over the same ground several times without seeming to get anywhere. Finally, the counselor said something like this:*

Counselor: Delia, I'd like to share a hunch with you. I'm beginning to think that your working conditions are not the central issue. It seems to be a bit deeper than that. It sounds to me like you really don't like the kind of work you're doing. You've got a lot of ability, and typing, even doing a good job typing, is just not that fulfilling.

Delia (pausing and looking surprised): This probably sounds stupid, but I had never thought of that. I've taken it for granted that this is "my" job. You mean there might be better jobs out there even for a single woman who's almost forty!

Delia and the counselor go on to explore the possibility of her getting a more fulfilling job. They also explore some of the negative ways she thinks about herself ("a single woman almost forty") and the ways in which such thinking keeps her aspirations low. In this case, the counselor's sharing a hunch helps Delia develop a *new perspective*, a new way of looking at herself and her problem situation. It is not just a static, self-contained insight, however. It is a dynamic insight, one that helps Delia see the possibility of some kind of problem-managing action. Given her talents, there well might be more fulfilling jobs available to her.

When clients explore their problem situations in terms of specific experiences, behaviors, and feelings in specific situations, they come to see more clearly *where they are*, which can be called Point A. The next step is to help them develop new perspectives on their problem situations so that they can see more clearly *where they want to be*, which can be called Point B. For instance, Point A for Delia is the disappointing and dissatisfying job she now has. Because she sees no hope for improvement in her present job, Point B is a new, more satisfying job. The new perspective that she may need in order to establish Point B as her goal is that there is no reason she must persist in a job she does not like. The counselor finds that Delia is hemming herself in by self-defeating beliefs and attitudes such as "I must always remain loyal to the company for which I work" and "For the sake of stability, it is better to stay in a job even though you don't like it." Once the counselor challenges her to examine and move beyond these disabling beliefs, Delia is able to set the goal of getting a new job. An inadequate examination of Point A leads to an inadequate conception of Point B.

The Goal of Stage II

The overriding goal of Stage II from the client's viewpoint is to set a goal—that is, to choose *to do something* that will help manage the problem situation more effectively. However, clients often cannot set such goals because they do not see the problem situation clearly or objectively enough. If this is the case, then counselors can help them develop the kinds of new perspectives that enable them to set reasonable goals. Helping clients develop new perspectives is a preparatory step in helping them set goals.

Given the overall goal of Stage II, there are two major cautions that relate to challenging and to developing new perspectives. The first is that challenging and developing new perspectives can be distorted if they are not seen in terms of the overall goal of Stage II. In the first part of Stage II, helpers challenge clients in a variety of ways to develop the kinds of perspectives needed to establish adequate goals. Therefore, challenging exists not for its own sake but for the sake of helping clients develop new perspectives on their problem situation. These new perspectives are meaningful if they help clarify the problem situation more fully. In this sense, challenging grows out of and complements the work of Stage I. Some helpers tend to act as if challenging clients were a goal in and of itself. Because I shall discuss the skills of challenging in some detail, it is important to keep in mind their purpose and to see them in the context of the entire helping process.

Second, the purpose of this part of Stage II is not merely to generate new perspectives for the sake of new perspectives. Rather, it is to generate the kinds of perspectives that carry with them suggestions of what may be done to handle a problem situation. In offering clients new perspectives or in challenging them to develop them themselves, helpers need to ask, "In what way does this insight point to some kind of action or behavioral change that will help the client handle this problem? Does this new perspective help the client clarify Point A (where he or she is presently) in such a way that Point B (where he or she wants to be) begins to be seen more clearly?"

What Greenberg and Kahn (1979, pp. 139–140) call the "stimulation phase in counseling" is one way of seeing Stage II. They note the need for perceptual change and "discovery" in the helping process.

> A view of the mind proposed by [William] James . . . provides a theoretical framework for understanding the function of stimulation in promoting discovery. In James's view, directing effort to take hold of some marginal impression in the mind, bringing this new information into the center of awareness, and attending fully will precipitate choice, decision, and action. By shifting one's attention and fully attending to some vague feeling, memory, sensory experience, or fleeting thought, people can expand their awareness of possibilities.

New perceptions can lead to new, problem-managing action.

Greenberg and Kahn (1979) see a two-stage process leading from exploration to action. The first stage is a process of *discovery* in which clients fully experience and accept specific feelings, thoughts, and sensations. For instance, Delia learns that she puts herself down a great deal—that is, she tells herself in a number of ways that she does not deserve more from life and that she should be satisfied with her lot. Discovery, which involves perceiving and then *owning* one's perceptions ("I *do* put myself down; I do it to myself"), is the first step toward action. But, according to Greenberg and Kahn, a second step is usually required because some discoveries are never acted on.

The second part of this process involves spelling out the *implications* of one's discovery. This leads to *goal-directed self-understanding.*

> The intention is not to place perceptual change or awareness in opposition with intellectual change or understanding and revive the long-standing argument on the importance of experiential insight versus intellectual insight. But rather to highlight that there are two different processes called discovery and dynamic self-understanding; the former relying on deep exploration and experiencing to construct a new perception, the latter relying on theme identification, recognition of similarities across situations, and social influence to achieve a new goal-directed understanding [Greenberg & Kahn, 1979, p. 144].

Once Delia discovers that she does put herself down in various ways, she can spell out what implications this has for her job. She is then ready to set some kind of goal. According to Greenberg and Kahn, then, helping clients have the kinds of experiences that lead to relevant discoveries is an important part of the helping process. As we shall see, many contemporary approaches to counseling and therapy provide methods to help clients make these kinds of discoveries.

Challenging Skills and the Development of New Perspectives

I use *challenging* instead of *confrontation* to describe the generic process of placing demands on clients or helping them place demands on themselves. *Confrontation* is loaded with negative connotations for some people. They picture people clawing at others or battering them verbally or making sudden, dramatic, and unreasonable demands on them. Its use will not be avoided in these pages; rather, it will be defined carefully and described as one possible skill in the challenging process.

Self-Challenge as an Ideal

One of the values I promote is client self-efficacy or self-responsibility. It sometimes happens that when people are listened to, understood, and helped to explore problem situations from their own frames of reference, they move naturally to challenging themselves.

Client (a 38-year-old woman who is coming to counseling because she has recently had a mastectomy): I can't believe what I've been learning here. When we began to look at how much support I have in terms of family and friends, this was the first time in my life that I reviewed my relationships with others so explicitly. I never realized how selfish and self-serving I can be. I control how others relate to me—we do things when I want to do them; we spend as much time as I want to spend. And now I could just see me using this operation as another tool to get what I want. Don't get me wrong. I don't want to exaggerate. And I don't think I'm a lousy human being. But there are some things about the ways I relate to others that need changing.

This woman made some discoveries about herself, owned them, and has begun to translate them into goal-directed self-understanding. This kind of self-challenging is refreshing, perhaps because most of us see so little of it (even in ourselves). However, helpers who wait for clients to make this move on their own may never get out of Stage I. Therefore, it is often necessary to challenge clients to move beyond their own limited frames of reference. However, because the ideal still remains self-challenge (a dimension of self-efficacy) rather than being challenged, it is useful to teach clients how to challenge themselves (training as treatment). Self-challenge is not a form of masochism, for neither self-challenge nor being challenged by others is a goal in itself. When challenge does become a goal in itself, it is almost impossible to avoid sadomasochistic exchanges. Challenge exists to help clients develop the kinds of new perspectives needed to set and clarify goals.

The Skills of Challenging

Because the skills of challenging are used to help clients explore themselves and their problem situations in terms of what they have not noticed or what they have chosen, at whatever level of consciousness, to ignore, these skills can have the effect of "strong medicine." A client who is already uneasy can become much more anxious when asked to examine overlooked aspects of his or her experiences, feelings, and behaviors. Strong medicine can be misused or abused, but it can also have dramatic healing effects. Helpers who respect their clients and who have a feeling for the movement of the problem-solving process will avoid indulging in any form of challenging merely for the drama that can accompany it. The skills of challenge are best when they are *invitational*—that is, they can be seen as ways of inviting clients to explore a problem situation more fully so that they can get to the business of doing something about it. The ideal is that once invited, they will collaborate in the process of challenging or, even better, become more and more self-challenging.

In Stage II, helpers use a variety of skills to help clients understand themselves more fully in order to see the need to act more effectively. Counselors not only help them piece together the data produced through the self-exploration process but also help them probe wider and look deeper in order to find the "missing pieces" they need to understand themselves and their problem situations better. Once clients begin to see themselves both as they are (Point A) and as they want to be (Point B), they are in a better position to set problem-managing goals. As noted, the goal of this stage is not any kind of self-contained insight but dynamic self-understanding, the kind of self-understanding that sits on the verge of action.

Here are a number of statements that indicate some kind of dynamic self-understanding on the part of the client.

Client A: I've been sitting around college waiting for someone to come give me an education. Well, I think I begin to see that no one is going to give me anything; no one's going to educate me but myself. These past two years I've alternated between anger over not being taught right and self-pity. I thought college should be like high school. If I'm honest with myself, I'd have to say that I've been wallowing in self-pity. I have to salvage the next two years, but I don't know how to go about it.

Client B: I'm losing out on most of my life by being so mousy. It's very hard for me to be assertive with others, especially with men. But I've had it; I can't be like this—especially if I'm interested in helping others. I just have to find ways to reach out to others.

Client C: What a revelation this group experience has been! I had no idea how manipulative I am. As I look back now, I see that I got better grades than I deserved in school by the way I "cultivated" my teachers. I'm still trying to do the same thing now that I'm out of school. I control my whole social life. At one time I actually thought it was altruism—I mean the way *I* would always be the one to seek others out. But now I see that this is just my way of controlling my involvement with others. (She turns to the group leader.) I even tried to manipulate you into counseling me the way I wanted to be counseled, but you wouldn't play my game.

Client D: I've been a clown so long that I'm not sure that there's a solid me left underneath for others to interact with. My blustering, my "wit," my bull-in-the-china-shop relationships with others—all a coverup. I tried to be just me this past week—no stream of jokes, no putting others down—and I was disoriented and even scared at times. I didn't know what to do and my friends didn't seem to know how to interact with a serious me.

Client E: Just for the hell of it, I tried to make last week altruism week. I did a lot of things for others, without being asked. I went over to my mother's and helped clean out the basement. I took some of my brother's kids to the zoo. I called up some friends and had a party Friday night. I just got out of myself in half a dozen ways—no big deal, just ordinary things. I've been sitting around discussing my self-centeredness to death. I think I found out more about getting out of myself last week than I have in all these sessions up to now. Last week I actually liked putting my own wants second. I think it was easy because it was so new, a kind of experiment.

These clients may not know *what* they want to do to handle their problems in living, but they have enough insight or understanding to realize that they want to do *something*. In the case of Client E, self-understanding *follows* action instead of preceding it. She had to experience altruistic behavior before being able to discuss her self-centeredness more concretely. This is an example of something said earlier, that the helping model in practice is not as logical and linear as presented in these pages. Her case illustrates concretely the need to be flexible in applying the stages of the model.

You should also note that all these clients are quite verbal and nondefensive. Their statements all indicate a degree of self-challenge. It would be misleading to let you believe that all clients are this verbal and this open to behavioral change.

Vague and abstract self-understanding is often equivalent to no understanding because it simply does not lead to action. Ideally, self-exploration yields concrete data; these data, when put together effectively, yield concrete self-understanding, the basis for specific, concrete action programs. Consider the difference between these two clients:

Client A: I think that I deal with my wife the way I deal with most women. The best word I can think of is *ambivalently*. I act in contradictory ways that mess up our relationship. It makes me think of the contradictory ways my mother and sisters related to me and how I gave the same back to them.

Here the client seems to understand something about himself that has some implication for the need to change, but the words are too vague. It is impossible to come up with any kind of solid goals based on his present understanding, even though it is new for him.

Client B: I think I can say that I love my wife. I work hard to see to it that she and I have a comfortable life together, and she does the same. I try to spend as much time as I can at home—working around the house, helping with the chores. I even go with her to places I don't particularly want to go because she wants to go—I mean out to dinner, and even to vacation spots she chooses. Yet, even as I say this, I realize that my heart isn't always in what I do. And I think that she knows that too. She can read my attitude toward her in the way I act when I'm with her. For instance, even though we are together a lot, I don't talk to her much. I'm around the house a lot, but I'm there and not there. I do things for her, but sometimes so reluctantly that it would be more honest not to do them. Even when we go where she wants to go on vacations, we end up doing what I want to do once we get there. I do very little to understand her, and she does very little to understand me. I think you know me better than she does in some ways. I keep giving her double messages—"I love you" and "I'm indifferent to you"—and she gives them right back to me. We have to do something to get our marriage back into shape. We've got to do something about the way we don't communicate with each other honestly. Otherwise what we do have will just die.

This client not only has explored his relationship with his wife but has been able to put the data together into a larger picture. He sees that he and his wife have begun to practice separation and are perhaps drifting toward divorce, without having a clear understanding whether this is what they want. He sees the need for action; he is motivated to act; and he has some idea of the direction his actions must take. He and his wife must take the steps necessary to achieve the kind of communication he has experienced in the counseling relationship.

In order to help the client reach dynamic self-understanding, the helper *shifts the perspective* of the counseling process in Stage II. In Stage I, helpers concentrate on their clients' frames of reference. They try to see the world from their clients' perspective rather than their own. Through primary-level accurate empathy and judicious probing, they try to help clients see this perspective as clearly as possible in terms of specific experiences, behaviors, and feelings.

In Stage II, however, there is a shift. The counselor now helps the client see the world from a more *objective* point of view. As Levy (1968) notes, if counselors see the world only as their clients see it, they will have little to offer them. The client's implicit interpretation of the world is in some ways distorted and unproductive, at least in the areas of life in which he or she is having problems. Helpers assume, however, that clients have the resources eventually to see the world, especially the world of their own behavior, in an undistorted way. This change in perspective is necessary if Stage II is to be a bridge between the data of Stage I and the action programs of Stage III. Disturbed, disorganized, and problematic people are often people in a rut. They keep blaming others for their problems, refuse to admit that they have any problems, or continue to apply solutions that don't work.

Let's consider the case of the client who comes to some kind of dynamic understanding of his relationship with his wife (Client B in the previous dialogue).

He did not start with those understandings. His data in Stage I looked quite different:

- I'm an easygoing person.
- I've been depressed lately.
- I've become less efficient at work.
- My wife is a nagger.
- I do not deserve my wife's treatment.
- I'm around the house a great deal.
- I help with chores.
- My present distress is caused by my wife's behavior.
- I provide well for my wife's needs and comfort.
- I let her have her way.
- My faults are insignificant compared to hers.

At this stage we can ask ourselves what are some of the ruts this client is in. Some of the possibilities are the following:

- I'm right; she's wrong.
- I try; she doesn't.
- I'm in pain; she's not.
- I keep acting maturely; she responds immaturely.

As we have seen in examining Client B's case, this client comes to a set of self-understandings different from the data in Stage I. His Stage II understandings are the following:

- I'm sending many double messages (such as like-dislike) to my wife.
- We're practicing separation or divorce.
- Some of my behavior is childish.
- The marital distress is not mine or hers: it's *ours*.
- There is little open, direct communication between us.
- We're in a downward spiral.
- We need to learn adult-to-adult communication skills.
- If at all possible, my wife and I should be here together.

This client has obviously come to a more objective perspective on his relationship with his wife.

We can now consider the skills that enable counselors to help their clients develop these kinds of new perspectives. Because all these skills are forms of challenging, you will notice some overlap. No attempt has been made to come up with pure forms of challenging, each separate and distinct from the other. I discuss three of the skills in this chapter and three in Chapter 7.

Summarizing as a Bridging Response

Counselors can use summarizing to help clients explore the problem situations with which they are dealing in Stage I in a more focused and concrete way. As such, it is a way of helping clients move from Stage I into Stage II. It can serve as a "bridging" response.

Brammer (1973) lists a number of goals that can be achieved by judicious use of summarizing: "warming up" the client, focusing scattered thoughts and feelings, closing the discussion of a particular theme, and prompting the client to explore a theme more thoroughly. Often, when scattered elements are brought together, the client sees the "bigger picture" more clearly. Thus summarizing can lead to new perspectives or alternate frames of reference.

In the following example, a trainer is giving a counselor trainee feedback in the form of a summary.

> *Trainer:* Let's see how all these pieces fit together. Overall you see yourself on the way to becoming an effective helper, but besides your obvious strengths, you also see some weaknesses. As to strengths, you are an enthusiastic learner; you care deeply about others; you are good at listening skills and the responding skills of Stage I. And yet you bog down when it comes to making the transition to Stage II. You feel uncomfortable in, well, "intruding" into others' lives. You're somewhat fearful of saying things that might make the client feel uncomfortable. At this point you feel tied up in yourself and sometimes you retreat back into Stage I.
>
> *Trainee:* That's it. I keep telling myself I'm "intruding." And I keep telling myself that it's "awful" for the client to feel discomfort.

The trainer, using a summary, pulls together the highlights of the trainee's self-exploration and lets them speak for themselves. A good summary is not a mechanical pulling together of a number of facts; it is a systematic presentation of *relevant* data. The helper makes some decisions as to what is relevant but bases this decision on listening to and understanding the client. So summaries, too, are social-influence processes.

In this example, the trainer, through the summary, helps the trainee focus more concretely on her misgivings about her "intrusiveness" (a fairly common problem for trainees and novice helpers). She has learned and feels comfortable with the skills of Stage I, but challenging skills, although making sense conceptually, are more difficult for her to learn and put into practice. They *are*, to some degree, intrusive, but it is an intrusiveness called for by the helping contract and carried out with the client's collaboration. The trainer's response helps her focus on her feelings of intrusiveness. She can explore this theme a bit more and decide how she wants to cope with it.

Let's look at another summary that helps a client understand himself more fully and see the need for action. The client is a 55-year-old man who is having problems with depression.

> *Counselor:* Let's take a look at what we've seen so far. You're down—not just a normal slump, but this time it's hanging on. You worry about your health, but you check out all right physically, so this seems to be more a symptom than a cause of your depression. There are some unresolved issues in your life. One that you seem to be stressing is the fact that your recent change in job has meant that you don't see much of your old friends anymore. Because you're single, you don't find this easy. Another issue—one you find painful and embarrassing—is your struggle to stay "young." You don't like facing the fact that you're getting older. A third issue is the way you—to use your own word—"overinvest" yourself in work, so much so that when you finish a long-term project, suddenly your life is empty.

> *Client* (Pause): It's painful to hear it all that baldly, but that about sums it up. As I listen to you, I can't help but think that it's time that I straighten out my values. I do overvalue being young.

This client, in the self-exploratory phase, produced data that pointed to certain painful conclusions: He is immature in some areas of life (for example, in his overvaluing of youth). He is "out of community" (his interpersonal life is at a low ebb). He is trying ineffective solutions to his problems (dealing with loneliness by a flight into work). The counselor's summary hits home—somewhat painfully. The client draws his own conclusion. He seems ready to consider the kinds of new perspectives that will help him establish problem-managing goals. Perhaps this summary would have been more effective if the helper had also summarized some of the client's strengths. This would have provided a more positive context for developing alternative frames of reference. As we shall see, an important part of counseling is helping clients identify the resources they can bring to bear on a problem situation.

Summaries, if effective, help a client focus more intensively on some important issue. Ineffective summaries—that is, summaries that are merely rehashes of many of the things clients have said—can distract rather than help focus. Summaries, though they can be used at any time to give focus and direction to the helping process, are especially useful at certain times: at the beginning of a new session, during a session when a client seems to be rambling, and when a client seems to have exhausted everything he or she has to say on a certain topic.

BEGINNING OF A NEW SESSION

When summaries are used at the beginning of a new session, they prevent clients from merely repeating what has already been said before. They put clients under pressure to move on. In the following example the client is a 65-year-old widower who has just retired.

> *Counselor:* Last week you talked about your loneliness and your fears of dying. You mentioned how these feelings are particularly intense in the evening and on weekends. You also talked quite a bit on how much you depended on your wife and how much you defined yourself through your job. At the end of the session you were discussing your feelings about being too old to do anything about all this. I'm wondering if this is how you saw our last session and whether you want to add anything to it.

Such a summary serves several purposes. It shows the client that the helper listened carefully to what he had to say and that she reflected on it after the session. It gives the client a jumping-off point for the new session. It gives the client an opportunity to add to or modify what was said. It prevents the client from merely repeating what had already been said. He might well add to or modify what was said, but it is less likely that he will merely repeat. It places the responsibility for moving on with the client. The client might well need help to move on, but it gives him the "first shot" at it. Summaries have a kind of "well, now what?" flavor built in. They are social-influence processes; they provide gentle pressure to move on. In this case, if the problem situation is clear enough, it suggests that it is time to begin to explore what might be done about it.

SESSIONS GOING NOWHERE

A summary can be used to give focus to a session that seems to be going nowhere. In the following example a young white ghetto resident who has had several run-ins with the police is talking to a black counselor associated with the probation office. The client is jumping from one topic to another and the counselor is having a hard time pulling it all together.

> *Counselor:* I'm not sure where we're headed here. Here's what I think I do understand. You're angry because your probation officer made you come see me. You feel it's a waste of time talking to me because I'm black. And you feel that we can't do much for you here. Talking about your problems doesn't make any sense when the whole system's got you boxed in.
>
> *Client:* You got it. Where do we go from here?

The counselor presents the central issues as he thinks the client sees them. It doesn't produce any magical change, but it does stop the rambling process and gives both of them a chance to say "What do we do now?"

WHEN A CLIENT GETS "STUCK"

Summaries can be used when clients seem to have exhausted everything they have to say about a particular issue and seem to be stuck. A summary of the principal points they *have* made can help them see the "bigger picture" more clearly and therefore help them move to dynamic self-understanding. In the following example, a young woman has been talking about her difficult relationship with her father. She has revealed a great deal about the history of that relationship and now stops dead and seems frustrated and confused.

> *Counselor A:* It's hard to pull all this together. You feel you don't really have much more to say about your relationship with your father.
> *Client:* Yeah, that's about where it stands. (The client remains silent.)

> *Counselor B:* Let's see if I can pull this together. Your father never had a good word for you when you were a kid, just criticism when you did something wrong. When you went to college, he seemed to resent it—perhaps because you, a woman, were getting more education than he had. He ridiculed the idea. Then his divorcing your mother was, for you, the last straw. Because you saw him as pretty much in the wrong, you were very angry and hurt; so you cut off all communication with him. That was over three years ago. Now he's gotten in contact with you once more. He seems to want to reestablish a relationship, almost as if nothing happened. He's taking a "let bygones be bygones" approach, and that doesn't satisfy you at all.
> *Client:* No, I have to get all this off my chest to him. I don't know whether he knows why I stopped talking to him. This is like a rock on my chest.

Counselor A makes the wrong choice here: his use of primary-level empathy does not help. Counselor B sees that this is a good time for a summary. She pulls together the salient facts in the client's experience with her father. Her response is to indicate something that she feels she needs to *do*. That is, the summary helps her see the need for some kind of action. Later in the counseling session (this is an actual case), the counselor role-played the client's father and had the client say directly what she wanted to say. This "rehearsal" was part of an action program that culminated in the client's actually speaking directly to her father.

Summaries often help clients get more involved in the helping process. Once the counselor presents a summary, the ball is in the client's court. The client can choose where to move. From time to time the counselor can also ask the *client* to summarize—that is, the helper can both model summarizing and train the client to do it.

> *Counselor* (at the beginning of a new session): You probably thought a bit about what you said last session. I wonder whether you could briefly outline what you think were the most important points you made last week.

Brammer (1973, see p. 94 for his guidelines for using summaries) says that the main purpose of summarizing is to give the client a feeling of movement. This movement, in terms of the developmental problem-management model, is toward the kind of problem clarification that leads to goal setting. Once clients learn to do their own summarizing, they will be more in touch with movement or the lack of it in the helping process.

New Perspectives through Information

Sometimes clients are not able to explore their problems fully because they lack information. If this is the case, then a simple challenging skill is to provide the needed information or help clients get it from some other source. Berenson and Mitchell (1974) call this "didactic" confrontation. Selby and Calhoun (1980, p. 236) call it "psychodidactics."

> Conveying information about the psychological and social changes accompanying a particular problem situation (e.g., divorce) may be a highly effective addition to any therapeutic strategy. This psychodidactic component has been neglected as an explicit part of treatment in spite of evidence indicating the therapeutic value of information about the client's problem situation.

It includes both giving information and correcting misinformation on the part of the client.

This skill or strategy is included under challenging skills because it helps clients develop new perspectives on their problems. In some cases, the information can be confirming and supportive. For instance, a parent who feels responsible following the sudden death of a newborn baby may experience some relief through an understanding of the features of the "sudden infant-death syndrome" (Selby & Calhoun, 1980, p. 239). The client in this case gets a new perspective that helps him or her handle self-blame.

The new perspectives clients get from information can be relieving, but they can also place demands on them. Consider the following example.

> *Troy was a college student of somewhat modest intellectual means. He made it through because he worked very hard. In his senior year he learned that a number of his friends were going to graduate school. He, too, applied to a number of graduate programs in psychology. He came to see a counselor in the student services center after being rejected by all the schools to which he had applied. In the interview it soon became clear to the counselor that Troy thought that many, perhaps even the majority, of college students went on to graduate school. After all, the people he knew were. The counselor shared with him the statistics of what could be called the educational "pyramid"—the decreasing percentage of students attending school at higher levels. Troy did not realize that the fact that he*

> *was finishing college made him part of an "elite." Nor was he completely aware of the extremely competitive nature of the graduate programs in psychology to which he had applied. He found much of this relieving, but then he found himself suddenly faced with what to do now that he was finishing school. Up to this point he had not thought of what he might do after finishing school. He felt disconcerted by the sudden need to look at the world of work.*

In this case, Troy is both relieved and challenged by what he learns.

Even the offer of information can challenge clients to examine issues they may have been avoiding. For instance, a young college woman has been exploring her fears about sexuality with a counselor at the center for student development.

> *Counselor:* Janie, you have talked a number of times about your fear of getting pregnant almost as if it were inevitable. I'm not sure whether you are aware of different contraceptive methods or how you feel about contraception at all.
>
> *Client:* I realize I'm ignorant about all that. My parents have never really said anything. I'd like to talk about methods, but I also want to talk about the religious questions involved. My parents are very strict Catholics.

This counselor is offering information to Janie, but she's not telling her whether or how to experiment sexually or pushing her own views on contraception. Rather, the offer of information moves the client to address an issue that is important for her.

Giving information is especially useful when ignorance is either one of the principal causes of a problem situation or it is making an existing problem worse.

> *Vivian got a job as a waitress in a large and busy restaurant. Everyone there seemed to be too busy to give her any hints. She did not understand how the system worked and remained ignorant of all the unwritten rules relating to the roles there—cook, bartender, busboy, waitress, kitchen manager, dining room supervisor, cashier, hostess, and so forth. For instance, she would ask a cook what she thought was an innocent question and get nothing but a dirty look. She became more and more anxious. A minister helped her see that she didn't know the "system" and was therefore being ground up by it. He helped her develop enough assertiveness to ask people for the kind of information that would enable her to fit in better.*

Some simple hints on how the system worked and the restrictions relating to roles helped greatly.

You need some cautions with respect to giving information. Do not over-whelm the client with information. Make sure it is clear and relevant to the client's problem situation. Do not confuse information giving with advice giving. The latter is seldom useful. Finally, do not use information giving as a subtle way of pushing your own values. For instance, do not immediately tell a client with an unwanted pregnancy what she has to do to get an abortion.

Advanced Empathy as a Bridging Response

Accurate empathy is central to the entire helping model, with primary-level accurate empathy predominating in Stage I and a combination of primary and advanced accurate empathy in Stage II. In the following example, the client, a soldier doing a five-year hitch in the army, has been talking about failing to be promoted. As he talks, it becomes fairly evident that part of the problem is that he is so quiet and unassuming that it is easy for his supervisors to ignore him. He is the kind of person who keeps to himself and keeps everything inside.

> *Client:* I don't know what's going on. I work hard, but I keep getting passed over when promotion time comes along. I think I work as hard as anyone else and I work well and efficiently, but all my efforts seem to go down the drain. I don't know what else I can do.
>
> *Counselor A:* It seems unfair to do the kind of work that merits a pro-motion and still not get it.
>
> *Counselor B:* It's depressing to put out as much effort as those who get promoted and still get passed by. I wonder if you see anything in your style that makes it easy for others not to notice you, even when you're working very efficiently.

Counselor A tries to understand the client from the client's frame of reference. She deals with the client's feelings and the experience underlying these feelings. Counselor B, however, probes a bit further. From the context, and from past interchanges, from the client's manner and tone of voice, he picks up something that the client does not state overtly: the client is so unassuming that his best efforts go unnoticed. His tendency to swallow his emotions completes the pic-ture. Counselor B uses a combination of primary and advanced empathy to help the client develop a new perspective, but one that is also based on the data of the self-exploration process. Advanced accurate empathy, then, goes beyond the expressed to the implied. If the helper is accurate, however, and if his timing is good, this kind of communication helps the client move beyond self-exploration to self-understanding. Let's take a look at the client's response to each counselor.

> *Client* (to Counselor A): I suppose there's nothing I can do but wait it out. (A long silence ensues.)

Client (to Counselor B): You mean I'm so quiet I could get lost in the shuffle? Or maybe it's the guys that make more noise, the "squeaky wheels" my dad called them, they're the ones that get noticed.

In his response to Counselor A, this client merely retreats more into himself. In his response to Counselor B, on the other hand, he begins to see that his non-assuming, nonassertive style may contribute to the problem situation. Once he begins to see what *he* does or does not do, he is in a position to change.

Primary-level accurate empathy gets at relevant *surface* (not to be confused with *superficial*) feelings and meanings; advanced accurate empathy gets at feelings and meanings that are somehow buried, hidden, or beyond the client's immediate reach. It is not suggested here that every client will react as positively as this one to the helper's challenges. The point is that different kinds of helper responses can have different effects on how clients view themselves and explore their problems in living.

Stage II is the phase in which "piecing together" takes place so that the client can see a bigger picture, and advanced accurate empathy is one of the principal tools in this process. Even when helpers see the world from their clients' point of view, they often see it more clearly, more widely, more deeply, and more cogently. They not only understand the client's perspective but also see the *implications* of this perspective for effective or ineffective living. The communication of advanced accurate empathy is the helper's way of sharing his or her understanding of these implications with the client. As such, it is a *bridging* response. It helps clients move from Stage I understanding of themselves and their problems to Stage II understanding—that is, from their own limited perspectives to wider, more goal-related perspectives.

Advanced empathy is a way of *sharing useful "hunches"* with your clients. There is something interpretive about it, therefore; but if you are attending and listening, your interpretations will be based on cues you receive from your clients. You will not be pulling them out of thin air. Of course, each hunch will have a different degree of probability, and you can expect clients to react strongly if you share hunches with low degrees of probability as if they were facts. I'll say more about this later when I deal with the *manner* in which skilled helpers challenge clients. Advanced accurate empathy can be communicated in a number of ways. Let's consider some of them.

EXPRESSING WHAT IS ONLY IMPLIED

The most basic form of advanced accurate empathy is to give expression to what the client only implies. In Stage I, helpers, for reasons already discussed, generally limit themselves to stating only what the client states. In Stage II, once rapport has been established and the client is exploring his or her experiences, behaviors, and feelings, the helper can begin to state or point out what the client implies but does not say directly. In the following example the client has been discussing ways of getting back in touch with his wife after a recent divorce, but when he speaks about doing so, he expresses very little enthusiasm.

> *Client:* I could wait to hear from her. But I suppose there's nothing wrong with calling her up and asking her how she's getting along.
> *Counselor A:* You see nothing wrong in taking the initiative to find out if everything is well with her.
> *Client* (somewhat drearily): Yeah, I suppose I could.
>
> *Counselor B:* You've been talking about getting in touch with her, but, unless I'm mistaken, I don't hear a great deal of enthusiasm in your voice.
> *Client:* To be honest, I don't really want to talk to her. But I feel guilty, guilty about the divorce, guilty about seeing her on her own. I'm taking care of her all over again. And that's one of the reasons we got divorced. I mean my constant "taking care of her" when she was more interested in independence.

Counselor A's response might have been fine for Stage I, but it misses the mark here and the client grinds to a halt. In Stage II, the counselor needs to help the client dig deeper. Counselor B bases her response not only on the client's immediately preceding remark but on the entire context of the self-exploration process. Her response hits the mark and the client moves forward. As with primary-level accurate empathy, the sign of an effective stab at advanced accurate empathy by the counselor is the way the client responds. As with primary-level empathy, there is no such thing as a good advanced empathic response in itself. The question is whether it helps the client clarify the issue more fully so he or she begins to see the need to act differently.

In the following example, the client is talking about a relationship that seems to be going sour. She keeps discussing what is going wrong in terms of experiences—that is, what the other person does to her. She seldom talks about her own behaviors.

> *Client:* I don't know why she acts the way she does. One day she will be chattering away on the phone in the most engaging way. She's carefree and tells me all that's happening. She's great when she's in that mood. But at other times she's actually rude to me and moody as hell—and it seems so personal. I mean not just that she's in a bad mood generally, but that somehow it is directed at me.
> *Counselor A:* It seems so unfair when she makes you a victim of her moods.
> *Client:* Right. For instance, it was only yesterday when she. . . .

> *Counselor B:* It's unsettling not to know where you stand with her. I'm
> not sure that you're saying that when you look at your own behavior, you just
> don't find anything that might bother her.
>
> *Client* (after a pause): Well, I suppose I do some things that bother her.
> For instance, yesterday. . . .

Counselor A at this stage might well, by the continued use of primary-level
empathy, merely reinforce the client's sense of being a victim. Counselor B, by
sharing a hunch without accusing the client of anything, elicits the kind of
exploration that could help the client understand *her* part in the deteriorating
relationship.

In the following example, the client, a high school student, is not coming to
grips with his problem because he is attempting to sweep some important
feelings under the rug.

> *Student:* Don't get me wrong; I really like my teacher. Everybody in the
> whole school admits that she's about the best. She makes English and history
> come alive, not like the others. But still I can't talk to her the way I'd like to.
>
> *Counselor:* You really like her and are glad that you are in her class; but
> it seems that you might be a bit resentful because she doesn't show you much
> personal attention.

The counselor has been listening to all the client's messages, both verbal and
nonverbal, and is therefore able to bring to center stage feelings the client has
been pushing back into the wings.

Advanced accurate empathy is part of the social-influence process; it places
demands on the client. Counselors are no longer merely responding to clients
as they did in Stage I; they are now demanding that the clients take a deeper
look at themselves. The genuineness, respect, understanding, and rapport of
Stage I have created a power base. Helpers now use this power to influence clients
to see their problems from a more objective frame of reference. These demands
are still based on an accurate understanding of the client and are made with
genuine care and respect, but they are demands nevertheless. The nonassertive
and unskilled helper can find it difficult to make such demands on his or her
clients.

IDENTIFYING THEMES

Advanced accurate empathy also includes helping clients identify and explore
behavioral and emotional *themes* in the data presented in Stage I. Themes are
self-defeating patterns of behavior and emotion. For instance, without stating
it explicitly, a client, through what she reveals about her feelings, experiences,
and behaviors and by the way she acts in the helping sessions, has indicated that

she is a fairly dependent person (a behavioral theme in the client's life). The counselor asks her to consider a self-defeating behavioral theme that she does not identify explicitly.

Counselor: It seems that letting others make decisions for you has both a positive and a negative payoff. It makes your life at work easier; there are very few hassles. But it also makes it easy for others both to ignore you and sometimes to take advantage of you. For instance, you work more overtime than anyone else in the office.

Poor Self-Image. A client may hint that he often operates from a poor self-image.

Counselor: As I listen, this thought is beginning to strike me: in growing up, you seem to have learned one lesson well, and that is, "I am not a worthwhile human being." You seem to say this to yourself at work, in your relationships with your friends, and even when you're alone with yourself.

Dominance. A client may intimate that she acts as a parent toward her husband almost constantly.

Counselor: I'd like to pull a few things together. If I understand it correctly, you take care of the household finances. You are usually the one who accepts or rejects social invitations. And now you've asked him to move because of the location of your new job. You see all of this as a way of making life better or easier for him. I wonder how he sees it. You think he's ungrateful. Maybe he just doesn't want to be your child anymore.

Fear of Intimacy. The client may indicate that he retreats from social involvement whenever there is any threat of intimacy.

Counselor: Let's see if this makes any sense to you. On the one hand, you feel quite lonely; but on the other hand, you are reluctant to get close to others. You mentioned, for instance, that your friend talked more intimately with your brother when you visited him than you ever have. It's as if getting close to others might demand a price that you're not sure you're ready to pay.

In each of these cases, the counselor goes beyond what the client has said explicitly. The thematic material might refer to feelings (such as themes of hurt, depression, or anxiety), to behavior (such as themes of controlling others, avoiding intimacy, blaming others, or overwork), to experiences (such as themes of being a victim, being seduced, being feared, or failing), or to combinations of these. Once you recognize a self-defeating theme or pattern, your task is to communicate your perception to the client in a way that enables him or her to see it, too. This task demands a high degree of accurate empathy, tact, and initiative. If you try to force thematic material on clients prematurely, they will most likely balk and you will have to retrace your steps. If you are accurate in identifying themes and tactful in communicating them, you can help clients see themselves in a new light. To some, the counselor's remarks in the previous examples might sound too direct or premature. These remarks, however, are taken out of context—both the context of the rapport-building Stage I behaviors that have preceded and the communication context itself, which included important paralinguistic and nonverbal behaviors.

Overly abstract themes borrowed from schools of therapy probably do little to help clients develop dynamic self-understanding:

> *Counselor:* Your inferiority complex contaminates much of what you do. Your will to fail runs much deeper than your will to community.

Such a statement is obviously a caricature, but the point is clear: themes need to be based solidly on an accurate understanding of the client's feelings, experiences, and behaviors and must be communicated as concretely as possible in language that makes sense to the client.

CONNECTING ISLANDS

This metaphor suggests another approach to advanced accurate empathy. The helper attempts to build "bridges" between the "islands" (Ivey, 1971; Ivey & Authier, 1978) of feelings, experiences, and behaviors the client reveals in the self-exploration stage. For instance, the following client talks about being progressively more anxious and tired in recent weeks. Later he talks about getting ready for his marriage in a few months and about deadlines for turning in papers for current courses. Still later he talks about his need to succeed, to compete, and to meet his parents' and grandparents' expectations.

> *Counselor:* John, it could be that your growing fatigue and anxiety have relatively simple explanations. One, you are really working very hard. Two, competing as hard as you do and striving for excellence have to take their physical and emotional toll. And three, the emotional drain of getting ready for your marriage can be enormous. Maybe it would be more useful to look at these factors before digging around for "deeper" causes.

John talked about these three islands as if they were unrelated to one another. Once he was willing to explore their interrelatedness, he explored his tendency to do too much and began to see that he tended to overvalue achievement and competition.

Advanced accurate empathy means helping the client fill in the missing links in the data produced in the self-exploration process. For instance, if the client presents two separate islands of behavior—(1) his disagreements with his wife about sex, training the children, and arranging household finances and (2) his heavy drinking—the missing link might be that he is using his drinking as a way of punishing his wife.

> *Counselor:* I wonder what the relationship is between your drinking and your disagreements with your wife, Bill. At least at first glance, it seems like a fairly good way of punishing her. What do you think?

The client has presented these two problems as separate. The counselor, in listening to the client, has a hunch that they are not separate. She suggests the concept of punishment as a possible bridge between the two.

Of course, counselors need to be accurate in the connections or relationships they propose. Counselors who work from a controlling rather than from a collaborative model of social influence might well be able to force clients to accept interpretations of their behavior that are not valid. But interpretations that are not based solidly on the client's experience and behavior simply do not help. They lead the client into blind alleys and in general do more harm than good. For instance, a counselor may convince a client that he is the sole cause of trouble in his marriage. If he would stop drinking, communication between him and his wife would get better. On the supposition that the man's wife is adding her share of irresponsibility to the marriage, such an interpretation simply would not help.

HELPING CLIENTS DRAW CONCLUSIONS FROM PREMISES

Still another way of conceptualizing advanced accurate empathy is to help clients draw their own conclusions from premises. Very often, in the data produced in the self-exploration process, there are certain implied premises from which certain logical conclusions can be drawn.

> *Client:* I really don't think I can take my boss's abuse any longer. I don't think she really knows what she's doing. She thinks she is doing me a favor by pointing out what I do wrong all the time. I like the work and I'd like to stay, but, well, I just don't know.
>
> *Counselor A:* What makes this really frustrating is that your boss might never realize what she's doing to you.
>
> *Counselor B:* The alternatives, then, are limited. One is to stay on the job and just "take it." But you feel it has become too painful. Another is to talk with your boss directly about this whole destructive relationship. A third is to start thinking about changing jobs, even though you like the work there. We really haven't talked about the second possibility.

Counselor A's primary-level accurate empathy might help the client probe more deeply into her feelings, but the assumption here is that she has already done that. It is a question of moving forward. Counselor B combs through what has been said in their interaction up to this point and draws some conclusions from the premises the client lays down. Perhaps the client is avoiding the subject of a direct confrontation with her boss. At some level of her being, she might realize that she, too, has some responsibility with respect to this unproductive relationship. This possibility would have to be investigated.

In certain cases, the counselor may draw a tongue-in-cheek conclusion from clients' premises in order to show them that the arguments they are constructing are leading nowhere. Beier (1966) calls this response an "asocial" response because it is not what the client expects. For instance, suppose that a married man has been describing his wife's faults at great length. After a while, the counselor responds as follows:

> *Counselor:* It was a mistake to marry such a woman, and maybe it's time to let her go.

This is not at all what the client has in mind, but because it *is* a logical conclusion to the case the client has been constructing against his wife, it pulls the client up short. He realizes, perhaps, that he has gone too far, that he is making things sound worse than they really are.

> *Client:* Well, I don't think things are that bad. She does have her good points.

Beier claims that such asocial responses make the client stop and think. They provide what he calls "beneficial uncertainty" for the client. Asocial responses, obviously, can be overused, can be too facetious, and—in the hands of the inept counselor—can sound actually sarcastic (in expression if not in intent). The counselor who is uncomfortable with this kind of communication can get the same result by using a social rather than an asocial response. For instance, the counselor in the last example might have said the following:

> *Counselor:* I'm not sure whether you are trying to say that your wife has no redeeming qualities.
> *Client:* Oh! Well, I didn't mean to be too hard on her.

Some clients, in a relationship that is not working out, have to make the other person the scapegoat in order to reduce their own culpability, at least initially. In this example, the counselor realizes that the client is engaging in hyperbole, and he helps the client understand what he is doing. The goal of Stage II should always be kept in mind. The asocial response and the state of beneficial uncertainty it causes are useful only to the degree that they help clients understand themselves and their problem situations more clearly—that is, clear enough to set reasonable goals.

FROM LESS TO MORE

Another way to look at advanced accurate empathy is to see it as helping clients move from the less to the more. If clients are not clear about some issue or if they speak guardedly, then the helper speaks directly, clearly, and openly. For instance, a client might ramble, touching on sexual issues lightly as he moves along. The counselor helps him face these issues more squarely.

> *Counselor:* George, you have alluded to sexual concerns a few times. My guess is that sex is a pretty touchy issue for you to deal with. But it also seems like a pretty important one.

Through advanced accurate empathy, the helper states clearly what the client says confusedly. What is said half-heartedly is stated cogently; what is said vaguely is stated specifically and concretely; and what the client presents at a superficial level is re-presented by the helper at a deeper level. In doing this, helpers interpret their clients' behavior, but their interpretations are based on what clients reveal about their own experiences, behaviors, and feelings and how the client acts during the counseling sessions—*not* on abstract psychodynamics.

OFFERING ALTERNATIVE FRAMES OF REFERENCE

As Levy (1963, 1968) pointed out, the same set of facts and data is open to a variety of interpretations. Sometimes clients do not change because they are locked into unproductive interpretations of certain experiences, behaviors, and feelings. For instance, Fred has had strong affectional feelings for some of his classmates at a boys' school. On a couple of occasions he has engaged in sexual play with other boys. He has begun to be bothered by the idea that he is homosexual. The counselor can offer Fred some alternative frames of reference.

> *Counselor:* I realize you've had these feelings and experiences, Fred. I'm not so sure that the only conclusion is that you are homosexual. You are very needy of love and affection—you don't get much of that at home. It could be that you get it when and how you can. And you have also told me that you are shy generally, but especially with girls. It's hard for you to go up and talk to a girl.

Suggesting alternative interpretations or frames of reference gives Fred room to move. He is not locked in to a single view of his sexuality. Although this form of helper behavior is a kind of social influence, it is not the same as trying to talk someone out of something.

The purpose of suggesting alternative interpretations is to help clients control their behavior more effectively: "To sum up, psychological interpretation, viewed as a behavior . . . consists of bringing an alternate frame of reference or language system to bear upon a set of observations or behaviors, with the end in view of making them more amenable to manipulation" (Levy, 1963, p. 7).

The categories described here are neither exhaustive nor meant to be completely distinct. There is obviously a great deal of overlap. What they have in common is that they are all different kinds of hunches that, when shared with clients, can help them see a problem situation more clearly. The kind of clarity needed, of course, is the kind that helps clients move toward action.

Principles Underlying Effective Challenging

Now that you have at least an initial understanding of some challenging skills that can help clients develop the kinds of perspectives they need to move on toward problem-managing action, it will be helpful to pause a moment and review the conditions under which challenging is most likely to have a beneficial impact on clients. After reviewing these conditions or principles, we will go on in the next chapter to consider three more challenging skills and the reason for challenging itself—that is, goal setting.

Principles Common to All Forms of Challenging

The following seven principles apply to all forms of challenging. They include both cautions and hints on how to challenge well. The first is *keeping the goal in mind.* Challenge must be integrated into the entire helping process. Keep in mind that at this stage of the counseling process the goal is to help clients develop the kinds of alternative perceptions and frames of reference they need to clarify problem situations and to come to the kind of understanding of themselves and of the situation that leads to goal setting. Challenging for the sake of challenging can cause the helping process to deteriorate into a power struggle.

The second is *allowing for self-challenge.* Give clients ample opportunity to challenge themselves. If they fail to do so, it may be, in part, that your skill of primary-level accurate empathy and/or your ability to use probes is falling short of the mark. Do not immediately blame the client for lack of progress. You can provide clients with probes and structures that help them engage in self-challenge.

> *Counselor:* I wonder whether you are beginning to see any "blind spots" in your relationship with your son.

Or the same client might be asked to list three things he thinks he does right and three things he needs to reconsider in his relationship with his son (see Greenberg & Higgins, 1980; Greenberg & Kahn, 1979; and Bernstein & Lecompte 1979, for ways of helping clients engage in self-challenge).

The third is *earning the right to challenge*. Berenson and Mitchell (1974) suggest that many people don't have the right to challenge others because they are not living very effectively themselves. They discuss some of the factors involved in earning this right:

- *Quality of the relationship.* Challenge only if you have spent time and effort building a relationship with your client. If your rapport is poor or you have allowed your relationship with the client to stagnate, then deal directly with what is happening (or not happening) between the two of you. The skill of immediacy, to be discussed in the next chapter, will help you do so.

- *Understanding the client.* Challenge only after spending an adequate amount of time trying to understand the client. Effective challenge is built on understanding and flows from it. Only when you see the world through the client's eyes can you begin to see what he or she is failing to see. Furthermore, if clients feel that you do not understand them, they will probably not listen to your challenges anyway.

- *Being open to challenge.* Don't challenge unless you are open to being challenged. If you are defensive in the counseling relationship, do not expect your clients to set aside their defensiveness. It is unrealistic to expect to deal with others' vulnerabilities without at the same time letting yourself be reasonably vulnerable.

- *Living fully.* Only a person who is striving to live fully according to his or her value system has the right to challenge others, for only such persons are potential sources of human nourishment. In other words, don't challenge unless you challenge yourself to develop physically, intellectually, socially, and emotionally.

The fourth is *the manner of challenging.* Once challenge seems appropriate, the way you go about it is important.

- *Delivering challenges tentatively.* Challenges delivered with a high degree of authoritarianism tend to put clients off. Challenge is not an opportunity for the helper to play God.

    Counselor A (responding to a teacher who is having trouble with both fellow teachers and the administration; they have been exploring his dislikes): You don't really "swallow" your anger. It comes dribbling out unproductively all the time.

Counselor B: From what you say, it sounds like the anger you "swallow" at faculty meetings doesn't always stay down. It seems to leak out at times in cynical remarks directed to "no one," in some aloofness, and occasionally in uncooperative behavior. I wonder whether this picture makes sense to you or not.

Counselor A's challenge is simply an accusation. The way Counselor B qualifies her statement allows the client to amend it without feeling he is arguing with her. Good challenges do not pin clients down; they still leave them room to move. On the other hand, challenges that are delivered with too many qualifications either verbally or through the helper's tone of voice sound apologetic and are easily dismissed by clients.

- *With care.* All I have described in the section on respect must be applied to any given instance of challenging. It includes being sensitive to the client's *present* ability to hear and respond to a challenge. If a client is disorganized and confused at the moment, it does little good to add to his or her disorganization by further challenging. A good sense of timing in interpersonal situations is part of social intelligence. Care also excludes motivation to be right or put clients in their place.
- *Building on successes.* High-level helpers do not demand everything from clients all at once and try to keep clients from doing the same. Rather, they help clients place more and more demands on themselves and in the process help them appreciate and celebrate their successes.

     Counselor A: You're still not as assertive as you need to be.
     Counselor B: Moira, your voice was much stronger that time. I noticed that the members of the group seemed to sit up and take notice. But there are still hints of hesitancy in your voice.

Counselor A does not reinforce the client for her accomplishment, however small it might be. Counselor B does.

- *Being concrete and specific.* Your challenges will hit the mark if they are concrete and specific. Clients don't know what to do about vague challenges. They may feel they should do *something*, but because they don't know what, they are confused.

     Counselor A: You're too passive, Ted. You have to go out and seize life if you expect others to pay attention to you.

The concept "passive" is too general, and the solution offered is too vague for Ted to seize. "Being active" needs to be broken down into specific behaviors that can be learned and put into practice gradually.

Counselor B: Ted, it could be that one reason people overlook you is that you don't assert yourself very much. If you always hang back, soon no one is noticing you. For instance, your voice is so soft and quiet that sometimes it's hard to hear you.

Counselor B realizes that Ted probably needs some help or training in being more assertive. He confronts the client with a general view of his behavior but gets explicit immediately.

The fifth is *challenging strengths rather than weaknesses.* Berenson and Mitchell (1974) discovered that successful helpers tend to challenge clients' strengths rather than their weaknesses. Confrontation of strengths means pointing out to clients the assets and resources they have but fail to use or to use fully. In the following example, the helper is talking to one of the members of a counseling group.

Group counselor: Rick, I'd like to comment on the *quality* of your interactions here. The times you've interacted with me, I've listened very carefully because your voice and your nonverbal behavior have told me that you are totally present. You listen and understand very well. I guess I'm not sure why you don't seem to be available like that to more people in the group and perhaps more consistently. Your interactions with me are so rewarding that when you retire for an extended period, I miss you. The *quantity* of your interaction in the long run affects the quality of your presence here. I wonder whether you notice this, too.

The helper places a demand on Rick—one that is implicit in the group contract—to *use* his assets.

On the other hand, as the name implies, weakness confrontation dwells on the deficits of the person being confronted. In the following example, the helper is talking to a woman living on welfare who has been accused of child neglect.

Counselor: You nagged at your husband and kept a sloppy house until he left. And now it's the kid's turn. You seem to think of only yourself. Life is a rat race and you're its principal victim.

In rare instances when the relationship between client and helper is strong and there is a history of respect, "blasts" like this might do some good. But ordinarily they are dead ends. Ineffective helpers do not know how to help clients mobilize their resources; so in their frustration, they resort to various modes of punishment, even though they know that punishment is ordinarily a poor motivator.

Realistically, most challenges have *something* negative about them. Even when you confront others' strengths, you are doing so because they are *not* using them effectively. However, the unintended punitive effects of challenge are mitigated greatly by emphasizing strength and potential.

The sixth is *challenging clients to clarify values*. Challenge clients to clarify their values and to make reasonable choices based on them. Be wary of using the challenging process to force clients to accept your values.

> *Client* (a 21-year-old woman who is a junior in college): I have done practically no experimentation with sex. I'm not sure whether it's because I think it's wrong or if I'm just plain scared.
>
> *Counselor A:* A certain amount of exploration is normal. Maybe it would be good to give you some basic information on contraception. That may help allay your fears a bit.
>
> *Counselor B:* It sounds like you're saying that maybe it's time to find out which it is.

Counselor A begins with a pronouncement and edges toward making some choices for the client; Counselor B challenges her gently to find out what she really wants. Genuineness demands that counselors be up front with their values without forcing them on clients. This is not always an easy thing to do. "What values am I pushing here?" is a question that counselors can profitably ask themselves throughout the helping process.

The client's values should not be challenged unless a "value" is patently inhuman—for instance, sadistic pleasure derived from punishing others. Rather, the behavioral implications of his or her values may need to be challenged. Let's consider a case in which the counselor confronts a value the client holds.

> *Counselor:* Bill, it seems obvious that you invest too much of yourself in work. Work doesn't really enhance your life any more; it imprisons you. You don't own your work; it owns you.
>
> *Bill:* It's my life and it's what I like to do. Do I have to be like everyone else?

Work is a legitimate value, and if the counselor attacks it directly, he can expect the client to react defensively. A more effective tactic is to challenge Bill to probe his own values in the area of work, see how he translates them into behavior, and work out the relationship of his work values to the other values in his life. Value *conflicts* rather than values themselves are the proper object of challenge.

The seventh is *remaining positive*. Challenging clients can involve helping them see the self-defeating consequences of some behavior patterns. If this is the case, then try to point out more constructive behaviors.

> *Group counselor A:* Elwood, often enough when another group member spends some time exploring a problem, you tend to "drop out" of the group.

You're physically here, but it's fairly obvious that mentally you're far away. If I'm the one talking and you do this, I feel cheated.

Group counselor B (Nancy is talking): Could I interrupt a minute, Nancy. . . . (Turning to Elwood) Elwood, I have the feeling that your mind has wandered off somewhere. I've noticed that happen a couple of times, usually when some other member is exploring a problem. When you do listen and get involved, you're usually quite perceptive.

Nancy: I agree. I'd like your help.

Counselor A's timing is poor. He is giving the client a lecture after the fact. Counselor B's timing is on the mark, and she emphasizes resources rather than deficits. Effective helpers instinctively look for a client's resources.

Reluctance to Challenge: The "MUM Effect"

Initially, some counselor trainees are reluctant to place demands on others or, preferably, help others place demands on themselves. They become victims of what may be called the "MUM effect," which refers to people's tendency to withhold bad news from others even when they know it is in others' interest to hear this news (Rosen & Tesser, 1970, 1971; Tesser & Rosen, 1972; Tesser, Rosen, & Batchelor, 1972; Tesser, Rosen, & Tesser, 1971). In ancient times the person who bore bad news to the king was sometimes killed. This obviously led to a certain reluctance on the part of messengers to bring such news. Bad news, and by extension the kind of "bad news" involved in any kind of challenging, arouses negative feelings in the *challenger*, no matter what he or she might think the reaction on the part of the receiver might be. If you are comfortable with the supportive dimensions of the helping process but uncomfortable with helping as a social-influence process, you are in danger of falling victim to the MUM effect, and your communications with your clients might remain watered down and safe.

Reluctance to challenge is not a bad starting position; it is far better than being too eager to challenge. However, all helping, even the most client-centered (Rogers, 1951), involves social influence. It is important for you to understand your reluctance (or eagerness) to challenge—that is, to challenge yourself on the issue of challenging and on the very notion of helping as a social-influence process. When trainees examine how they feel about challenging others, these are some of the things they discover:

- "I am just not used to challenging others. My interpersonal style has had a lot of the 'be and let be' in it. I have *misgivings about intruding into other people's lives.*"

- "If I challenge others, then *I open myself to being challenged.* I may be hurt or I may find out things about myself that I would rather not know."
- "I might find out that I *like* challenging others and that the floodgates will open and my negative feelings about others will flow out. I have some fears that deep down I am a very angry person."
- "I am afraid that I will *hurt* others, damage them in some way or other. I have been hurt or I have seen others hurt by heavy-handed confrontations."
- "I am afraid that I will delve too deeply into others and find that they have problems that *I cannot help them handle.* The helping process will get out of hand."
- "If I challenge others, they will no longer *like me.* I want my clients to like me."

Exploring your feelings about challenging is part of a larger exploration process—that is, taking a good look at why you want to be a helper in the first place. It is assumed that this is one of the issues you will explore while in training. From time to time, irrational elements will surface in your relationships with clients. For instance, as was mentioned earlier, they will use you and the helping process to play out relationships they have with other significant people in their lives, past or present. You will tend to do the same and to react to the feelings they are projecting on you. These phenomena have been called "transference" and "countertransference" (see Luborsky & Spence, 1978, pp. 343–347, for bibliographical references and a summary of the research on transference and countertransference). The skill of immediacy, which will be discussed in the next chapter, is an important challenging skill that will help you deal with transference and countertransference and, indeed, all that happens between you and any given client.

The Challenged Client's Response

Even when one form of challenge or another is a response to a client's plea to be helped to live more effectively, it can precipitate some degree of disorganization in the client. Different writers refer to this experience under different terms: "crisis," "disorganization," "a sense of inadequacy," "disequilibrium," and "beneficial uncertainty." However, counseling-precipitated crises *can* be beneficial for the client. Whether they are or not depends, to a great extent, on the helper's skill.

As we have seen, social-influence theory suggests that people who feel inadequate are often open to being influenced to a greater degree than people not in crisis. Challenge, because it usually induces some sense of inadequacy in clients, can render them more open to influence. However, some clients can resist being influenced and respond defensively even to responsible challenge. One way of looking at the way clients sometimes resist challenge is from the point of view of cognitive-dissonance theory (Festinger, 1957). Challenge, as we have seen, can induce dissonance (discomfort, crisis, disequilibrium or whatever name is given to it). Because dissonance is an uncomfortable state, the client will try to get out of it. According to dissonance theory, there are five typical ways people experiencing dissonance attempt to rid themselves of this discomfort.

One way is to *attempt to discredit challengers*. The challenger is confronted and discredited. Some attempt is made to point out that they are no better than anyone else.

> *Client* (who has been discussing her marital problems and has been challenged by the helper): It's easy for you to sit there and suggest that I be more "responsible" in my marriage. You've never had to experience the misery in which we live. You've never experienced his brutality. You probably live in one of those "nice" middle-class marriages.

This is a common strategy for coping with challenge—counterattack. Counselors who elicit this kind of response from their clients may merely be the victims of their clients' attempt to reduce dissonance. However, it is best not to jump to that conclusion immediately. The client might be airing a legitimate gripe. It may be that the counselor has been inaccurate or heavy-handed in his or her challenge.

Second, *attempts are made to persuade challengers to change their views*. In this approach, challengers are reasoned with; they are urged to see what they have said as misinterpretations and to revise their views. In the following example, the client pursues this strategy by using rationalization.

> *Client:* I'm not so sure that my anger at home isn't called for. I think that it's a way in which I'm asserting my own identity. If I were to lie down and let others do what they want, I would become a doormat at home. I think you see me as a fairly reasonable person. For instance, I don't get angry here because there is no reason.

Sometimes a client like this will lead an unwary counselor into an argument about the issue in question. A client who is highly committed to rationalization is difficult to deal with, but arguing with him or her may not be the answer.

A third way is *devaluing the importance of the issue at hand*. This is another form of rationalization. For instance, if the client is being challenged about her sarcasm, she points out that she is rarely sarcastic, that "poking fun at others" is a minor part of her life and not worth spending time on. The fact that clients themselves run from topics that are too painful emphasizes the necessity of an accurate understanding of the client's feelings, experiences, and behavior. The client has a right to devalue a topic if it really isn't important. The counselor has to be sensitive enough to discover which issues are important and which are not.

Fourth, *support is sought elsewhere for the views being challenged.* Some clients leave one counselor and go to another because they feel they "aren't being understood." They try to find helpers who will agree with them. This is an extreme way of seeking support of one's own views elsewhere. But a client can remain with a counselor and still offer evidence that others do contest the helper's point of view.

> *Client:* I asked my wife about my sarcasm. She said she doesn't mind it at all. And she said she thinks that my friends see it as humor and as a part of my style.

This is an indirect way of telling the counselor she is wrong. The counselor might well be wrong, but if the client's sarcasm is really dysfunctional in his interpersonal life, the counselor should find some way of pressing the issue. If the counseling takes place in a group, it is much more difficult for clients to use this approach to reducing dissonance.

> *Juan:* Does anyone else here see me as biting and sarcastic?
> *Susan:* I think you do get sarcastic from time to time. The reason I've said nothing about it so far is that you haven't been sarcastic with me. And I'm a bit afraid of you.

Because Juan can get direct feedback on his behavior from the group, it is harder for him to play games.

Fifth, the client can *change cognition to correspond to that of the confronter.* The client can agree with the counselor. However, the purpose of challenging is not to get clients to agree with their helpers; it is to help them reexamine their behavior in order to develop the kinds of perspectives *they* need to clarify the problem situation and establish goals. Therefore, when clients "agree" with their challengers, this may be nothing more than a game.

> *Client:* I think you're right. I'm much too blunt and forward when I speak; I should try to think what impact I'm going to have before I open my mouth.

This response may be mere capitulation rather than self-exploration. Clients can agree with the challenges of helpers in order to get them "off their back." If such confessions do not lead to goal-setting behavior, however, they may be merely one more way of handling dissonance and not a move toward constructive behavior change.

If clients are challenged in keeping with the principles outlined here, they will be more likely to accept the invitation to reexamine their experiences, behaviors, and feelings. Consider this example, in which the counselor is challenging a man about the way he relates to his son:

Counselor: Whenever your son explains how he feels about his relationship with you, you tend to explain what he's said in a way that agrees with your own views of the relationship. I'm not sure that you listen to him intently because what you're saying sounds so different from what he's saying.

Client: You mean it sounds like I'm trying to put my words into his mouth so that I can say "See, we're really saying the same thing!"

This client does what few people spontaneously do when they are challenged: he first checks to see whether he has an accurate understanding of what the counselor is saying. However atypical this response might be in everyday life, it is one that counselors can help their clients develop. This is the first step in helping clients learn how to challenge themselves.

In the following example, we hear a client who has been challenged to be more assertive in the helping relationship itself.

Client: In the last half hour I've begun to do what I'm always doing outside: I've become an obedient mouse. I've been trying to talk with you in a way that will please you rather than help me. I'm constantly looking for cues in your behavior that tell me whether I'm doing the "right thing" or not.

This client catches himself in unproductive behavior and confronts himself. Once he recognizes unproductive behavior, he can explore it with the helper and try to come up with measures to prevent its recurrence.

Now that some principles for effective challenge of clients have been outlined, let us return to the consideration of the remaining three skills, specifically, confrontation, helper self-sharing, and immediacy.

Chapter

7

Stage II:
Developing New Perspectives
and Setting Goals

Part Two:
The Skills of Confrontation, Counselor Self-Sharing, and Immediacy; the Task of Setting Goals

This chapter deals with the following topics:

There are at least three more principal ways of helping clients develop the kinds of new perspectives that enable them to move toward the kind of action that helps them manage problem situations: confrontation, helper self-disclosure, and immediacy.

Confronting the Client

Confrontation is a word that inspires fear in many people, for they have seen or imagined themselves or others devastated by irresponsible personal assault. They see confrontation as an attack, and sometimes even a vicious attack, on another person, though the attacker often says that it is for this person's "own good." If confrontation is actually an attack, then it seems to help the confronter get a load off his or her chest rather than help the other person live more effectively. Although some think that even "attack therapy" might encourage growth if it takes place in the context of a supportive community (Maslow, 1967), this is not what I mean by confrontation in this chapter. There is such a thing as responsible and caring confrontation. The purpose of this section is to help you understand the nature and techniques of confrontation as one form of challenging and help you integrate it into your overall counseling style. It is very important to keep in mind that confrontation, too, needs to be related to developing new perspectives and to moving on to goal setting, program development, and action.

Put most simply, confrontation, like other forms of challenge, is an invitation to *examine* some form of behavior that seems to be self-defeating or harmful to others and to *change* the behavior if it is found to be so. Through confrontation clients develop alternate frames of reference with regard to their experiences, behaviors, and feelings, whether overt or covert or a combination of both.

Berenson and Mitchell (1974) describe five types of confrontation. I have already touched on three—"strength confrontation" and "weakness confrontation" in the section on general principles of challenging and "didactic confrontation" in the section on information giving. I review the two other types here.

Confronting Experientially

As you involve yourself more deeply with your clients, you will notice that at times you experience them (their experiences, feelings, and behaviors) *differently* from the ways they experience themselves. While avoiding making your own experience normative, you can invite them to examine these differences. For instance, Alicia, a woman in her late twenties, has been talking about herself as "unattractive" in a group counseling session.

> *Group counselor:* You say that you're unattractive, and yet I know that you get asked out a lot. I don't find you unattractive myself. And, if I'm not mistaken, I see people here react to you in ways that say "I like you." I can't put all of this together with your being "unattractive."
>
> *Alicia:* Okay. What you say is true, and it helps me clarify what I mean. First of all, I'm no raving beauty, and when others find me attractive, I think they mean they find me intellectually interesting, a caring person, and things like that. At times I wish I were more physically attractive, though I hate to admit it. The fact is that much of the time I *feel* unattractive. And sometimes I feel most unattractive at the very moment people are telling me directly or indirectly that they find me attractive.
>
> *Group member:* So you've gotten into the habit of telling yourself in various ways that you're unattractive.
>
> *Alicia:* Yeah. It's a lousy habit.

Because the counselor's experience of Alicia is so different from her experience of herself, he invites her to explore the difference in the group. Her self-exploration clarifies the issue greatly. Getting rid of the habit of telling herself that she's unattractive might well be a goal.

There are a number of sources of differences in experiencing. For instance, discrepancies, distortions, evasions, games, tricks, and smoke screens all contribute to clients being experienced differently by others from the ways they experience themselves. Most of us occasionally fall prey to one or more of these, but significant and long-term discrepancies and distortions contribute to self-defeating life patterns. Let's take a closer look at these categories.

CHALLENGING DISCREPANCIES

Confrontation can zero in on discrepancies between what clients think or feel and what they say, between what they say and what they do, between their views of themselves and others' views of them, between what they are and what they wish to be, and between their expressed values and their actual behavior. These discrepancies can refer to their behavior in the counseling sessions or outside. For instance, a helper might challenge the following discrepancies that take place outside the counseling sessions:

- Tom sees himself as witty; his friends see him as biting.
- Minerva says that physical fitness is important, but she overeats and underexercises.
- George says he loves his wife and family, but he is seeing another woman and stays away from home a lot.
- Penny says she hates her work, but she does nothing to look for a new job.
- Leo says he wants to be more assertive, but he does not spell out what "being assertive" means concretely for him.
- Clarissa makes promises to her daughter but does not keep them.

> *Counselor* (after summarizing what Clarissa had said about how she relates to her 11-year-old daughter): If I were your daughter, I'd be angry because you didn't do what you said you'd do. I might misbehave a lot to let you know just how I feel. Does what I'm saying sound unfair?
>
> *Clarissa:* I keep thinking that she's a little kid and that fooling her a bit isn't that bad. After all, she's only 11. I think I keep my word better with adults. (Pauses) Now that I've said that, it sounds stupid.

A counselor might challenge the following kinds of discrepancies that take place inside the counseling sessions:

- Mary is obviously confused and hurt, but she says she feels fine.
- Bernard says yes with his words, but his body language says no.
- Evita says she wants help, but she refuses to disclose herself enough to clarify the problem situation.

> *Counselor:* Evita, you came complaining about serious family problems, but it seems that *neither* you nor I think that what we've talked about so far is that serious. I'm not sure whether there's more and, if there is, what might be keeping you from talking about it.
>
> *Evita:* There's a lot more, but I'm embarrassed to talk about it.

The counselor is properly tentative in pointing out this discrepancy and the client moves forward. The client needs support and some help to overcome her embarrassment.

CHALLENGING DISTORTIONS

Some clients cannot face the world as it is, and therefore they distort it in various ways. For instance:

- Arnie is afraid of his supervisor and therefore sees her as aloof; in reality, she is a caring person.

- Edna sees her counselor in some kind of divine role and therefore makes unwarranted demands on him.
- Eric sees his stubbornness as commitment.
- Nancy sees herself as a sexual victim, but this is only partially true because she flirts and seduces.

> *Counselor:* Nancy, I realize that the sexual demands made on you by your older brother have had a profound impact on you, but your continuing to put most of the responsibility for your sexual problems on others seems to be self-defeating. It also seems too convenient.
>
> *Nancy:* It seems that I'm not going to be able to seduce you.

The counselor bluntly but caringly invites Nancy to examine her blaming behavior with a view to replacing it with something more constructive. The overriding goal is that Nancy become responsible for her own sexual behavior. To do this, she must break the tyranny of the past. When clients don't want to act or are afraid to act, they often say in one way or another that they are *unable* to act.

CHALLENGING SELF-DEFEATING ATTITUDES AND BELIEFS

As you talk to clients and help them explore their problem, it might soon become clear to you that clients have attitudes and beliefs that keep them locked into their problem situations. Ellis (1962, 1971, 1973, 1974; Ellis & Harper, 1975) in his rational-emotive therapy and Meichenbaum (1974, 1977; Meichenbaum & Genest, 1980) in his cognitive-behavior modification point out that the inner or covert experiences and behavior that sustain self-defeating patterns of overt behavior have to be challenged. They have both developed methodologies for helping clients come to grips with what can be called self-defeating self-talk or self-dialogue.

> *Client:* I've decided not to apply for that job.
> *Counselor:* How come?
> *Client:* Well, it's not exactly what I want.
> *Counselor:* That's quite a change from last week. It sounded then as if it was just what you wanted.
> *Client:* Well, I've thought it over. (Pauses)
> *Counselor:* I've got a hunch based on what we've learned about your style. I think you've been saying something like this to yourself: "I like the job, but I don't think I'm good enough for it. If I try it, I might fall flat on my face and that would be *awful*. So I'll stick to what I've got, even though I don't like it very much." Any truth in any of that?
> *Client:* Maybe more than I want to admit.

Challenging clients' self-limiting attitudes and beliefs can be one of the most powerful methodologies for behavior change at your disposal. One possible danger, however, is that such confrontation can be used as a way of discrediting a client's reasonable values because they don't appeal to you.

Some of the common beliefs that Ellis (1962, 1971, 1974; Ellis & Harper, 1975) says get in the way of effective living are the following:

- *Being liked and loved.* I *must* always be loved and approved of by the significant people in my life.
- *Being competent.* I *must* always in all situations demonstrate competence, and I must be talented and competent in some important area of life.
- *Having my way.* I *must* have my way and my plans must always work out.
- *Being hurt.* People who do anything wrong, and especially those who harm me, are evil and should be blamed and punished.
- *Being in danger.* If anything or any situation is dangerous in any way, I must be anxious and upset about it.
- *Being problemless.* Things should not go wrong in life, and if by chance they do, there should be quick and easy solutions.
- *Being a victim.* Other people and outside forces are responsible for any misery I experience, and I therefore cannot be expected to control my feelings.
- *Avoiding.* It is easier to avoid facing life's difficulties than to develop self-discipline; making demands of myself should not be necessary.
- *Tyranny of the past.* What I did and especially what happened to me in the past determines how I act and feel today.
- *Passivity.* I can be happy by avoiding, by being passive, by being uncommitted, and by just enjoying myself.
- *Catastrophizing.* If any of the previous principles are violated in my life, it is terrible, awful, and catastrophic.

Clients can be infected to varying degrees with what Alcoholics Anonymous groups have called the "stinkin' thinkin' " involved in these principles.

Artis, a man in his mid-thirties, has recently lost a well-paying job. He can easily get another job, but not one as plush as the one he has lost. To make things worse, he has just been told that he needs an operation for hemorrhoids. He has been catastrophizing over the loss of his job, and now he feels that he is being completely done in by this new catastrophe. The counselor has spent some time helping him explore the problem situation and communicating support through empathy.

> *Client:* I just can't stand the way life is ganging up on me! I'm getting more than my fair share.
>
> *Counselor A:* It's downright unfair that all this is happening at once.

Counselor B: What's happening is lousy, but handling it by saying to yourself that it shouldn't be happening and that it's just awful seems to be making things even worse. I mean, it seems to be keeping you from looking for practical ways of coping with all of this.

Counselor A is merely empathic. What he says might well reinforce the client's complaining without helping him move on. Counselor B is still empathic, but she also confronts the client's self-defeating thinking and suggests an alternate—that is, exploring coping possibilities.

The work of Ellis and Meichenbaum is too important to be given summary treatment here. You are encouraged to read it and to review evaluations of it (see Patterson, 1980, for a starter).

CHALLENGING GAMES, TRICKS, AND SMOKE SCREENS

If clients are comfortable with their delusions and profit by them, they will obviously try to keep them. If they are rewarded for playing games, inside the counseling sessions or outside, they will continue a game approach to life (Berne, 1964; Harris, 1969; James & Jongeward, 1971). For instance, Clarence plays "Yes, but. . . ." He presents himself as one in need of help and then proceeds to show his helper how ineffective the help he is getting is. Dorita makes herself appear helpless and needy when she is with her friends, but when they come to her aid, she is angry with them for treating her like a child. Kevin seduces others in one way or another and then becomes indignant when they accept his implied invitations. The number of games people can play in order to avoid the work involved in facing the tasks of life squarely is seemingly endless. Clients who are fearful of changing will attempt to lay down smoke screens in order to hide from the helper the ways in which they fail to face up to life. Such clients can use communication in order not to communicate (Beier, 1966).

One function of Stage I is to set up an atmosphere that discourages clients from attempting to play games with you. This is one meaning of a good working relationship. If clients do try, skilled helpers do not get "hooked" into their games. For instance, effective helpers don't start out by giving advice; so they prevent clients from playing the "yes, but . . ." game. However, if a client does attempt to play some game or to lay down diversionary smoke screens during the helping interviews, the counselor challenges this behavior. Beier (1966) suggests that some clients play one kind of game or another to attempt to *restrict* the helper's response in some way. The helper thus "engaged" is easy to sidetrack.

The following client has just begun to explore a sensitive area—how he manipulates an older brother into coming to his aid financially. He takes financial risks because he knows he can talk his brother into bailing him out.

Client: I really like what you've been doing in these sessions. It feels good to be with such a strong person.

Counselor A (in an angry voice): See, that's exactly what I've been getting at. Now you're manipulating me and not even trying to be subtle!

Counselor B: Thanks. I think that it's important that we respect each other here. And perhaps that's the issue with your brother—respect.

Counselor A gets angry and lets himself be sidetracked, but Counselor B uses the client's game to refocus on the issue at hand.

Helpers can also challenge the games that clients play outside the counseling sessions. In the following example, Sophie, a 55-year-old woman, has been exploring her relationships with her married children. She has her own game. She "confides" in one of them some kind of negative information about herself— for instance, that she can't seem to manage things at the house as well as she used to—and then counts on that one to tell the others. The payoff is that she remains the center of attention much of the time without seeming to do much to demand it. Lately, however, her children seem to be on to her game. She tries to see their behavior as "indifference." She is talking to her pastor about her "loneliness." The pastor has spent a good deal of time exploring the whole problem situation with her.

Pastor: I'd like to make a bet with you.

Sophie (a bit surprised): About what?

Pastor: If I've listened carefully to what you've been saying, you've gotten a lot of attention from the kids by playing one off against the other. Nothing evil, mind you, just a bit clever. Maybe just a bit too clever. My bet is that you could relate to them straight and get all the human contact you need. And I think my bet is safe because I see you as a resourceful woman.

Sophie (cautiously): Tell me more about this bet.

The helper calls her game. But he challenges her strengths rather than her weaknesses. Casting his challenge in the form of a bet adds tentativeness. By exploring the bet together, they can come up with a goal that will have something to do with restructuring her relationships with her children. Dreikurs (1967) suggests that clients use their symptoms to cover up their real intentions. He sees this as a game that needs challenging: "As Adler pointed out, one of the most effective therapeutic means [of challenging clients' games] is 'spitting in the patient's soup.' He can continue what he's doing, but it no longer 'tastes so good' " (p. 230).

Using Descriptions in Confronting Clients

One of the most important practical hints for confronting others is one suggested by Wallen (1973): *describe* in concrete terms what you see as counterproductive behavior in clients, and *describe* the impact you think it has on them and others. As Wallen notes, there is a strong tendency in interpersonal transactions to use negative forms of verbal behavior, such as commanding, judging, labeling, accusing, questioning, and being cynical or sarcastic instead of more neutral describing. It is assumed that helpers out of respect for their clients would not fall into this trap. However that assumption is not always borne out. In the following example, the client is a 30-year-old male who is very resistant to change. He has been discussing problems in interpersonal relations. He sees his bluntness and sarcasm as honesty.

Counselor A: You're really insensitive! You rage around like a bull in a china shop and then can't understand why people aren't nice to you.

Counselor B: Let's see if I understand what you're saying. What you say to others very often seems to put them off. When this happens, your tendency is to see it as their problem. For instance, you say to yourself that they are too sensitive. Still, two things seem to happen—others feel hurt, and when they turn on you, you feel isolated. It seems that you exercise a lot of power in your relationships. I wonder whether you think this power might be channeled more effectively.

Counselor A becomes exasperated and accuses the client. Counselor B not only describes the client's behavior and its effects but also tries to focus on the client's strength rather than just his weakness.

Caricatures of Confrontation

Gordon (1970), in teaching parents ways of being effective in their relationships with their children, describes a number of categories of ineffective parental behaviors. These behaviors are caricatures of perversions of confrontation. They are ways helpers become ineffectually "parental" with their clients. The following is a checklist of these behaviors. Some of the categories overlap, and some of these behaviors might at times be useful, provided they are not your way of taking over responsibilities that belong to the client. Can you suggest situations in which some of these behaviors might be changed enough so that they are constructive?

- *Commanding, ordering, directing.* "Go back to your wife and tell her what we've talked about."
- *Warning, admonishing, threatening.* "If you keep on being dependent, you're going to end up a very lonely woman. I've seen it happen before."
- *Exhorting, moralizing, preaching.* "Try to be more sensitive to her needs. Sensitivity is very important in intimate relationships."
- *Advising, giving suggestions, offering solutions.* "If I were you, I'd quit your teaching job as soon as possible and take one in the business world."

- *Lecturing, giving logical arguments.* "She's not going to give in and neither are you. The conclusion seems to be to end the relationship."
- *Judging, criticizing, disagreeing, blaming.* "If you can admit that getting fired was your own fault, then you'll be in a position to start thinking of new jobs."
- *Approving, praising, agreeing with.* "Telling your mother-in-law off was the best thing you could have done. It was your way of regaining your manhood."
- *Name-calling, ridiculing, shaming.* "I can't believe that you'd just drop him without letting him know why. What an awful way to treat someone."
- *Reassuring, consoling, sympathizing.* "Don't let this get you down. He probably didn't know he was hurting you this much."
- *Questioning, interrogating.* "How do you feel right now? What is bothering you the most? What other relationships are going wrong?"
- *Humoring, distracting.* "I bet you can see the humor in all this mess. You're the kind that doesn't let her sense of humor die."

Turning clients into children is not only showing them a lack of respect; it is just not an effective way of helping them grapple with change.

Encouraging Action

By encouragement to action, another form of confrontation, Berenson and Mitchell (1974) mean that clients are encouraged to act upon their world in some reasonable, appropriate manner and are discouraged from taking a passive stance toward life. Effective helpers are reasonably assertive people who are not afraid to call clients to action, especially when clients say they want to act but fail to do so. There is an element of encouragement to action in every kind of challenge—that is, clients are being called to change both their covert and overt behavior to more constructive patterns.

Changes in covert behavior are usually meaningless unless they are followed by changes in overt behavior.

> *Client:* These sessions have been very useful. I understand myself a lot better now.
>
> *Helper:* What about your relationship with your wife? In what ways is that better?
>
> *Client:* I can't think of any major way in which that has improved, but it does not bother me much any more.

If counseling has merely helped this client to anesthetize himself to the problem situations of his life, then it may have been for the worse. Feeling better about himself is certainly good, but not if it makes him content to live less effectively than he might. It would be a different story if he had come to feel better about himself because he had struggled to do something about this important relationship.

Perhaps helping is too often seen as a process through which we encourage clients to think themselves into better ways of acting instead of encouraging them to act themselves into better ways of thinking and feeling.

> *Client:* Well, I've been quite faithful to the physical fitness program we outlined together a month ago. I run and do the other exercises every day. I'm eating and sleeping sensibly.
>
> *Helper:* You sound very positive.
>
> *Client:* I'm actually proud of myself. I'm not depressed. I feel I've got a lot more energy to face my other problems. In fact, some of the things you said about the self-defeating ways I relate to others are beginning to make sense to me. I'd like to go over some of that with you.

This client has acted himself into better ways of thinking and feeling. It is an example of the nonlinear nature of helping. Moving ahead to an action program has put him in a better position to see his problems in living more clearly.

ENCOURAGING CLIENTS TO ACT IN THE HELPING SESSIONS

More will be said about encouraging clients to act outside the helping sessions when we get to Stage III. However, some clients need to be encouraged to participate in the helping sessions themselves. Without knowing it, clients sometimes impede the helping process in two ways. One relates to the sense of self-defeat that brings them to helpers in the first place. The second relates to self-responsibility. Because these are ways in which movement in the helping process itself is impeded, they need to be challenged.

FAILURE TO STATE PROBLEMS SO THEY APPEAR SOLVABLE

One of the games clients play (with ineffective helpers) is to state problems in a way that makes them seem insoluble. This game often elicits the counselor's pity and sympathy, which may be precisely the payoff the client is looking for.

> *Insoluble problem:* "In sum, my life is miserable now because of my past. My parents were indifferent to me and at times even unjustly hostile. If they had only been more loving, I wouldn't be in this present mess. I am the unhappy product of an unhappy environment."

Clients may not use this rather stilted language, but the message is still the same. The point is that the client's past cannot be changed. Therefore, because she defines her problem in terms of the past, her problem cannot be solved. "You certainly had it rough and are suffering from it now" might be the kind of response that such a statement is designed to elicit.

> *Soluble problem:* "Over the years I've been blaming my parents for my misery. I still spend a great deal of time feeling sorry for myself. As a result, I sit around and do nothing—I don't make friends; I don't involve myself in the community; I don't take any constructive steps to get a better job."

Again, the language is stilted, but this message is different from the previous one. The problem, stated this way, can be managed. The client can stop blaming his parents because he cannot change them; he can increase his self-esteem and therefore stop feeling sorry for himself; and he can acquire the interpersonal skills he needs to enter more effectively into relationships with others.

A problem cannot be solved if it is stated in vague terms or defined in terms of forces beyond the client's control.

> *Insoluble problem:* "The world is going to seed. No matter what the politicians say, there's always the possibility of nuclear warfare. It's frightening. You almost wonder why you keep going on."

The client cannot change the complexity of the world or the possibility of atomic war. Because an atomic holocaust is a possibility, some concern and fear is realistic. But if the client believes that his present anxiety and passivity are due to the possibility of nuclear warfare, there is no solution.

> *Soluble problem:* "I'm overly anxious and tend to blame my anxiety on things that happen to me—like the mess the world is in. I think I should blame myself much more—the ways I act and the ways I fail to act. I'm too passive; I say that I'm overwhelmed because I can't change the world, but I don't lift a finger to change what I can change. For instance, I gripe about politicians, but I haven't even voted in the last three elections. I don't work in any community projects. I just watch the TV news and gripe."

Because of the way the client states her problems, the counselor has a much better chance to help her begin to take charge of her life in a more active way. For instance, when the client begins to do things (such as involve herself in community projects), she will probably find herself less anxious because she will be less preoccupied with herself.

Clients state problems in insoluble ways when they say "I can't" instead of "I don't."

Unsolvable: "I can't get her out of my mind. And I can't start thinking of going out with other women."

Solvable: "I don't tell her what I feel. And then I expect her to know anyway."

Saying "I can't" instead of "I don't" may seem to be just a language problem, but often the language suggests some underlying, self-defeating attitude.

FAILURE TO OWN THE PROBLEM

This is a special case of stating a problem in insoluble terms. Clients who state their problems in terms of what others do or fail to do are whistling in the wind. Clients can manage some kind of direct control over their own overt and covert behavior; they don't have that kind of control over others' behavior.

Not owned: "I live in a racist society. It even rubs off on me."

Owned: "I am a racist. I live in a neighborhood that excludes minority groups, especially blacks. And I begin to see that this is only one way in which I express my prejudices."

Not owned: "My friends don't seem to care for me really. They keep me on the margin of their social life."

Owned: "I'm biting and cynical when I'm with my friends. I think sometimes they just say 'ugh' quietly and wish I weren't there. I alienate them. I don't listen well to others. I can hardly blame people for not inviting me to their parties and on vacations."

Not owned: "My husband is a drunk and I can't do much to change him, though I try. He has ruined the home, and our children suffer a great deal. He should get out of the house, out of our lives."

Owned: "I haven't learned how to cope with my husband's excessive drinking. I know that I've done things that merit having a drunk for a husband. I've always nagged, even before he started drinking. When the children were born, I showed them much more interest than I showed him. I've put the entire blame for our misery on his drinking, but I share the blame."

When two human beings find themselves in conflict, it is rare for one of them to be blameless. A wife cannot directly change her husband, but she can change her own behavior. Even when a client has to face a situation that is patently unjust or unfair, such as a boss who is sarcastic and aggressive, she can still decide how to act toward him.

In sum, a problem situation is not clear until the client owns it in some way. If the client is hesitant to own it, then the helper can encourage him or her to do so.

Helper Self-Sharing

Another way of challenging your clients is to share with them something about yourself. Like other forms of challenging, helper self-disclosure is not an end in itself. It must contribute something to getting the work of helping done. Helper self-disclosure can have two principal functions.

First, it can be a form of *modeling* and, as such, a way of showing clients how to disclose themselves and a way of encouraging them to do so. Most of the research on helper self-disclosure stresses this function: "Overall . . . the research weighs in favor of the conclusion that therapist modeling of self-disclosure can be an effective method of denoting . . . for clients what is to take place behaviorally in psychotherapy" (Doster & Nesbitt, 1979, p. 204). It is most useful with clients who don't know what to do or who are reluctant to talk about themselves in an intimate or personal way. Therefore, this kind of helper self-disclosure would seem to be most useful early in the helping interviews, but it could also be used any time a client gets "stuck" and is having difficulty revealing himself or herself. Both Jourard (1968, 1971a, 1971b) and Mowrer (1973a; Mowrer & Vattano, 1976) were pioneers in urging this kind of helper self-disclosure. Self-help groups (Gartner & Riessman, 1977; Hurvitz, 1970) such as Alcoholics Anonymous use modeling extensively as a way of showing new members what to talk about and of encouraging new members to talk freely about themselves and their problems.

Second, helper self-disclosure can help clients develop the kinds of new perspectives needed for goal setting and action. If your experience can help clients develop useful alternate frames of reference, then sharing yourself seems to be a question of common sense.

> *Ben is a counselor in a drug rehabilitation program. He was an addict for a number of years but "kicked the habit" with the help of the agency where he is now a counselor. It is clear to all addicts in the program that the counselors there had been addicts and are not only rehabilitated but intensely interested in helping others both rid themselves of drugs and develop a kind of lifestyle that helps them stay drug-free. Ben freely shares his experience, both of being a drug user and his rather agonizing journey to freedom.*

Ex-alcoholics and ex-addicts can make excellent helpers in programs like this. Sharing their experience is central to their style of counseling and is accepted by their clients.

Weigel, Dinges, Dyer, and Straumfjorn (1972) found evidence suggesting that helper self-disclosure can frighten clients or make them see helpers as less well adjusted. In view of this and other difficulties, it seems that helper self-disclosure should follow certain principles. Helper self-disclosure can be part of the contract. Derlega, Lovell, and Chaikin (1976) found that helper self-disclosure can well be misunderstood by naive or uninformed clients and prove counterproductive. However, if, as in the case of the drug counselors just mentioned, it is clear from the start to clients that "high self-disclosure by the therapist is part of the professional role and is appropriate for effective treatment" (Doster & Nesbitt, 1979, p. 204), then clients are not put off by it. In short, if you don't want clients surprised about your sharing your experience with them, let them know that you might do so.

Sharing yourself is *appropriate* if it helps clients achieve the treatment goals outlined in this helping process—that is, if it helps them talk about themselves, if it helps them talk about problem situations more concretely, if it helps them develop new perspectives and frames of reference, and if it helps them set realistic goals for themselves. Helper self-disclosure that is exhibitionistic or engaged in for "effect" is obviously inappropriate. Here are some principles to be followed to ensure that self-sharing is appropriate.

1. *Selective and focused.* Helper self-disclosure is appropriate if it keeps clients on target and does not distract them from investigating their own problem situations.

    Counselor (talking to a graduate student in psychology): Listening to you brings me right back to my own days in graduate school. I don't think that I was ever busier in my life. I also believe that the most depressing moments of my life took place then. On any number of occasions I wanted to throw in the towel. For instance, I remember once toward the end of my third year when. . . .

    It may be that selective bits of this counselor's experience in graduate school might be useful in helping the student get a better conceptual and emotional grasp of her problems, but he has wandered off into the kind of reminiscing that meets his needs rather than hers.

2. *Not a burden to the client.* Helper self-disclosure is appropriate if it does not add another burden to an already overwhelmed client. One counselor thought that he would help make a client who was sharing some sexual problems more comfortable by sharing some of his own experiences. After all, he saw his sexual development as not too different from the client's. However, the client reacted by saying, "Hey, don't tell me your problems. I'm having a hard enough time dealing with my own. I don't want to carry yours around, too!" This novice counselor shared too much of himself too soon. He was caught up in his own willingness to disclose rather than its potential usefulness to the client.

3. *Not too often.* Helper self-disclosure is inappropriate if it is too frequent. This, too, distracts the client and shifts attention to the counselor. Research (Murphy & Strong, 1972) suggests that if helpers disclose themselves too frequently, clients tend to see them as phony and suspect that they have ulterior motives.

In summary, then, even though the research on helper self-disclosure is somewhat ambiguous (DeForest & Stone, 1980; McCarthy, 1979; Nilsson, Strassberg, & Bannon, 1979), it is still a skill or response that should certainly be part of any helper's repertory. That is, helpers should perhaps be *willing* and able to disclose themselves, even deeply, in reasonable ways, but actually do so only if it is clear that it will contribute to the client's progress.

The Skill of Immediacy: Encouraging Direct, Mutual Talk

It has been suggested that many, if not most, clients who seek help are having trouble with interpersonal relationships. This is either a central problem or part of a wider problem situation. Some of the difficulties clients are having in their day-to-day relationships also appear in their relationships to helpers. If they are compliant outside, they are often compliant in the helping process. If they become aggressive and angry with authority figures outside, they often do the same with helpers. Therefore, the client's interpersonal style can be examined, at least in part, by examining his or her relationship with the helper. If counseling takes place in a group, then the opportunity is even greater, for the relationship of each client not only to the helper but to each of the other members can be explored. The skill or "package" of skills that enables either counselor or client to initiate this kind of exploration has been called "immediacy" (Carkhuff, 1969a, 1969b; Carkhuff & Anthony, 1979), "direct, mutual communication" (Higgins, Ivey, & Uhlemann, 1970; Ivey, 1971; Ivey & Authier, 1978), and "you-me talk" (Egan, 1976, 1977). It is a person's ability to explore with another person what is happening in his or her relationship with that other person. There are two types: relationship immediacy and here-and-now immediacy.

Relationship immediacy refers to your ability to discuss with a client where you stand in relationship to him or her. The focus is not just on the transaction at hand but on the way the relationship itself has developed. In the following example, the helper, a 44-year-old woman working in a community mental health agency, is talking to a 36-year-old man she has been seeing once a week for about two months.

> *Counselor:* We seem to have developed a good relationship here. I feel we respect each other. I have been able to make demands on you and you have

made demands on me—there has been a great deal of give and take in our relationship. You've gotten angry with me, but we've worked it out. I'm wondering what our relationship has that is missing in your relationship to your supervisor.

    Client: Well, for one thing, you listen to me, and I don't think she does. On the other hand, I listen pretty carefully to you, but I don't think I listen to her at all and she probably knows it.

The counselor is reviewing her good relationship with the client to help him develop some new perspectives on a difficult relationship outside.

    Here is another example. Lee, a 38-year-old trainer in a counselor training program, is talking to Carlos, 25, one of the trainees.

    Trainer: Carlos, I'm a bit bothered about our relationship. When you talk to me, I get the feeling that you are being very careful. When you speak to me, you talk slowly—you seem to be choosing your words, sometimes to the point that what you are saying sounds almost prepared. You have never challenged me on anything in the group. When you talk most intimately about yourself, you seem to avoid looking at me. I find myself giving you less feedback than I give others. I've even found myself putting off talking to you about all this. Perhaps some of this is my own imagining, but I want to check it out with you.

    Carlos: I've been putting it off, too. I'm embarrassed about some of the things I think I have to say.

Carlos goes on to engage Lee in a dialogue about their relationship and how it is affecting his pursuit of the training goals in the group. Again, it is not just some immediate incident that is being discussed, but rather the overall *patterning* of their relationship.

    Here-and-now immediacy refers to the helper's ability to discuss with clients what is happening between them in the here-and-now of any given transaction. The entire relationship is not being considered, but only this specific interaction. In the following example, the helper, a 43-year-old woman, is a counselor in an alcoholic rehabilitation program. Agnes, a 49-year-old woman, has stopped drinking and is now taking a look at her current interpersonal lifestyle. Agnes seems to have withdrawn quite a bit, and the interaction has bogged down.

    Counselor: I'd like to stop a moment and take a look at what's happening right now between you and me.

    Agnes: I'm not sure what you mean.

    Counselor: Well, our conversation today started out quite lively and now it seems rather subdued to me. I've noticed that the muscles in my shoulders have become tense and that I feel a little flush. I sometimes tense up that way when I feel that I might have said something wrong.

Agnes: What could that have been?

Counselor: Agnes, is it just me or do you too feel that things are a bit strained between us right now?

Agnes: Well, a little.

Counselor: We were discussing how you can control your friends with your emotions. This gets you what you want, but the price you pay can be too high. For instance, you describe some of your friends as becoming more and more "wary" of you. Now all of a sudden you've gone a bit quiet and I've been asking myself what I might have done wrong. To be truthful, I'm feeling a bit controlled, too. I'm obviously giving my perspective, and I'd like to hear yours.

The counselor does two things. First, she deals with the impasse in the session by examining what is happening in the here-and-now of the relationship. Second, she begins to explore the possibility that what the client is doing here and now is an example of her self-defeating approach to interpersonal relationships in her day-to-day life. She is tentative in what she says and invites the client to present her perspective.

A Complex Skill

People often fail to be immediate with one another in their interactions. For instance, a husband feels slighted by something his wife says. He says nothing and "swallows" his feelings. But he becomes a little bit distant from her the next couple of days, a bit more quiet. She notices this, wonders what is happening, but says nothing. Soon little things in their relationship that would ordinarily be ignored become irritating. Things become more and more tense, but still they do not engage in direct, mutual talk about what is happening. The whole thing ends in a game of "uproar" (see Berne, 1964)—that is, a huge argument over something quite small. Once they've vented their emotions, they feel both relieved because they've dealt with their emotions and guilty because they've done so in a somewhat childish way.

Immediacy is a difficult, demanding skill. One reason people such as the couple in the example just presented do not engage more readily and more opportunely in direct, mutual talk is that they have never learned to do so. Like other human-relations skills, immediacy or you-me talk has three components: awareness, technological skill or know-how, and assertiveness.

AWARENESS

If you are going to talk to a client about what is happening between the two of you—either in your overall relationship or in the here-and-now of *this* interaction—you have to *know* what is happening. You have to be able to read cues in both yourself and the other. For instance, if you do not read the clues that indicate that the client feels hurt or if you do not notice the tenseness in your own body, you cannot be immediate. Effective helpers, although not overly self-conscious about relating to clients, still *monitor* what is happening in these relationships.

KNOW-HOW

Once you notice something in your relationship to a client that is related to or affecting the helping process, you face the issue of how to communicate your perceptions. Immediacy is a communication skill formed from a combination of three other skills: empathy, self-disclosure, and confrontation.

Empathy. You must not only perceive what is happening between you and the client, but you must be able to put your perceptions and understandings into words. Very often immediacy calls for *advanced* accurate empathy because what is happening in the relationship may not be expressed openly and directly. For instance, if you begin to notice that a client is "engaging" you by using mild flattery ("I like your style. I like your directness.") and that you are letting yourself be distracted by it, then immediacy calls for checking out your perceptions.

Self-Disclosure. Being immediate involves revealing how you think and feel about what is happening in your relationship with the client. You are listening not only to the client but also to yourself. Self-disclosure means putting yourself on the line.

> *Counselor:* I find you an affable, engaging person; so I don't think I make as many demands of you as I would of someone toward whom I feel more neutral.

Immediacy is not a way of "dealing with" the client. Rather, it is an exercise in mutuality, an expression of the give and take of the helping relationship. The self-disclosure element of immediacy conveys the message "I want to be open in my relationship to you." Of course, the principles governing helper self-disclosure in general are also applicable here.

Confrontation. Immediacy often means pointing out discrepancies, challenging games, exploring distortions, and the like. In immediacy, however, helpers confront not just the discrepancies they find in their clients but also those they find in themselves. They invite their clients and themselves to discuss the nonfacilitative dimensions of the relationship.

Counselor: Here's what I think has been bogging us down. See if it makes sense to you. I feel that I have let myself gradually adopt the role of "daddy" and that you have gradually let yourself adopt the role of "little girl." I find myself talking to you the way I actually talk to my little girl at home. I think our interactions here lack the kind of "robust caring" found in adult-to-adult relationships. I let myself picture you as brittle and then become overcareful. How do you feel about all this?

Client: It's been very comfortable. But we are moving slowly. And I'm not as brittle as I make myself out to be.

Immediacy requires mutuality. It is important to invite clients to explore the relationship. However, if the clients do not have the kinds of communication skills required for immediacy, they will find the invitation hard to accept. This is another reason for making training a part of the helping process. If you expect clients to involve themselves, make sure they have the working knowledge and skills they need to do so.

ASSERTIVENESS

Immediacy is not an easy skill for many people, even when they have the kinds of awareness and know-how required by it. Primary-level accurate empathy can be easy because, in a sense, it is giving a gift to the other. The other challenging skills discussed here can be relatively easy because the focus remains on the client. Immediacy is difficult because it is by its nature very self-involving. Helpers who are struggling with intimacy in their own lives can expect to have trouble with this skill.

In the following example, a 17-year-old high school student is talking to the school counselor. He's bright but failing several subjects. This is the third interview.

Client: I don't know why I keep coming here. I keep talking about myself, but nothing happens. I still hate school, and I can't wait to get out.

Counselor: You do talk about yourself, but I'm not sure that I'm helping talk about what's really important to you. You talk about classes you don't like, teachers you don't like, rules you don't like. But you don't talk a lot about yourself. My bet is that you resent being here because you were sent. But more important, my hunch is that you still don't trust me very much. At least not enough to talk about yourself very deeply.

Client: I don't know if it's you. "Shrinks" turn me off.

Counselor: Well, if I'm still a "shrink" to you, then something's going wrong between you and me. If I'm just another "shrink" to you, then it's pretty easy to write me off. If I'm being written off, I'd like to know why. It may be that I just don't like not being liked. Then it's my problem.

Client: Okay. It's not you. (Pause) But why *should* I trust you? The adults in my life haven't been exactly charmers. Why don't you analyze my parents. That'd be a real challenge for any shrink. (He gets up and walks over and looks out the window.)

They go on to explore the client's messy home life. An unskilled helper might have continued to encourage the kind of unproductive self-exploration in which the client was engaged, and eventually such a helper might have terminated the session on the presumption that the client was not "motivated" to work. This counselor, however, is attentive to the cues that the relationship itself is not going right. He uses immediacy to help break through the impasse.

Situations Calling for Direct, Mutual Communication

The skill of immediacy can be most useful in the following situations:

- When a session is *directionless* and it seems no progress is being made: "I feel we're bogged down right now. Perhaps we could stop a moment and see what we're doing right and what's going wrong."
- When there is *tension* between helper and client: "We seem to be getting on each other's nerves. It might be helpful to stop a moment and clear the air."
- When *trust* seems to be an issue: "I see your hesitancy here and I'm not sure whether it's related to me or not. It might still be hard for you to trust me."
- When there is *social distance* between helper and client in terms of social class or widely differing interpersonal styles: "There are some hints that the fact that I'm black and you're white is making both of us a bit hesitant."
- When *dependency* seems to be interfering with the helping process: "You don't seem willing to explore an issue until I give you 'permission' to do so. And I seem to have let myself slip into the role of 'permission giver.' "
- When *counterdependency* seems to be blocking the helping relationship: "It seems that we're letting this session turn into a struggle between you and me. And if I'm not mistaken, both of us seem to be bent on winning."
- When *attraction* is sidetracking either helper or client: "I think we've liked each other from the start. Now I'm wondering whether that might be getting in the way of the work we're doing here."

Immediacy is the skill needed by the helper to handle the issues that deal with the relationship between helper and client, including the "transference" and "countertransference" issues mentioned earlier. Moreover, if clients are to engage in direct, mutual talk with their helpers, they, too, need this skill. Training in immediacy can be part of an overall training-as-treatment program.

Immediacy, of course, is not a goal in itself. The goal of the helping process is not to establish and enjoy relationships but to explore and work through problem situations. Immediacy, if allowed to become a goal in itself, distracts both helper and client from the goal of the helping process. Immediacy at its best can do two things. First, it can provide new perspectives on the counseling relationship and help client and counselor work more effectively together. Second, what clients learn about themselves in their interactions with helpers can provide new perspectives on how they relate to people outside.

Box 7–1 summarizes the challenging process.

BOX 7–1:   A SUMMARY OF THE PROCESS OF CHALLENGING

There are several reasons for challenging:

1. Help clients participate more fully in the helping process
2. Help them clarify problem situations more fully
3. Help them develop the kinds of new perspectives needed to set reasonable goals

The following skills are needed for effective challenging:

1. *Summarizing.* This skill enables you to help clients view their problem situations in a more focused way; it also places them under pressure to clarify their problems more fully and/or to begin to set goals.
2. *Information giving.* This skill enables you to help clients acquire the kind of information that enables them to see their problem situations in a new light and see how they might act to handle them.
3. *Advanced empathy.* This skill involves your sharing "hunches" with clients about their experiences, behaviors, and feelings. These hunches are useful if they have a fair degree of accuracy and if they actually help clients see problem situations more clearly.
4. *Confrontation.* This skill enables you to challenge the discrepancies, distortions, smoke screens, and games clients use, knowingly or unknowingly, to keep themselves and others from seeing their problems clearly and to keep themselves from problem-managing action.
5. *Helper self-sharing.* This skill enables you to share your own experience with the client both as a way of modeling nondefensive self-disclosure and of helping clients see their own problem situations more clearly.

(Box 7–1 continues)

BOX 7–1 *(continued)*

6. *Immediacy.* Through this skill you engage in direct, mutual talk about what is happening between you and the client in the counseling relationship so clients can overcome blocks to more effective involvement and see more clearly both the productive and unproductive ways they tend to relate to others.

As a helper, you must first take a look at your own *remote* preparation for challenging others. Here are some guidelines for challenging clients in a facilitative way:

1. *Effective living.* Ask yourself how willing you are to grapple with your own problems in living.
2. *Helper self-challenge.* Examine your ability to challenge yourself and your openness to being challenged.
3. *Capacity for intimacy.* Examine your willingness to enter deeply into the lives of others.

You must also look at your *immediate* preparation for challenging— that is, how prepared you are to challenge *this* client.

1. *The purpose of challenge.* Keep in mind that you are challenging this client in order to help him or her develop new perspectives and set goals.
2. *Earning the right.* Make sure you have earned the right to challenge the client by establishing rapport, being genuine, showing respect, and providing understanding.

Finally, be careful of the *way* in which you challenge the client.

1. *Self-responsibility.* Give clients an opportunity to challenge themselves.
2. *With care.* Ask yourself whether you are challenging the client right now because you care or because you are annoyed.
3. *Tentatively.* Do not make pronouncements or accuse clients; deliver your challenge in such a way as to give them room to move.
4. *Strengths.* Challenge the strengths of clients rather than their weaknesses; help them see what positive behaviors can take the place of negative ones.
5. *Gradually.* Do not demand everything all at once. Challenge clients first in areas where the probability for success is relatively high; help clients build on their successes.

Gaining New Perspectives through Action

I have already suggested that for some clients an action program is one of the best ways of gaining the kinds of new perspectives needed to handle a problem situation. Such clients are acting their way into new ways of thinking.

> *Woody, a college sophomore, came to the student counseling service with a variety of interpersonal and somatic complaints. He felt attracted to a number of women on campus but did very little to become involved with them. After exploring this issue briefly, he said to the counselor, "Hell, I just have to go out and do it." Two months later he returned and said that he had run into disaster. He had gone out with a few women, but none of them really interested him. Then he did meet someone he liked quite a bit. They went out a couple of times, but the third time he called, she said that she didn't want to see him any more. When asked why, she muttered something vague about his being too preoccupied with himself and ended the conversation. He felt devastated and so returned to the counseling center. He and the counselor took another look at his social life. This time, however, he had some experiences to probe. He wanted to find out what "too preoccupied with himself" meant. They could stop talking hypothetically and talk about what actually happened or did not happen.*

This student put into practice Weick's (1979) dictum that chaotic action is preferable to orderly inaction. Some of his experiences were painful, but now there was a chance of examining his interpersonal style much more concretely.

Training Clients in Challenging Skills

The communication skills we have seen so far—especially attending; listening; responding with accurate empathy; exploring a problem situation concretely; and challenging through advanced accurate empathy, self-sharing, confrontation, and immediacy—are also the basic skills needed in effective interpersonal relationships. They are, therefore, often precisely the skills clients lack. Just as you are now developing a working knowledge of and being trained in these skills, so also can you instruct and train clients in them. If you suspect that clients will need to acquire or improve these skills in order to achieve the goals they are now ready to set, then some kind of training in them seems mandatory. If you ask clients to pursue goals for which they have neither the skills nor the resources, the outcome is predictable.

How Long Does It Take to Get to Goal Setting?

No time frame can be established for Stages I and II because problem situations differ radically from one another even in the same person. A person may quickly analyze a problem situation related to his or her job and yet need to spend much more time clarifying problem situations related to interpersonal relationships. Problem situations need to be explored adequately enough to set meaningful goals. Poorly clarified problem situations lead to goals that, even if achieved, do little to help the client. On the other hand, ineffective helpers allow or even encourage clients to spend too much time clarifying problems.

Setting Problem-Managing Goals

The helping process has until now focused on the work of helping the client get involved with and own the process and on the work of problem definition and clarification. But once a problem is clearly defined, it is time to move on. The problem-solving process is organic and cumulative. It is successful if it leads to *problem-handling action.* Listening for the sake of listening, exploring for the sake of exploring, and challenging for the sake of challenging are all useless. The work to this point is successful if it leads to the kind of problem clarification that contributes to the establishment of realistic, problem-handling goals. The importance of helping clients set clear, workable goals cannot be overstressed (Bucker, 1978; Carkhuff & Anthony, 1979; Erez, 1977; Flowers, 1978; Hill, 1975; Latham & Rinne, 1974; Smith, 1976).

Goals, if they are to be translated into problem-managing action, need to be clear and specific. In the following example, George has concluded that drinking is doing him no good. In the beginning of counseling, he saw himself as a "social drinker" and was not ready to see himself as a "problem drinker." The helper challenges him to explore the effects of drinking on his life. He is now ready to decide what he wants to do about drinking.

> George, with the help of Evelyn's consultation, realized that he could set various goals with respect to drinking. For instance, he could stop drinking completely. Or he could decide to stop drinking for a certain period of time, let us say six months. Or he could cut down on his drinking, allowing himself only a certain amount of alcohol in any given day. Or he could choose to restrict his drinking to certain times of the day or week. The goal he chooses is the elimination of drink from his life for a period of at least six months. A six-month "dry" period does not sound as drastic to him as stopping completely. He wants to see what his life will be like without

> *alcohol. Evelyn and he both think that his goal fulfills the requirements for being effective. At this stage George feels quite satisfied with his relationship to Evelyn. He feels that she is both understanding and, when necessary, "tough." She does not make decisions for him, but she does challenge him to make his own. He is feeling more and more responsible for the helping process and he appreciates Evelyn as an important and skillful human resource.*

Let us take a closer look at goals and the skills counselors need to help clients engage in goal setting in such a way as to raise the probability of problem-managing action.

Shaping: Helping Clients Set Concrete and Specific Goals

The concept of shaping was considered briefly in Chapter 1. It is used here in its wider sense—that is, a step-by-step process leading to some rewarding accomplishment. Some clients, once they develop new perspectives, know exactly what they want to do about a problem situation. For others this is not as clear. There are at least three different steps toward what may be termed a "working" goal. Because clients start in different places, not all need all three steps.

DECLARATION OF INTENT

Some clients, once they see a problem clearly, also see the need to do something about it. In the following example, the client, Jon, has been discussing his relationship to his wife and children. The counselor has been helping him see how they view some of his behavior negatively. Jon is open to be challenged and is a fast learner.

> *"Boy, this session has been an eye-opener for me. I've really been blind. My wife and children don't see my investment—rather, my overinvestment—in work as being for them. I really have to switch my priorities."*

This statement certainly seems to be well intentioned. However, it is not yet a goal. It is rather *a statement of intent*, an indication on the part of the client that he wants to do something about a problem that has been clearly defined.

The following example deals with a 48-year-old woman, Laureen, who has discovered that she has breast cancer and will need a mastectomy. She has had a couple of sessions with a self-help group composed of women who have had to face the same problem.

> *"As I listen to all of you 'tell your stories,' I've begun to see how passive I've become since I found out the diagnosis. I feel that I'm surrendering myself*

> *to doctors and to the whole medical establishment. No wonder I feel so depressed. I'm ordinarily an active woman. I usually take charge of my life. Well, I want to take charge of it again."*

Note again, she does not say *what* she is going to do to handle her passivity, but she is determined to do something. This is a declaration of intent.

AN AIM

An aim is more than a declaration of intent. It is a declaration of intent that identifies the area in which the client wants to work and makes some general statement about it. In the following example, we return to Jon, who has been talking about his being overinvested in work at the expense of family life.

> *"I don't think that I've got so taken up with work deliberately. That is, I don't think I'm running away from family life. But family life is deteriorating because I'm just not around enough. I want to spend more time with my wife and kids."*

This is more than a declaration of intent because it includes in some general way what Jon wants to do—"spend more time with my wife and kids." But it still does not say *precisely* what he wants to do. The problem with aims is that their very vagueness makes it too easy to put them off. All of us are familiar with the New Year's Eve resolutions phenomenon. Lots of people indicate in vague ways how they are going to get better the coming year. "I'm really going to get into shape this year." We also know that few people actually carry out such resolutions. Vague aims are not really goals. They are often merely wishes of one kind or another. However, it is useful to help clients move from mere statements of intent to aims. Aims are closer to goals. This is part of the shaping process.

If a problem is defined fairly clearly, then aims begin to emerge. For instance, Laureen, the woman about to undergo a mastectomy, realizes that she has become passive in various ways. "I used to be careful about my personal appearance, but I notice that I've been letting myself go." One aim, then, might be to reinvest herself in her personal appearance. "I'm going to force myself to take care of how I look." This is not a statement of *precisely what* she wants to do or of *how* she wants to do it, but it is more than a general statement of intent.

GOALS

Goals are clear statements of what a person wants to do concretely and specifically to handle a problem situation or some part of it. For instance, Jon says, "I'm consistently going to spend three out of four weekends a month at home. During the week I'll let myself work no more than two evenings." Notice how much more specific this is than "I'm going to spend more time with my family." Your job is to help the client engage in this shaping process. Notice that this is not the same as setting goals *for* the client.

Helping Clients Set Workable Goals

The shaping process is complete if you help clients set goals with the following characteristics: stated as accomplishments, clear and specific, measurable or verifiable, realistic, adequate, owned by the client, in keeping with the client's values, and set in a reasonable time frame. Let's consider each of these separately.

ACCOMPLISHMENTS

Workable goals are accomplishments that help manage a problem situation. They are not the processes that lead up to these accomplishments. For instance, if a client says, "My goal is to get some training in interpersonal communication skills," then she is stating her goal as a process rather than an accomplishment. However, her goal is achieved only when these skills are *acquired, practiced, and actually used* in interpersonal situations. The processes that lead up to accomplishments are called programs, and these will be considered in the next chapter. The goal of a person who is drinking too much is not to join Alcoholics Anonymous. This is a program. This person has reached his or her goal when the drinking has *stopped*. You can help clients develop this "past participle" (drinking *stopped*, skills *acquired, practiced, and used*, the number of marital fights *decreased*, anger *controlled*) approach to goal setting. Stating goals in terms of accomplishments (or at least developing accomplishment-oriented ways of thinking about goals) is not just a question of language; it is a question of the accomplishments toward which behavior is directed rather than the behavior itself. For instance, it makes little sense if a person works hard (behavior) if he or she doesn't work smart enough to accomplish something that is valued (see Gilbert, 1978).

CLEAR AND SPECIFIC

In some way, the client should be able to visualize the accomplishment. "I want to get into physical shape" is not as clear as "Within six months I will be running a mile under nine minutes at least four times a week." The former is an aim; the latter is a goal. The client can actually see himself or herself doing something. Notice that this goal is also stated as an accomplishment—that is, it is stated in terms of an exercise pattern that is *in place* and consistently pursued.

As we have seen, some goals are never accomplished because they are never stated explicitly enough.

Abstract: "I want to change the world for the better."

Concrete: "I want to work toward getting more frequent rubbish collection service in the 50th ward as a way of controlling rodents. This would mean that during the rodent-control program, rubbish would be collected twice a week."

Note that this is expressed as an accomplishment. It is achieved when the rubbish collection program is in place.

Abstract: "We want to relate to each other better."

Concrete: "We try to solve our problems about family finances by fighting and arguing. We'd like to reduce the number of fights we have and increase the number of times we make decisions about money by talking them out."

To set concrete goals, clients have to be helped to move from declarations of intent, to aims, and finally to behavioral goals.

MEASURABLE OR VERIFIABLE

Clients must be able to tell whether they have achieved their goals or not. Therefore, the criteria for the accomplishment of goals must be clear to them. "I want to have a better relationship with my wife" is an aim, not a goal, because it cannot be verified. Clients have to be helped to ask themselves "How will I know that I have achieved my goals?"

Clients can't know whether they are making progress if they do not know where they started. If a couple wants to reduce the number of fights they have per week, then they need to know how often they fight in the first place. Collection of what behaviorists call base-line data is part of the process of problem clarification.

Husband: To our horror, we discovered that we were having about two or three good fights per *day*. I mean, our marriage was really deteriorating. Now we might have about three rather nasty arguments per week. The picture has changed quite a bit. Both of us are much less tense than we used to be.

The word *verifiable* is used here because it is not always necessary to count things in order to determine whether a goal has been reached, though sometimes this is helpful. For instance, a couple might say something like: "Our relationship is better, not because we've found ways of spending more time together, but the quality of our time together has improved. By that we mean that we listen better; we talk about more personal concerns; we are more relaxed; and we feel better about what we're doing the rest of the day."

REALISTIC

A goal is realistic if the resources necessary for its accomplishment are available to the client, the external circumstances do not prevent its accomplishment, the goal is under the client's control, and the cost is not too high. Let's take a brief look at each of these.

Resources. It does little good to help clients develop clear and verifiable goals if the resources are not available for their accomplishment.

Unrealistic: John decides to go to graduate school but has neither the financial nor academic resources needed to do so.

Realistic: John decides to work and to take one graduate course at night in rehabilitation counseling to see whether he is really interested in this field and to determine whether he is capable of the work.

Goals are unrealistic if they are set too high.

Unrealistic: "I've never had a course in German, but this summer I want to learn to speak it fluently."

Realistic: "In the past I have been fairly good at picking up languages. I want to learn as much German as possible this summer—at least enough to be somewhat comfortable on my three-week trip to Germany this fall."

Clients sabotage their own efforts if they choose goals beyond their reach. Sometimes it is impossible to determine beforehand whether the personal or environmental resources needed are available. If this is the case, it might be best to start with goals for which the resources are certainly available and then move on to those that are more questionable in this regard.

Environmental Obstacles. A goal is not really a goal if there are environmental obstacles that prevent its accomplishment—that is, obstacles that cannot be overcome by the use of available resources.

Jessie feels like a second-class citizen at work. He feels that his supervisor gives him most of the dirty work and that generally there is an undercurrent of prejudice against Hispanics in the plant. He wants to quit and get another job. However, the country is deep into a recession and there are practically no jobs available in the area where he works. For the time being his goal is not workable. He needs another interim goal that relates to coping with his present situation.

Sometimes an interim goal can be to find a way around an environmental obstacle. For instance, it may be that there are openings in other plants but not in Jessie's specialty. So Jessie goes to night school and becomes qualified in a trade similar to his own. Once qualified, he gets a job in a different plant.

Under the Client's Control. Sometimes clients defeat their own purposes by setting goals that are not under their control. For instance, it is common for people to believe that their problems would be solved if only other people would not act the way they do. In most cases, however, we do not have any direct control over the ways others act.

> *Cybelene wanted a better relationship with her parents. She said that the relationship would be better if only they would make fewer demands on her now that she was married and had her own career and home to attend to. It was under her control to let her parents know some of her needs, but there was relatively little she could do to make her parents respect these goals. For instance, she wanted her parents to come to her new home for either Thanksgiving or Christmas. Her parents, however, insisted that she and her husband come to their house because both of these celebrations were "traditional" and therefore best spent "back home." She refused to go home for both and her parents kept telling her how much they were hurt.*

Clients, however, usually have much more freedom in changing their own behavior. Consider the following example.

> *Tony, a 16-year-old boy, felt that he was the victim of his parents' inability to relate to each other. Each tried to make him a pawn in the struggle, and at times he felt like a Ping-Pong ball. A counselor helped him see that he could do little to control his parents' behavior but that he might be able to do quite a bit to control his own behavior and his reactions to his parents' attempts to use him. For instance, when his parents started to fight, he would simply leave instead of trying to "help." If either tried to enlist him as an ally, he would say that he had no way of knowing who was right. He worked at creating a good social life outside his home. This helped him weather the tension he experienced there.*

Clients should know that statements that either say directly or imply "My goal is to have him or her. . ." are statements that have a high probability of impeding the helping process.

Not Too Costly. Some goals can be accomplished, but the cost is too high or the payoff is too low. It may sound overly technological to ask whether any given goal is "cost effective," but the principle remains important. Skilled counselors help clients squire rather than squander resources.

> *Enid discovered that she had a terminal illness. In talking with several doctors, she found out that she would be able to prolong her life a bit more*

> *through a combination of surgery, radiation treatment, and chemotherapy.*
> *However, no one suggested that these would lead to any kind of cure. She*
> *also found out what each of these three forms of treatment and each*
> *combination would cost, not so much in terms of money, but in terms of*
> *added anxiety and pain. She ultimately decided against all three because*
> *none of them and no combination promised much in terms of the quality*
> *of the life that was being prolonged.*

It goes without saying that another patient might have made a different decision. The words *cost* and *payoff* are relative. Some clients might value an extra month of life no matter what the cost.

ADEQUATE

Goals are unrealistic if they are, for one reason or another, set too high. Goals are inadequate if they are set too low. To be adequate, the accomplishment of a goal must contribute in some *substantial* way to managing the problem situation or some part of it. If a client drinks two fifths of gin a week and one can of beer, her drinking problem will not be effectively handled if she eliminates the can of beer. If the quality of the time spent by a man at home is not good, then merely increasing the time spent at home will do little to help him develop a better relationship with his family. If the problem is not clearly defined, it can be impossible to determine whether any given goal is adequate.

> *Aaron was extremely anxious and depressed when he learned that he*
> *would have to undergo major surgery for the removal of a brain tumor.*
> *There was no way of telling whether it was malignant or benign until the*
> *surgery had been performed. A minister talked to him in rather general*
> *terms about "the love of God" and suggested that he pray more. Aaron*
> *became more and more agitated and finally took his own life.*

In crisis situations such as this, it can be terribly difficult to help a client identify some goal that might contribute substantially to handling the emotions felt. However, suggesting stylized goals that have no meaning for the client might only make things worse.

OWNED BY THE CLIENT

It is essential that the goals chosen be the client's rather than the helper's or someone else's goals. Various kinds of probes can be used to help clients discover what *they* want to do in order to manage some dimension of a problem situation more effectively. For instance, Carl Rogers, in a film of a counseling session, is asked by a woman what she should do about her relationship to her daughter. He says to her: "I think you've been telling me all along what you want to do." She knew *what* she wanted to do, but she was asking for his approval. If he had given it, the goal would in some way have become his instead of hers. At another time he asks, "What is it that you wish that I would tell you to do?" This puts the responsibility for goal setting where it belongs: on the client's shoulders.

> Cynthia was dealing with a lawyer because of an impending divorce. They had talked about what was to be done with the children, but no decision had been reached. One day she came in and said that she had decided on mutual custody—that is, both she and her husband would have legal custody. She wanted to work out such details as which residence would be their principal one, where they would live when, and so forth. The lawyer asked her how she had reached a decision. She said that she had been talking to her husband's parents—she felt she was still on very good terms with them—and that they had suggested this arrangement. The lawyer challenged Cynthia to take a closer look at her decision. He felt that he did not want to help her carry out a decision that was not her own.

Clients tend to work harder for their goals. Choosing goals that are not their own also enables them to blame others if they fail to reach these goals or if they find out that reaching them does little to help them manage a problem situation.

CLIENT'S VALUES

Although helping is, as we have seen, a process of social influence, it remains ethical only if it respects the client's values. Helpers may challenge clients to reexamine their values, but they should in no way encourage clients to actions that are not in keeping with their values. For instance, the Garzas' son is in a coma in the hospital after an automobile accident. He needs a life-support system to remain alive. They are experiencing a great deal of uncertainty, pain, and anxiety. They have been told there is very little chance that their son will ever come out of the coma and that if he does, it is most likely he will be severely handicapped. A counselor should not urge that they terminate his life-support system if this is counter to their values. However, a counselor might well help them explore and clarify the values involved. For instance, the counselor might suggest that they talk it over with their minister. In doing so, they find out that the termination of the life-support system in this case would not be against the tenets of their religion. Now they are free to explore other values that relate to their decision.

If clients are to make reasonable decisions in terms of realism, adequacy, and values, they may need help exploring the *consequences* of different goals.

REASONABLE TIME FRAME

Reasonable time frames for the accomplishment of goals need to be determined. Goals that are to be accomplished "sometime or other" never seem to be achieved. If Jon says, "I'm going to spend three out of every four weekends and five out of every seven evenings at home with my family and do so consistently *whenever business conditions stabilize again*," then he violates this condition because the time frame is not clear. If his business is bad and needs a great deal of attention, then the deteriorating relationship with his family will have to be managed in some way other than spending more time at home. For instance, another aim might be to increase the quality of the time he does spend there. This, however, is merely an aim and would have to be made much more concrete and specific in order to be a goal.

This, then, is what is meant by workable goals. A goal, to be workable, must meet all these requirements. If one is missing, it may prove to be the fatal flaw in a client's movement toward action.

The Centrality of Goal Setting

Goal setting is the central point of the helping process. On the one hand, everything done up to this point has been preparatory. The relationship has been established to help the client explore and clarify the problem situation. The client has been challenged in order to develop new perspectives. New perspectives clarify the problem to the point where it begins to become clear that something needs to be done to manage it. New perspectives also help clients see, at least in some general way, what needs to be done. Goal setting completes this process. On the other hand, everything that takes place from this point on, program development and implementation, is done to see that these goals are actually accomplished.

Sometimes clients want to skip the goal-setting part of the process. Once they see some problem fairly clearly, they want to do something about it immediately.

> *Harry was a sophomore in college who was admitted to one of the state mental hospitals because of an "acute schizophrenic episode" at the university. He was a disc jockey for the university radio. He came to the notice of college officials one day when he put on a rather bizarre performance that included a lengthy presentation of some grandiose religious ideas. In the hospital, it was soon discovered that this pleasant, likable young man was actually a loner. Everyone who knew him at the university thought he had a lot of friends, but in fact he did not. The campus was large and this went unnoticed. Harry was soon released from the hospital but returned weekly for therapy. The helper discussed with him his lack of contact with women. Once it became clear to him that his meetings with women were perfunctory and almost always took place in groups—he had actually thought he had a rather full social life with women—Harry rushed headlong into a program of dating. This ended in*

disaster because he lacked some basic social and communication skills. With the help of the therapist, he returned to the problem clarification and new perspectives part of the helping process and then established some goals that proved to be more realistic. One of them was to examine his interpersonal style and acquire some communication skills in a safe setting. He accomplished this goal by joining an interpersonal skills group offered by the university communication department.

Harry's leaping from problem clarification to action without taking time to set some reasonable goals is an example of the nonlinear nature of helping. His lack of success in dating, even though it involved a fair amount of pain, actually helped him see his problem with women more clearly. He then had to backtrack, set some realistic goals, and move more slowly.

The Difference between Goals and Programs

The example of Harry points out the difference between a goal and a program. A goal is a client's way of saying "This is *what* I want to do in order to manage the problem situation more effectively." The client still might not know exactly *how* he or she is going to do it, but at least the *what* is clear. A program spells out *how* a goal is to be accomplished. For instance, one of the things Jon, the man who wants to improve the quality of his family life, must do in order to accomplish the goal of spending more time at home is train someone to take care of evening and weekend emergencies at work. This, then, is one of the steps of an overall program that will lead to the accomplishment of his goal.

An Objection to Setting Goals

Clients can be helped to move from vague statements of intent to setting clear and specific goals. However, some people see the helping process at this point as becoming too "technological." Some suggest that the client's goals be allowed to "emerge" in some kind of natural way. There are two ways emergence could be productive—that is, contribute to the management of a problem situation or some part of it. First, it could mean that once clients are helped, through a combination of probing, empathy, and challenge, to clarify a problem, they begin to see more clearly what they want to do to manage the problem. Second, it could mean that some clients, like Harry, must first act in some way before they find out just what they want to do. These kinds of emergence pose no problem. However, if emergence means that clients should wait around until "something comes up" or if it means that clients should try a lot of different programs in the hope that one of them will work, then emergence can be self-defeating, however common it might be.

Haphazard problem solving is not to be equated with spontaneous living.

You will find clients have been trying these two kinds of emergence, and part of the problem is that such emergence is not working for them. They are spinning their wheels. Setting concrete and specific goals may not be part of a client's ordinary style, but this does not make it either unnatural or overly technological. In my experience, helping clients set clear and realistic goals has been one of the most useful parts of the helping process. The problem with leaving goal setting to chance is that people skip goal setting entirely and keep trying one program after another. Failure to set goals can lead to a kind of "tyranny of programs." The client who says "I've tried everything and nothing works" may well be a victim of such tyranny.

Clients can be trained to shape their own goals directly. That is, training clients to set goals that have the previously outlined characteristics can be a part of a training-as-treatment approach to helping. A client who has goal-setting skills has more freedom—that is, he or she can decide whether to set specific goals or to let them emerge, in some positive sense of this term. The "technology" presented here, both helping clients set goals and training them in goal-setting skills, can be as human as the person using it.

Box 7–2 summarizes what you need to know and do about goal setting. Setting goals ends the work of Stage II and leads into Stage III, immediate preparation for and implementation of action. Box 7–3 summarizes the work of Stage II.

BOX 7–2:   A SUMMARY OF THE PRINCIPLES INVOLVED IN GOAL SETTING

DEFINITION

A goal is a behavioral accomplishment that contributes to managing a problem situation or some part of it.

SHAPING

Shaping is used to help clients move toward clear and specific goals. Many clients, even after they are helped to clarify a problem situation, still don't know what they can do to manage it. There are three stages here.

- *Declaration of intent.* This is an indication on the part of the client that he or she wants to *do* something to handle the problem. This can be taken as a positive indication of a client's willingness to commit resources.
- *Aims.* Help the client to move from a declaration of intent to some general statement of what he or she would like to do to handle the problem.

(Box 7–2 continues)

BOX 7–2 *(continued)*

• *Goals.* Help the client refine his or her aims until they have the following characteristics:

1. They are clear and specific.
2. They are measurable or verifiable.
3. They are realistic in terms of client resources, environmental conditions, ability to control, and cost.
4. They are adequate—that is, contribute in some substantial way to managing the problem.
5. They are in keeping with the client's values.
6. They are set in a reasonable time frame.

In all of this, make sure that the goals chosen are the client's and not yours.

BOX 7–3:   A SUMMARY OF THE WORK OF STAGE II

Keep in mind the primary objective of Stage II: helping clients establish workable goals—that is, ways of managing the problem situation or some part of it.

If clients have blind spots that prevent them from seeing a problem situation clearly enough to set reasonable goals, then challenge them to develop the kinds of new perspectives they need to do so.

Use whatever mix of challenging skills seems appropriate to *this* client in *this* situation—summarizing, helping the client get new information, sharing hunches about the client and his or her behavior (advanced accurate empathy), sharing your own experience, confronting, and being immediate.

Challenge clients to "own" problems—that is, to define them in terms of what *they* do or don't do instead of what others do or don't do.

Use the skill of immediacy to help clients "own" the helping process—that is, participate more fully in it.

Help clients shape workable goals—help them move from mere statements of intent to more concrete aims to specific problem-managing goals.

Make sure they see goals as statements of precisely *what* they are going to do to manage a problem situation or part of it more effectively.

Help clients set goals that are stated as accomplishments, clear and specific, measurable or verifiable, realistic, adequate, owned by them, in keeping with their values, and set in a realistic time frame.

Chapter

8

Stage III:
Action

Part One:
The Development
and Sequencing of Programs

This chapter deals with the following topics:

Examples of a client who needs and of a client who does not need help in
  Stage III
The five tasks of Stage III
Task 1: Helping clients identify program possibilities
Helping clients engage in divergent thinking
The requirements for creativity
Brainstorming as a program-development skill
Using prompts to help clients identify program possibilities
Task 2: Helping clients choose programs
The balance-sheet method
Program sampling
The criteria for choosing a program
Four strategies for choosing programs
Task 3: Helping clients order program steps
Shaping: Developing subgoals and subprograms
Hints for effective sequencing of program steps
Helping clients develop contingency plans
Problems associated with program development

Some clients, once they have a clear idea of *what* they want to do to manage some problem situation, mobilize their own and whatever environmental resources are necessary to achieve their goals. Other clients, however, even though they have a fairly good understanding of the problem situation and know what they want to do to handle it (goals), still do not have a clear idea of *how* to achieve these goals. They still need your help. Consider the following example.

Jeff had been in the army for about ten months. He found himself both overworked and, perhaps not paradoxically, bored. He had a couple of sessions with one of the educational counselors on the base. During these sessions, he began to see clearly that not having a high school diploma was working against him. Because he had not finished high school, he was in a number of ways considered a second-class citizen in the army. Someone mentioned that he could finish high school while in the army. He then realized that this had been pointed out to him during the orientation talks, but he hadn't paid any attention to it. He had joined the army because he wasn't interested in school and couldn't find a job. He decided that he would get a high school diploma as soon as possible. He got the authorization he needed from his company commander to go to school. He found out what courses he needed and enrolled in time for the next school session. It didn't take him long to finish school. Once he received his high school degree, he felt better about himself and found that opportunities for more interesting jobs opened up for him in the army. Achieving his goal of getting a high school degree helped him manage the problem situation.

Jeff was one of those fortunate ones who quickly found out what he needed to do to manage a problem situation and then went out and did it.

Jeff's experience is quite different from that of the client in the following example. She needs much more help than he did.

As long as she could remember, Grace had been a fearful person. She was afraid of being rejected and afraid of failure. As a result, she had a rather impoverished social life and had had a series of jobs that were safe but boring. She became so depressed that she made a halfhearted attempt at suicide, probably more a cry of anguish and perhaps a cry for help than a serious attempt to get rid of her problems by getting rid of herself.

During her stay in the hospital, she had a few therapy sessions with one of the psychiatric staff. The staff member was supportive and helped her handle both the guilt she felt because of the suicide attempt and the depression that had led to the attempt. Just talking to someone about things she usually kept to herself seemed to help. She began to see her depression as a case of "learned helplessness." She saw clearly how she had let her choices be dictated by her fears. She also began to realize that she was a person who had a number of unused or underused resources. For instance, she was intelligent and, though not good looking, was still attractive in other ways. She had a fairly good sense of humor, though she seldom gave herself the opportunity to use it. She was also sensitive to others and basically caring.

After she was discharged from the hospital, she returned for a few out-patient sessions. She got to the point where she wanted to do something about her general fearfulness and her passivity, especially the passivity in her social life. The counselor taught her relaxation and thought-control techniques that helped her reduce her anxiety. Once she felt less anxious, she was in a better position to do something about establishing some relationships. With the help of the counselor, she set a goal of acquiring a couple of friends and of becoming a member of some social group. However, she was at a loss as to how to go about this because she thought that friendship and a fuller social life were supposed to happen "naturally." She soon came to realize that many people had to work at acquiring a more satisfying social life, that for some people there was nothing automatic about it at all.

The counselor helped her identify different kinds of social groups she might join. She was then helped to see which of these would best meet her needs without placing too much stress on her. She finally chose to join an arts and crafts group at a local YMCA. This gave her an opportunity to begin developing some of her talents and to meet people without having to face demands for intimate social contact. It also gave her an opportunity to take a look at other more socially oriented programs sponsored by the Y. She began using the relaxation techniques regularly and finally joined the Y program. She met a couple of people she liked and who seemed to like her in the arts and crafts program. She began having coffee with them once in a while and then an occasional dinner.

She still needed support and encouragement from the counselor but was gradually becoming less anxious and feeling less isolated. Once in a while Grace would let her anxiety get the better of her. She would skip a meeting and then lie to the counselor about having attended. However, as she began to let herself trust the counselor more, she revealed this more or less self-

defeating game. The counselor helped her develop coping strategies for those times when anxiety seemed to be higher.

Grace's problems were more severe than Jeff's and she did not have as many immediate resources. Therefore, she needed both more time and more attention to develop goals and the programs to achieve these goals.

A careful examination of Grace's case shows that Stage III includes the following tasks:

1. *Identifying program possibilities.* Once goals are clear, it is necessary to identify the different ways each one might be accomplished. For instance, Grace's aim was to establish some kind of nonthreatening social life. This was translated into the goal of joining some kind of social group in which she could both develop some of her interests and make contact with others. The counselor helped her take a census of the different possibilities.

2. *Choosing programs.* Once a number of program possibilities are identified, they must be evaluated in terms of their realism. That is, they must fit the client's resources and the restrictions of the client's environment. In Grace's case, this meant choosing a program that fit her interests, that provided some kind of social contact, and that was not too threatening.

3. *Sequencing programs.* Choosing a program also implies clarifying precisely both what steps are necessary and the order in which these steps are to be accomplished. For instance, it was important for Grace to get some practice at relaxation skills before joining the Y program.

4. *Implementing programs.* Once any given technique is chosen and the steps are clear, then the program is to be implemented. It often happens that a number of obstacles arise and that the client needs guidance, support, and encouragement to stick to the program. As we have seen, Grace still felt a bit "rocky" as she joined the YMCA program. However, the counselor helped her find ways to reduce her anxiety and provided her with support and encouragement.

5. *Evaluating programs.* As programs are being implemented, clients can be helped to monitor the quality of their participation in them with a view to either increasing the quality of participation or of making some changes in the program itself. In Grace's case the program seemed all right, but at times she would fail to use the strategies she had learned to cope with her anxiety. This was interfering with her participation. Once she shared this problem with the counselor, they worked together at finding ways to prevent anxiety rather than merely coping with it once it had already arisen.

These, then, are the tasks of Stage III. The first three tasks will be considered in this chapter; the last two will be considered in the next.

Helping Clients Identify Program Possibilities

Sometimes goals are not achieved because clients rush off and try the first program that comes to mind.

> *Elmer injured his back and underwent a couple of operations. After the second operation, he felt a little better but then his back began troubling him again. The doctor told him that further operations would not help; so Elmer was faced with the problem of handling chronic pain. It soon became clear that his psychological state affected the level of pain. When he was anxious or depressed, the pain always seemed much worse. He was talking to a counselor about all of this when he read about a pain clinic located in a Western state. Without consulting anyone, he signed up for a six-week program. He was back within ten days, feeling more depressed than ever. He went to the program with extremely high expectations because his needs were great. The program was a holistic one that helped the participants develop a more realistic lifestyle. It included programs dealing with nutrition and quality of interpersonal life. Group counseling was part of the whole picture, and the groups included a training-as-treatment approach. For instance, the participants were trained in behavioral approaches to pain management. Elmer arrived at the clinic, which was located on a converted farm, with unrealistic expectations. He expected to find "marvels of modern medicine" that would somehow magically help him. He was extremely disappointed when they talked about reducing and managing rather than eliminating pain. He was not prepared for the kind of program he found.*

Elmer's aim was the elimination of pain, and he refused to see that this might not be possible. A more realistic aim would have been the reduction and the management of pain. He did not spend enough time setting up a realistic goal and spent no time taking a census of the possibilities available to him.

Taking a census of program possibilities is not an end in itself. The research on problem solving (D'Zurilla & Goldfried, 1971; Heppner, 1978) suggests that the quality and efficacy of a program tends to be better if it is chosen from among a number of possibilities. Let us consider the case of Carlita, who has come to realize that heavy drinking is ruining her life. Her goal is to stop drinking. She feels that it simply would not be enough to cut down. She has to stop. To her the program seems simple enough: whereas before she drank, now she won't drink. Because of the novelty of not drinking, she is successful for a couple of days and then falls off the wagon. This happens a number of times until she finally realizes that she needs some help. Stopping drinking, at least for her, is not as simple as it seemed.

A counselor at a city alcohol and drug treatment center helps her explore various techniques that can be used in a stop-drinking program. Together they come up with the following possibilities:

- Join Alcoholics Anonymous
- Move someplace declared "dry" by local government
- Take Antabuse, a drug that causes nausea if followed by alcohol
- Replace drinking with other rewarding behaviors
- Join some self-help group other than Alcoholics Anonymous
- Get rid of all liquor in the house
- Take the "pledge" not to drink; to make it more binding, take it in front of a minister
- Join a residential hospital detoxification program
- Do not spend time with friends who drink heavily
- Change social patterns; for instance, find places other than bars and cock-tail lounges to socialize
- Try hypnosis to reduce the drive for alcohol
- Use behavior modification techniques to develop an aversion for alcohol—for instance, pair painful but safe electric shocks with drinking or even thoughts about drinking
- Change self-defeating patterns of self-talk—such as "I have to have a drink" or "One drink won't hurt me"
- Become a volunteer to help others stop drinking
- Read books and view films on the dangers of alcohol
- Stay in counseling as a way of getting support and challenge for stopping
- Share intentions of stopping drinking with family and a few close friends
- Stop on your own without help from anyone else
- Spend a week with someone you know who does a great deal of work with alcoholics and go on his rounds with him
- Walk around skid row meditatively
- Have a discussion with family members as to the impact of your drinking on them
- Discover things to eat that might help reduce your craving for alcohol
- Get a hobby or a vocation that you like that will call up a lot of your resources and take up a great deal of your attention
- Generally, make sure that stopping drinking does not leave a vacuum in your life; do another census on the ways you can fill this void

Although this is not an exhaustive list, it contains many more items than Carlita would have thought of had she not been stimulated by the counselor to take a census of program possibilities. One of the reasons that clients are clients is they have never been very creative in looking for solutions to their problems, or at least at the moment, whatever creativity they do have is not being used. Once goals are established, getting them accomplished is not just a matter of hard work. It also depends on how effective you are in helping clients stimulate their own creativity.

Helping Clients Engage in Divergent Thinking

One of the behavioral mechanisms that hold people in the grip of the "psychopathology of the average" is a failure to develop the ability to think "divergently." Let's consider an example. Picture a room with forty people in it. In the front of the room a woman holds up a red brick. She asks the people in the room to write down how that brick may be used. The odds are that there are people in that room who will write down only one answer—that it can be used in constructing some kind of building. They take the "one right answer" approach to the problem or question posed. This is called "convergent thinking." In a convergent thinking approach to problem solving, people look for the one right answer. It is not that such thinking is useless. If a person is faced with five electrical wires he or she must handle and is told that only one of them is live but that by tracing the circuits he or she can determine which one it is, then the one right answer is extremely important (on the assumption that the current cannot be turned off and the person must touch all five of the wires). However, many of the problem situations of life are too complex to be handled by convergent thinking. Such thinking limits the ways people use their own and environmental resources.

Let's return to the example of the woman with the brick. Some of the people in the room might have suggested that the brick could be used as a paperweight, to construct a bookcase, or ground up and used to give paint color and texture. There are all sorts of possibilities. This is divergent thinking. One problem with such thinking is that, however useful it might be, it is often not rewarded in our culture. Sometimes it is even punished. For instance, studies in creativity have shown that students who think divergently can be thorns in the sides of teachers (Guilford, 1962; Holland, 1961). Many teachers feel comfortable only when they ask questions in such a way as to get the "one right answer." When students who think divergently give answers that are different from the ones expected, even though these responses might be useful (perhaps more useful than the expected responses), they may be ignored or even punished. If this is the case, the offering of divergent responses, as might be expected, soon extinguishes. Students learn that divergent thinking is not rewarded, at least not in school, and they may generalize their experience and end up thinking that it is simply not a useful form of behavior. This is especially true when they see social dissent and other forms of divergent thinking ignored or even punished in society.

It is evident that divergent thinking can be extremely useful in problem solving. It is useful in developing new perspectives, in setting workable goals, in finding different ways to achieve these goals, and in searching for needed resources. Helping clients become better divergent thinkers can be a training-as-treatment method with great payoff potential. It is possible to challenge clients to move out of the ruts they have cut for themselves by constant convergent thinking. Einstein is said to have been such a creative scientist because he was not afraid to ask "impertinent" questions of nature. Clients can be helped to ask impertinent questions of themselves and their environment. Although some kind of balance between convergent and divergent thinking might be most useful, it is likely that most clients (and perhaps most helpers) you meet will be overbalanced on the convergent side.

> Quentin wanted to be a doctor; so he enrolled in the premed program at school. He did well, but not well enough to get into medical school. When he received the last notice of refusal, he said to himself, "Well, that's it for me and the world of medicine. Now what will I do?" When he graduated, he took a job in his brother-in-law's business. He became a manager and did fairly well financially, but he never experienced much career satisfaction. He was glad that his marriage was good and home life rewarding because he received little satisfaction at work.

Not much divergent thinking went into handling this problem situation. For Quentin, becoming a doctor was the one right career. He didn't give serious thought to any other career related to the field of medicine, even though there are dozens of interesting jobs in the allied health sciences.

The case of Miguel, who also wanted to become a doctor but failed to get into medical school, is very different.

> Miguel, too, failed to get into medical school. But he thought to himself, "Medicine still interests me; I'd like to do something in the field." With the help of a medical career counselor, he reviewed the possibilities. Even though he was in premed, he had never realized that there were so many careers in the field of medicine. He decided to take whatever courses and practicum experiences he needed to become a nurse. Then, while working in a clinic in the hills of Appalachia, where he found the experience invaluable, he managed to take an M.A. in family-practice nursing by attending part-time a nearby state university. He chose this specialty because he thought it would enable him to be closely associated with delivery of a broad range of services to patients and would also enable him to have more responsibility for the delivery of these services. When he graduated, he entered private practice as a nurse practitioner with a doctor

in a small Midwestern town. Because the doctor divided his time among three small clinics, Miguel had a great deal of responsibility in the clinic where he practiced. He also taught a course in family-practice nursing at a nearby state school and conducted workshops in holistic approaches to preventive medical self-care. His career satisfaction was very high.

A great deal of divergent thinking went into the elaboration of these goals and in coming up with the programs to fulfill them.

Requirements for Creativity

A review of the requirements for creativity (Robertshaw, Mecca, & Rerick, 1978, pp. 118–120) shows that people in trouble often lose or fail to use whatever creative resources they have. The creative person is characterized by the following:

- *Optimism and confidence,* while clients are often depressed and feel powerless
- *Acceptance of ambiguity and uncertainty,* while clients may feel tortured by ambiguity and uncertainty and want to escape from them as quickly as possible
- *A wide range of interests,* while clients may have a narrow range of interests or have had their interests severely narrowed by anxiety and pain
- *Flexibility,* while clients may have become quite rigid in their approach to themselves, others, and the social systems of life
- *Tolerance of complexity,* while clients are often confused and looking for simplicity and simple solutions
- *Verbal fluency,* while clients may not be verbally fluent at all
- *Curiosity,* while clients may not have developed a searching approach to life or may have been hurt by being too venturesome
- *Drive and persistence,* while clients may be all too ready to give up
- *Independence,* while clients may be dependent or counterdependent (the other side of the dependence coin) and fight efforts to be helped with "yes, but" and other games
- *Nonconformity or reasonable risk taking,* while clients may have a history of being very conservative, being conformist, or getting into trouble with others and with society precisely because of their particular brand of nonconformity

A review of some of the principal deterrents to creativity surfaces further problems. Innovation is hindered by the following:

- *Fear,* and clients are often quite fearful and anxious
- *Fixed habits,* and clients may have self-defeating habits or behavior patterns that may be deeply ingrained
- *Dependence on authority,* and clients may come to helpers looking for the "right answers" or be counterdependent
- *Perfectionism,* and clients may come to helpers precisely because they are tortured by this problem and can accept only ideal or perfect solutions

Therefore, it is easy to say that imagination and creativity are most useful at this point of Stage III, but it is another thing to help clients stimulate their own, perhaps dormant, creative potential. However, once you know the conditions that favor creativity, you can use responding and challenging skills to help clients awaken whatever creative resources they might have. You can also use training-as-treatment skills to help clients develop creativity-related techniques, such as brainstorming.

Brainstorming as a Program-Development Skill

Once clients are helped to set workable goals, they may need help in exploring how to achieve these goals. One excellent way of helping clients surface possible programs is *brainstorming* (Maier, 1970; Osborn, 1963), the technique used with Carlita. Brainstorming is a technique for generating ideas, possibilities, or alternate courses of action. The brainstormer tries, through divergent thinking, to identify as many ways of achieving a goal as possible. There are certain rules that help make this technique work (see D'Zurilla & Goldfried, 1971; Osborn, 1963). I explore six of them.

SUSPEND JUDGMENT

Do not let clients criticize the program possibilities they are generating and do not criticize these possibilities yourself (Bayless, 1967; Davis & Manske, 1966; Parloff & Handlon, 1964). There is some evidence that this rule is especially effective when the problem situation has been clarified and defined, which would, of course, be the case in a problem-solving approach to helping. In the following example, a man who is in pain because he has been rejected by a woman he loves is exploring ways of getting her out of his mind.

> *Client:* One possibility is that I could move to a different city, but that would mean that I would have to get a new job.
> *Helper:* Write it down. We'll take a more critical look at these later.

Having clients suspend judgment is one way of handling the tendency on the part of some to play a "yes, but" game.

"LET YOURSELF GO"

Encourage clients to include even wild possibilities. Later on it is easier to cut suggested programs down to size than to expand them (Maltzman, 1960). The wildest possibilities often have within them at least a kernel of an idea that will work.

> *Helper:* So you need money for school. Well, what are some wild ways you could go about getting the money you need?
> *Client:* Well, let me think. . . . I could rob a bank . . . or print some of my own money . . . or put an ad in the paper and ask people to send me money.

Clients often need "permission" to let themselves go, even in such a harmless way.

ENCOURAGE QUANTITY

Help clients develop as many alternatives as possible. This increases the possibility of finding useful ideas. Studies show that some of the best ideas come along later in the brainstorming process (Maier & Hoffman, 1964; Parnes, 1967).

> *Client:* Maybe that's enough. We can start putting it all together.
> *Helper:* It didn't sound like you were running out of ideas.
> *Client:* I'm not. It's actually fun.
> *Helper:* Well, let's keep on having fun for a while.

PIGGYBACK

Help clients, without criticizing any of their proposals, both add on to ideas already generated and combine different ideas to form new possibilities. In the following example, the client is trying to come up with ways of increasing her self-esteem.

> *Client:* One way I can get a better appreciation of myself is to make a list of my accomplishments every week, even if this means just getting through the ordinary tasks of everyday life.
> *Helper:* Anything else you might do with that?
> *Client* (Pause): And I could star the ones that took some kind of special effort on my part and celebrate them with my husband.

CLARIFY ITEMS ON LIST

Without criticizing their proposals, help clients clarify them. When a proposal is clarified, it can be expanded.

College student (talking about financial support now that he has moved out of the house and his parents have cut off funds): And I suppose there might be the possibility of loans.

Counselor: Are there different kinds of loans?

Client: Well, my grandfather talked about "putting a stake" in my future, but at the time I didn't need it. (Pause) And then there are the low-interest state loans. I usually never think of them because none of the people I know use them. I bet I'm eligible. I'm not even sure, but the school itself might have some loans.

Two basic assumptions of brainstorming are that the suspension of judgment increases productivity and that quantity breeds quality. For our purposes, the evidence supporting these assumptions seems to be substantial enough (Brilhart & Jochem, 1964; Meadow, Parnes, & Reese, 1959; Weisskopf-Joelson & Eliseo, 1961; see D'Zurilla & Goldfried, 1971, and Heppner, 1978, for reviews of this research).

CONCRETENESS IN BRAINSTORMING

Brainstorming is not the same as free association. Although clients are encouraged to think of even wild possibilities, these possibilities still must in some way be stimulated by and relate to the client's problem situation and the goals that have been established to manage it. Therefore, brainstorming itself is influenced by the way in which the problem situation has been defined and the clarity and concreteness of the goals that have been set. Concreteness and specificity are as important in this program-census step as they are in the problem-clarification and goal-setting stages (Crutchfield, 1969; D'Zurilla & Goldfried, 1971; Goldfried & D'Zurilla, 1969; Hackman, 1967; Maier, 1960, 1970).

Using Prompts

Without taking over responsibility for the program census, you can use certain prompts to stimulate your client's imagination. For instance, Jason T. has terminal cancer. He has been in and out of the hospital several times over the past few months or so, and he knows he probably will not live more than a year. He would like the year to be as full as possible and yet he wants to be realistic. He hates being in the hospital, especially a large hospital where it is so easy to be anonymous, and one of his goals is to die outside the hospital. He would like to die as benignly as possible and be in possession of his faculties as long as possible. How is he to achieve this goal?

You can use the following interrelated and overlapping prompts to help him identify possible programs or elements of programs:

PERSONS

What people might help him achieve his goal? Jason has heard of a *doctor* in Wisconsin who specializes in the treatment of chronic pain. He teaches people how to use a variety of techniques to manage pain. He says that perhaps his *wife and daughter* can learn how to give simple injections to help him control the pain. Jason thinks that talks every once in a while with a *friend* whose wife died of cancer, a man he respects and trusts, will help him find the courage he needs.

MODELS

Does the client know people who are presently doing what he or she wants to do? One of Jason's fellow workers died of cancer at home. Jason visited him there a couple of times. That's what gave him the idea of dying at home or at least outside the hospital. He noticed that his friend never allowed himself "poor-me" talk. He refused to see dying as anything else but part of living. This touched Jason deeply at the time, and now reflecting on that experience may help him develop realistic attitudes.

PLACES

Are there particular places that might help? Jason immediately thinks of Lourdes, the shrine where believers flock with all sorts of human problems. He doesn't expect miracles, but he feels that he might experience life more deeply there. It's a bit wild, but why not a pilgrimage? He still has the time and also enough money to do it.

THINGS

What things exist that can help the client achieve the goal? Jason has read about the use of combinations of drugs to help stave off pain and the side effects of chemotherapy. He notices that the use of marijuana by terminal cancer patients to help control nausea has just been legalized in his state.

ORGANIZATIONS

Are there any organizations that help people with this kind of problem? Jason knows there are mutual-help groups composed of cancer patients. He heard of one at the hospital and believes there are others in the community.

PROGRAMS

Are there any ready-made programs for people in the client's position? A hospice for the terminally ill has just been established where Jason lives. They have three programs. One helps people who are terminally ill stay out in the community as long as they can. A second makes provision for part-time residents. The third provides a residential program for those who can spend little or no time in the community. The goals of these programs are practically the same as Jason's.

THE CLIENT'S SKILLS, WORKING KNOWLEDGE, AND INNER RESOURCES

What resources does the client have that can be used to achieve this goal? Jason knows something about the principles of behavior, such as reinforcement, aversive conditioning, and shaping. He has read that these principles can be used in pain management (Fordyce, 1976). He also has strong religious convictions that can help him face adversity. These resources relate to possible courses of action.

If a client is having a difficult time coming up with programs, the helper can "prime the pump" by offering a few suggestions. This can be done in such a way that the principal responsibility for the program census stays with the client.

Helping Clients Choose Programs

Some clients, once they are helped to see different program possibilities, move forward on their own—that is, they put together a program that fits their needs and implement it. Others, however, still need help in putting together a viable program. If this is the case, then once program possibilities have been identified, the counselor helps the client choose those programs or program elements that provide the best "fit," the programs that are most in keeping with the client's values, resources, and circumstances. In order to do this, helpers need, above and beyond the communication skills that enable them to provide continuing support and challenge, the skills of program construction. As we have just seen, clients are encouraged to think of as many different ways of accomplishing their goals as possible. However, having a large number of possible solutions can be a problem in its own right because individuals then have a hard time picking the best (Johnson, Parrott, & Stratton, 1968). It is useless to have clients brainstorm if they don't know what to do with the possibilities they generate.

If a goal is what a client wants to accomplish in order to manage some problem situation, then program construction can be seen as coming up with an effective strategy for accomplishing the goal.

The Balance Sheet

The decision balance sheet is a decision-making aid counselors can use to help clients choose the kinds of programs that best fit their needs. Janis and Mann (1977) offer it as a way of helping clients examine the consequences of different programs in the light of both usefulness and values. The balance sheet deals with the question of *utility*—"Will this course of action get me where I want to go?"—and *acceptability*—"Can I live with this course of action?" It helps clients consider not just themselves but also significant others and the social systems of their lives. Benefits or gains and losses or costs are considered in the balance sheet.

BENEFITS OR GAINS

If I choose this program or follow this course of action, what benefits or gains are in it for me, for significant others in my life, and for the social systems of which I am a member?

In each case, these potential benefits or gains are *acceptable* to me because: *my* gains are acceptable because . . . , the gains of *significant others* are acceptable because . . . , or the gains for *relevant social settings* are acceptable because. . . .

In each case, these potential benefits or gains are *unacceptable* to me because: *my* gains would be unacceptable because . . . , the gains for *significant others* would be unacceptable because . . . , or the gains to *relevant social systems* would be unacceptable because. . . .

LOSSES OR COSTS

If I choose this program or follow this course of action, what losses or costs can I expect to incur for myself, for significant others, and for relevant social systems?

In each case, these potential losses are *acceptable* to me because: *my* losses are acceptable because . . . , the losses to *significant others* are acceptable because . . . , or the losses to *relevant social systems* are acceptable because. . . .

In each case, these potential losses or costs are *unacceptable* to me because: *my* losses or costs are unacceptable because . . . , the losses or costs to *significant others* are unacceptable because . . . , or the losses or costs to *relevant social systems* are unacceptable because. . . .

Some examples will help make the use of the balance sheet clear. Let's return to Carlita, the woman who has admitted that she is an alcoholic and whose goal is to stop drinking.

If I choose alternate course of action #_____:

Gains for self:	Acceptable to me because:	Not acceptable to me because:
Losses for self:	Acceptable to me because:	Not acceptable to me because:
Gains for significant others:	Acceptable to me because:	Not acceptable to me because:
Losses for significant others:	Acceptable to me because:	Not acceptable to me because:
Gains for social setting:	Acceptable to me because:	Not acceptable to me because:
Losses for social setting:	Acceptable to me because:	Not acceptable to me because:

Figure 8–1. The decision balance sheet

One program possibility discovered in the brainstorming process is to spend a month as an inpatient at an alcoholic treatment center. This possibility intrigues Carlita. Because choosing this possibility would be a serious decision, the counselor helps her use the balance sheet (Figure 8–1) to weigh possible costs and benefits. The counselor explains the sheet to her and Carlita fills it out at home. He tells her to mark the spots she feels she needs to discuss after filling it out. She returns with the following:

BENEFITS OF CHOOSING THE RESIDENTIAL PROGRAM

For me

It would help me because it would be a dramatic sign that I want to do something to change my life. It's a clean break, as it were. It would also give me time just for myself; I'd get away from all my commitments to family, relatives, friends, and work. I see it as an opportunity to do some planning. I'd have to figure out how I would act as a sober woman.

For significant others

I'm thinking mainly of my family here. It would also give them a breather, a month without an alcoholic wife and mother around the house. I'm not saying that to put myself down. I think it would give them time to reassess family life and make some decisions about any changes they'd like to make. I think something dramatic like my going away would give them hope. They've had very little reason to hope for the last five years.

For relevant social settings

I can't think of many benefits for social settings apart from the family. I'd probably be more "with it" in my part-time job, but they've never had any real complaints.

ACCEPTABILITY OF BENEFITS

For me

I feel torn here. But looking at it just from the viewpoint of acceptability, I feel kind enough toward myself to give myself a month's time off. Also something in me wants very strongly to have a new start in life.

For significant others

I think that my family would have no problems in letting me "take off" for a month. I'm sure that they'd see it as a positive step from which all of us would benefit.

For relevant social settings

This does not seem to be an issue at work. They like me now. I might be more efficient and most likely I'd be more personable, less moody.

UNACCEPTABILITY OF GAINS

For me

Going away for a month seems such a luxury, so self-indulgent. Also, taking such a dramatic step would give me an opportunity to change my current lifestyle, but it would also place demands on me. My fear is that I would do fine while "inside" but that I would come out and fall on my face. I guess I'm saying it would give me another chance at life, but I have misgivings about having another chance. *I need some help here.*

For significant others

The kids are young enough to readjust to a "new" me. But I'm not sure how my husband would take this "benefit." He's more or less worked out a lifestyle that copes with my being drunk a lot. Though I have never left him and he has never left me, still I wonder whether he wants me "back," sober, I mean. Maybe this belongs under the cost part of this exercise. *I need some help here.* I notice that some of my misgivings relate not to a residential program as such but to a return to a lifestyle free of alcohol. Doing this exercise helped me see that more clearly.

For relevant social settings

As far as I can see, there's nothing unacceptable about my being more efficient or more personable at work.

COSTS OF CHOOSING A RESIDENTIAL PROGRAM

For me

Well, there's the money. I don't mean the money just for the program, but I would be losing four weeks' wages. Some of that I use just for myself. The major cost seems to be the commitment I have to make about a lifestyle change. Also I guess the residential program won't be all fun. I don't know exactly what they do there, but some of it must be demanding.

For significant others

It's a private program and it's going to cost the family a lot of money. It's also going to disturb their patterns of living because the probability is that they're going to get a "new" me back and they'll have to learn to live with me all over again.

For relevant social settings

There may be one cost here. If I change my lifestyle, I may want a better job or I may make the decision not to work at all. In that case, they would lose someone they see as a good employee.

ACCEPTABILITY OF COSTS

For me

I have no problem at all with the money or with whatever the residential program demands of me physically or psychologically. I'm willing to pay. The demand the program places on me for a new life-style? Well, in principle, I'm willing to pay what that costs. *I need some help here.*

For significant others

They will have to make financial sacrifices, but I have no reason to think they would be unwilling. Still, I can't be making decisions for them. I see much more clearly the need to have a session with the counselor with my husband and children present. I think they're also willing to have a "new" person around the house, even if it means making adjustments and changing lifestyle. I want to check this out with them, but I think it would be helpful to do this with the counselor. I think they will be willing to come.

For relevant social settings

If getting better means not working or getting a different job, let it be. I can hardly base my decisions on what they will think at work.

UNACCEPTABILITY OF COSTS

For me

Although I'm ready to change my lifestyle, I hate to think that I will have to accept some dumb, dull life. I think I've been drinking, at least in part, to get away from dullness. I've been living in a fantasy world, a play world a lot of the time. A stupid way of doing it perhaps, but it's true. I have to do some life planning of some sort. *I need some help here.*

For significant others

>   It strikes me that my family might have problems even with a sober me
> if I strike out in new directions. I wonder if they want the traditional
> homebody wife and mother. I don't think I could stand that. *I need some*
> *help here.*

For relevant social settings

>   They can get along without me for a month at work. And if necessary,
> they can get along without me completely.
>   All in all, it seems like the residential program is a good idea. There is
> something much more "total" about it than an out-patient program. But
> that's also what scares me.

Carlita's use of the balance sheet helps her make an initial program choice,
but it also enables her to discover issues that she has not worked out completely
yet. By using the balance sheet, she returns to the counselor with work to do;
she does not come merely wondering what will happen next. This highlights the
usefulness of exercises and other forms of structure that help clients take more
responsibility for both what happens in the helping process and behavior outside.

Some clients find it easier to choose programs if they first *sample* some of the
possibilities.

>   Carlita, surprised by the number of program possibilities there were to
> achieve the goal of getting liquor out of her life, decided to sample some of
> them. She went to an open Alcoholics Anonymous meeting; she went to a
> meeting of a women's consciousness-raising group; she visited the hospital
> that had the residential treatment program; she joined a two-week trial
> physical fitness program at a YWCA; and she had a couple of "strategy"
> meetings with her husband and children. Although none of this was done
> frantically, it did occupy her energies and strengthened her resolve to do
> something about her alcoholism.

It goes without saying that some clients could use program sampling as a way
of putting off action. However, if a program is going to require a high cost in
terms of time, energy, and/or money, sampling it to see how it fits one's
resources, values, and preferences makes sense.

Criteria for Choosing a Program

The criteria for choosing a program do not differ from the criteria for
choosing a goal. These criteria are reviewed briefly here through a number
of examples.

CONCRETE AND SPECIFIC

Programs, like goals, need to be concrete and specific if they are to be translated into action. If Carlita would say, "My goal is to stop drinking. In order to achieve this goal, I'm going to lessen the amount of stress in my life. If I feel less stress, I won't be tempted to drink as much," she is violating this criterion. The principle she suggests may be sound, but her application of it is much too vague to be of any use. If Elmer's goal is to reduce and manage the pain from a chronic back condition, then learning to control his reaction to pain through a biofeedback program is a concrete and specific way of moving toward his goal. Note that being concrete and specific is important *throughout* the helping process—in clarifying and defining the problem situation, in setting goals, and now in elaborating programs.

MEASURABLE OR VERIFIABLE

The relationship between the program and the accomplishment of the goal must be capable of being verified.

> Susan intends to take some kind of communication course as a way of helping her be more assertive in class, in talking with her parents, and in her relationships with her peers. The course she takes, however, is a "sensitivity training" program that is characterized by "planned goallessness." She attends the meetings but does not know exactly what she is learning, if anything. There is no way of telling whether this program is helping her to be more assertive. Trish, on the other hand, has the same goal, but she takes a course in interpersonal communication skills. She is given a clear idea of what each skill is and how it can be used. She learns and practices the skills in the training group and is given help in transferring these to other settings. She knows what she is learning and how it contributes to her goal.

If a program is not capable of being verified, it is impossible to determine whether the client is participating in it or not.

REALISTIC

The program must be within the resources of the client, under his or her control, environmentally possible, and owned by the client.

> Destry is in a halfway house after leaving a state mental hospital. From time to time he still has bouts of depression that incapacitate him for a few days. He wants to get a job because he thinks that it will help him feel better about himself, become more independent, and manage his depression better. He answers want ads in a rather random way and keeps

getting turned down after being interviewed. He simply does not yet have
the kinds of resources demanded by the jobs he is seeking. The counselor
helps him explore some sheltered workshop possibilities. She helps him
find a workshop that is not a dead end, but rather a step toward a more
ordinary type of job. Destry does have the psychological resources to work
successfully in a sheltered workshop.

There is, of course, a difference between realism and selling a client short. Programs that make clients "stretch" for a valued goal can be most rewarding.

ADEQUATE

Programs must contribute in some substantial way to accomplishing the goal. Sometimes goals do not get accomplished because programs are not substantial enough or because they are not relevant even though substantial.

Stacy was admitted to a mental hospital because she had been exhibiting
bizarre behavior in her community. She dressed in a slovenly way and went
around admonishing the residents of the community for their "sins." She
was diagnosed as schizophrenic, simple type. She had been living alone for
about five years, since the death of her husband. It seems that she had
become more and more alienated from herself and others. In the hospital,
medication helped control some of her symptoms. She stopped
admonishing others and took reasonable care of herself, but she was still
quite withdrawn. She was assigned to "milieu" therapy, a euphemism
meaning that she followed the more or less benign routine of the hospital.
She remained withdrawn and usually seemed moderately depressed. No
therapeutic goals had been set and the nonspecific program to which she
was assigned was totally inadequate.

Sometimes programs are inadequate because the resources needed for an adequate one are not available. In this example, "milieu" therapy is a euphemism for a lack of adequate resources in the hospital.

IN KEEPING WITH CLIENT'S VALUES

Programs, like goals, may be in keeping with the values of the client or violate them.

Glenn was cited for battering his 2-year-old child. Mandatory counseling
was part of the suspended sentence he received. He had a violent temper—
that is, he got angry easily, did little to control it, and vented it on others,
including the child. The counselor discovered that Glenn and his wife were
having sexual problems and that sexual frustration had a great deal to do

with his anger. The counselor suggested that Glenn lower his frustration (and therefore control his anger) by engaging in sexual relations with other women. Glenn did this, but felt guilty and became depressed.

The counselor is in the wrong for suggesting a program without consideration of the client's values. He might be doing so because he thinks that Glenn's having sex with other women, if evil at all, is less evil than his abusing his child, but this is not his decision.

SET IN A REASONABLE TIME FRAME

This implies that clients have a clear idea of the steps of a program and know when they are to do what.

Tammy, after consulting her doctor, undertook a physical fitness program as part of an overall weight-reduction program. Her counselor gave her a book that outlined both a variety of exercises and a running schedule. The book indicated three different kinds of programs, slow, medium, and fast, and scaled each according to age groups. Tammy decided that she needed a taste of success. She chose the slow program for her age group. The book indicated each objective and the time allotted it. Each day Tammy had a very clear idea of just what to do. She stuck to the schedule and began feeling much better about herself.

If a client does not know what the steps of a program are and when each is to be accomplished, this militates against his or her starting it at all.

Risk and Probability of Success in Selecting Programs

In choosing programs, clients can be helped to evaluate the risk involved and to determine whether the risk is proportional to the probability of success. Estimating the risk involved in each alternative ties together personal values and the information gathered (Gelatt, Varenhorst, & Carey, 1972). The balance sheet helps clients identify both values and degree of risk. Gelatt and his associates suggest four strategies that deal with the factors of risk and probability.

First is the *"wish" strategy*. In the wish strategy, the client chooses a program that *might* (he or she hopes) lead to the accomplishment of a goal, regardless of risk, cost, or probability. For instance, Jenny wants her ex-husband to increase the amount of support he is paying for the children. She tries to accomplish this by constantly nagging him and trying to make him feel guilty. She does not consider the risk (he might get angry and stop giving her anything), the cost (she spends a lot of time and emotional energy arguing with him), or the probability (he does not react favorably to nagging; he sees that as one of the reasons for the divorce). In the wish strategy the client operates blindly, using some preferred means without taking its usefulness into account. Clients who "work hard" and still "get nowhere" might well be using the wish strategy—that is, they are persevering in using means they prefer but that seem to be of doubtful efficacy.

Second is the *"safe" strategy*. In the safe strategy, the client chooses only safe courses of action, ones that have little risk associated with them and with a high degree of probability of producing some kind of success. For instance, Liam, a man in his early forties, is very dissatisfied with his job but is afraid of losing it if anyone finds out that he is thinking of changing. He chooses only possibilities for which interviews are given in the evening, and he excludes those he thinks might be too competitive or too challenging. He simply wants a job different from the one he has. The trouble with this strategy is that it places limitations on the kinds of goals one can pursue. Goals have to be tailored to safe and probable means. Clients might well end up being safe but also sorry.

The *"escape" strategy* is the third one. It lets the client choose means that are likely to help him or her avoid *the worst possible result*; it minimizes the maximum danger. Let's say a client has had fits of violence. He commits himself to a mental hospital, for he feels there he will be protected from his own violence. The greatest danger for him is harming another person. By placing himself in custodial care, he minimizes this danger. The obvious problem with such a strategy is that it is an avoidance strategy based on negative reinforcement. It can prevent any new learning from taking place.

Fourth is the *"combination" strategy*, which allows the client to choose courses of action that, although they involve risk, both minimize danger and increase the probability of achieving a goal in the way and to the degree the client desires. This combination strategy is the most difficult to apply, for it involves the hard work implied in the comprehensive problem-solving methodology described in these pages: clarification of objectives, a solid knowledge of personal values, the ability to rank a variety of action programs according to one's values, plus the ability to predict results from a given course of action. Sometimes clients have neither the time nor the will for this kind of detailed work; sometimes helpers do not have the decision-making skills to help clients do this work.

Helping Clients Order Program Steps

Some programs are simple, and there is no need to help clients determine the steps and when they are to be accomplished. Others are more complicated, and clients need to get an overall picture of the steps and a clear idea of which step is to be taken first. Otherwise, they may become confused and give up. Some clients are able to do this kind of sequencing of steps on their own; others still need a counselor's help.

Moving toward a goal gradually, step by step, is one way of increasing the probability of reaching that goal. Because some action programs are not simple, one-step processes, they can be broken down into a series of steps. If any given step seems too complicated, it can be broken down into even simpler steps that the client can manage.

A very simple step in a multiple-step program can ease the tension of a serious problem. Consider the following example:

> Cary is having a great deal of trouble in his relationships with others. Part of his program is participation in a communication skills program one evening a week at a community college. One simple step in this training program is learning how to attend to others. Cary uses this simple skill outside the group, and it changes his whole stance toward others. Instead of moving into human contacts impulsively, awkwardly, fearfully, or belligerently, he now uses the skill of attending as a way of pausing and allowing other people to be present in their own way. It is a simple step, but it does a great deal in helping him relate to others.

We can now take a more systematic look at the process of helping clients put the steps of a program into some kind of facilitative sequence.

Shaping: Developing Subgoals and Subprograms

If a problem situation is complex, any given goal the client chooses may have a number of subgoals. A subgoal is a step toward a larger goal. For instance, if an automobile is to move smoothly down an assembly line, all sorts of subgoals need to be accomplished first. It does little good to have the chassis moving down the line if the other parts are not available for assembling. "Fenders *manufactured*, *shipped*, and *in place* for assembly" would be an important subgoal or objective. Without this subgoal, further goals would be impossible.

The simpler the programs, the better, provided that they help clients achieve their goals. However, simplicity is not an end in itself. The question is not whether any given program is complicated or not but whether it is well *shaped* or organized. If complicated programs are broken down into subgoals and subprograms, they are as capable of being achieved, if the time frame is realistic, as simpler ones. In schematic form, program shaping looks like this:

Subprogram #1 leads to subgoal #1
  Subprogram #2 leads to subgoal #2
    Subprogram #n (the last in the sequence) leads to the accomplishment of the major goal

Your job is to help clients identify subgoals—that is, *major steps* on the way toward the achievement of an important goal—and organize these subgoals into a *sequence* leading to the major goal. This can be applied to Wanda, a client who has set a number of goals in order to manage a complex problem situation. One of these goals is finding a job. She can divide the program leading to this goal into a number of steps. Another way of putting this is that each step leads to the accomplishment of a *subgoal*. The following subgoals are part of Wanda's job-finding program:

>Subgoal #1: job possibilities *canvased*
>Subgoal #2: best job prospects *identified*
>Subgoal #3: job interviews *arranged and completed*
>Subgoal #4: job interviews *completed*
>Subgoal #5: job *chosen*
>Major goal in total program: job *started*

If all this is accomplished, then the client achieves one of the major goals in her program, satisfactory employment.

For each of these subgoals, a program is established. For instance, the program for subgoal #1 might include reading the help wanted section of the local papers, contacting friends or acquaintances who might be able to offer jobs or provide leads, reading the bulletin boards at school, visiting employment agencies, and talking with someone in the job placement office at school. Remember that clients often tend to overlook program possibilities, and one of your tasks, even in the elaboration of subprograms, is to help them break out of overly narrow patterns of thinking. As usual, both support and challenge are still needed to help clients move beyond their own narrow perspectives. The communication skills discussed in earlier chapters are tools needed throughout the helping process to provide both support and challenge.

>*Wanda:* I'm beginning to panic. I've been reading the help wanted sections of the local paper and of a couple of the papers in nearby towns, but I haven't seen anything that seems right for me.
>*Counselor:* Newspapers seem to be only one source of job possibilities. Let's see if we can come up with other ways of finding out what kind of work is available. For instance, most people don't know that more jobs are obtained through word of mouth than through newspaper ads.
>*Wanda:* Well, I could call some places where I would like to work. I could ask some of my friends who are already working to keep their eyes open.

And she goes on to explore further possibilities.

Hints for Effective Program Sequencing

SUBGOAL QUALITY

The number of subgoals and subprograms will differ with the complexity of each problem situation. First of all, a subgoal must fulfill the same requirements as a goal; it must be

1. Stated as a clear, specific, behavioral *accomplishment.* "Job possibilities thoroughly canvased" is a goal that is stated as a clear accomplishment.
2. *Adequate*—that is, clearly related in some substantial way both to the next subgoal and to the major goal toward which it is directed. If Wanda does a good job at canvasing job possibilities, then she is ready to pick out the best prospects (the next subgoal in the program) and is moving toward her major goal of getting a job.
3. Within the *control* of the client and something the client rather than some-one else is to do. In the example, Wanda takes responsibility for canvasing job possibilities.
4. *Realistic*—that is, within the resources and capabilities of the client and in keeping with the environmental (social system) constraints within which the client is operating. Wanda needs some encouragement from the counselor, but she has the resources needed to search out job possibilities.
5. *Compatible* with other program subgoals and with the client's values. Job possibilities must first be discovered before Wanda can decide which ones look most promising and that she holds no values that would keep her from finding out what the job market has to offer.
6. Capable of being *verified.* It is evident both to Wanda and to the counselor whether she has done a reasonably adequate job in canvasing possibilities.
7. Assigned a reasonable *time frame* for completion. Wanda gives herself two weeks for this task and gets it done within that time.

Let us consider another example.

One of Leroy's problems is that he is "out of community"—that is, he has no close friend and no group with which he interacts regularly. It becomes clear that many of his other problems are related to having such an impoverished social life. Therefore, one major goal of his total program is "getting into community"—that is, participating in groups and establishing friendships. Although Leroy is somewhat fearful of making contact with others, he is lonely enough to want to do something about his social life. Through discussions with the counselor, he comes up with the following subgoals related to becoming a member of some kind of social group:

> *Group possibilities identified within two weeks*
>   *Best possibilities explored*
>   *Social group chosen*
>   *Social group joined*

Leroy has never thought of taking such direct action to improve his social life. He has been waiting for something to happen; and, predictably, nothing has happened. It seems that he has to make it happen. He evaluates each of these subgoals. For instance, he looks carefully at the subgoal "group possibilities identified." He finds that it is

1. *Stated as an accomplishment. He can picture himself with a list of possibilities in front of him.*
2. *Adequately and clearly related to the next subgoal, "group chosen," for it is better to choose from a number of possibilities, and to the ultimate goal of actually participating in a social group.*
3. *Within his control. Though he might need some suggestions from both the counselor and others, he can come up with a list of possibilities.*
4. *Realistic. He has the minimal skills needed to come up with a list.*
5. *Compatible. It doesn't interfere with any other goal or go against any value he holds.*
6. *Capable of being verified. He either has a list of possibilities or he does not.*
7. *Assigned a reasonable time frame. He judges two weeks to be an adequate amount of time.*

It is not necessary to apply each of these criteria explicitly to each subgoal. It can be immediately clear whether a subgoal meets most of these requirements or not.

SUBPROGRAM STEPS

Each step in a subprogram should have the characteristics of programs discussed earlier in this chapter—that is, each step should be

- *Clear.* The client should know exactly what to do.
- *Clearly related to the next step.* The progression of steps should be clear to the client.
- *Clearly related to the subgoal.* The client should see the steps as a more or less direct line toward the subgoal.
- *Not too large.* The "size" of a step should be related both to the client's actual resources and circumstances and to the client's feelings about any given step. What does he or she see as too large?

- *Not too small.* Although some helpers suggest there is no such thing as a step that is too small, some clients feel they are being treated like children if they are asked to do too little.
- *Reasonably scheduled.* There should be a realistic time frame for each step of the subprogram as well as each subgoal.

STEP SIZE

It is not enough to identify subgoals and establish subprograms. In setting up both programs and subprograms, there is one cardinal rule: *no step should be too large.* Watson and Tharp (1981) suggest helpers too often mistakenly attribute lack of will power to their clients. The problem, they say, is not lack of will power but poorly shaped programs—that is, programs that ask clients to do too much at one time. If any given step in a program seems too formidable for a client, he or she might balk or become disorganized. Any step that seems too large can be broken up into one or more smaller steps.

Jason T., introduced earlier, was dying of cancer. He felt a lot of the emotions that can sweep through cancer patients and people facing death—confusion, denial, rage, fear, isolation, hurt, and depression. He talked one day with a minister from his church who was on his weekly rounds in the hospital. The minister, after talking briefly with Jason, suggested he find someone with whom or some forum in which he could talk about his illness, his feelings, his values, and what he would like to do in the time he had left. This sounded good to Jason; but when the minister, who was somewhat rushed because he had a lot of patients to see, left, Jason had no idea what to do. Finding such a forum was too big a step for him because he was still struggling with his emotions. His brief conversation with the minister had done little to lessen his turmoil. After the minister left, Jason felt even more depressed than usual.

The next day a counselor from the pastoral ministry staff of the hospital stopped by. She provided support both by helping him explore his feelings and eventually by helping him find a forum for coming to grips day by day with the realities of living until he died. After helping him ventilate and explore his feelings about dying, she helped him identify a forum in which he could continue to discuss his feelings as a first subgoal or step toward the major goal of participating in some ongoing forum. A well-shaped program helped Jason become an agent rather than merely a patient. He now wanted to do something about his illness rather than merely endure it. "What do terminal cancer patients do for support?" he asked himself and, with the help of the counselor, began to identify some of the possibilities. There were more possibilities than he had suspected—for

> *instance, living-at-home programs, hospital-based mutual-help groups, one-to-one counseling, family counseling, group programs supported by various church agencies, and hospice-based programs. Exploring some of the possibilities included a visit to a hospice, and he ultimately decided to spend the rest of his time there.*

Initially, the counselor may have to take the responsibility of helping clients shape programs and subprograms. However, in doing so, the counselor can also train clients in the fundamentals of shaping so they can use them on their own.

Helping Clients Develop Contingency Plans

One important reason for helping clients choose a program from among alternates is the possibility that the chosen program, or part of it, might not work. It is thus wise to help clients determine backup or contingency programs.

> *Jason made plans to become a resident in the hospice he had visited. He thought this would be the best way for him and his family to handle his dying. Although he had visited the hospice and had liked what he had seen, he could not be absolutely sure it would work out. Therefore, with the help of the counselor, he drew up two other possibilities. One was living at home with some outreach services from the hospice. A third was spending his last days in a smaller hospital in a nearby town. This would not be as convenient for his family, but he would feel more comfortable there; he hated large hospitals. Jason came to these decisions after being helped to weigh the pros and cons by means of the balance-sheet approach.*

Contingency plans are needed, especially when clients choose a high-risk program to achieve a critical goal. Having backup plans also helps clients develop more responsibility. If they see that a plan is not working, they have to decide whether to try the contingency plan.

Some Program-Development Problems

RESISTING THE WORK

Some clients resist the work involved in setting up effective programs. Some people balk at it because it seems too complicated. They feel inept in the face of all this. They often come to counseling feeling disorganized and do not want this feeling intensified. If this is the case, you can lead them step by step through the process without revealing too much of what the next step is. Because you, as the helper, are aware of the logic involved in program development, you can use this logic in guiding clients who are too disorganized or too resistant to use it directly themselves. The point is that some systematic process should serve as a framework or guideline for choosing and elaborating programs. Although intuition can be a valuable resource, doing all this intuitively, especially in the case of complicated problem situations, is expecting too much of intuition. Put more positively, intuitions guided by the logic of the program-development process are likely to be more useful than "raw" intuitions.

GETTING LOST IN DETAILS

A common mistake made by novices who use program-development "technology" to help others is to become too detailed. If you keep using it in your own life to help yourself elaborate programs to achieve your goals, it will tend to become second nature to you. You can quickly learn the skill of breaking problems and goals into smaller parts and of "chaining" together the steps needed to accomplish both subgoals and major goals. Experience will teach you to avoid overloading clients and therefore running the risk of discouraging them and avoid causing them to "loaf" through the helping process and running the risk of giving it up because they see it as ineffectual. Learning and using program-development skills is like learning any other kind of skill. At first it feels awkward, but with practice the entire process becomes much easier.

A BALANCE BETWEEN TOO MUCH AND TOO LITTLE

Throughout the helping process, effective counselors remain sensitive to clients' needs and wants. Janis and Mann (1977) suggest that many people make poor decisions because they take a "minimal" approach to decision making—that is, they tend to make decisions that fulfill minimum requirements. For instance, let us say that a woman decides she wants a job that pays $175 per week and is within walking distance of her apartment. She accepts the first job that meets these minimum requirements and becomes secretary to the manager of a nearby laundry firm. It is not long before she becomes dissatisfied with the job and begins to realize there were other requirements she had not considered. For instance, she likes companionship at work but sees little of her boss and works alone all day. For her, a minimal approach has proved very inefficient (though it may have looked efficient at the time), for it has left her dissatisfied, and she now faces the prospect of searching for a new, more fulfilling job.

On the other hand, taking an "optimal" approach to decision making can be just as self-defeating. Optimizing means that a person continues looking for and evaluating options until she or he is completely satisfied that the decision being made is absolutely the "best" one. The problems with this approach to decision making are evident. Optimizing can be a way of never making a decision because any given course of action might not be the best one. It is also an expensive approach to decision making in terms of the client's time and the cost of counseling.

There is a continuum between minimal and optimal approaches. One of your tasks as a counselor is to help clients find the best place on this continuum for the decisions they must make. The best place depends on such variables as time available; the seriousness of the problem; the needs, wants, and resources of the client; and environmental constraints. However, too many people with problems fail to give *enough* consideration to decision-making processes. That is, clients, when they face problems in living, often drift toward the minimal end of the continuum.

CLIENT RESOURCES AND PROGRAM FIT

We have seen that part of listening to clients is listening for the resources they have, especially those they have but don't use. We have also seen that an important part of challenging is challenging clients to use the resources they already have. Nowhere is assessment of the client's personal, social, and environmental resources more critical than in program development. To help clients choose idealized programs for which they lack the resources turns helping into a self-defeating process for them. In a more positive vein, skilled counselors, precisely because they continue to help clients develop a broad picture of their resources and environmental possibilities and restrictions throughout the helping process, help clients choose programs that are best fitted to and make best use of their resources.

> Dermot, a college student, is developing a serious drinking problem. One of his teachers notices this and asks one of Dermot's friends to see if she can be of any help. She talks to him and eventually he decides to drop by the school counseling center. The counselor soon realizes that unused resources on Dermot's part play an important role in the problem situation. He is a very talented person, but he does little with his talents. In the program-development phase, one possibility identified is working as a volunteer in an alcoholic treatment center for teens. Dermot, who is majoring in psychology, discovers he can get field-study credit for this kind of volunteer work. More important is the fact that he mobilizes and uses such personal resources as his abilities to care about, to understand, and to make demands on others—abilities he has used relatively little and of which he has little appreciation. Working as a volunteer is a program that fits well with Dermot's resources.

If the counselor had Dermot get involved in a program for which he had few resources or in a program that demanded very little of him, the outcome might have been far different.

POSTDECISIONAL DEPRESSION

Sometimes people get depressed after making a relatively important decision, like buying a house or a car or choosing a course of action to face up to some problem situation (see Janis & Mann, 1977). They keep asking themselves whether they could have made a better one. They feel sad that their resources are now committed. In a sense, they have given up some of their freedom, and they mourn this. The best way to help clients avoid this trap is to help them start implementing the courses of action they have chosen.

In the next chapter, the two final tasks of Stage III will be considered: the implementation and evaluation of programs.

Chapter 9

Stage III:
Action

Part Two:
Implementing
and Evaluating Programs

This chapter deals with the following topics:

Strategies for helping clients implement programs
Using force-field analysis to discover obstacles and resources
The use of "check" or "think" steps in implementing programs
Training clients to be assertive in implementing programs
Using the principles of behavior in implementing programs
Helping clients use self-contracts
Helping clients get feedback on performance
Helping clients evaluate the helping process
The reasons for evaluation
A method of evaluation
The need to recycle the helping process
The function of Stage I skills in Stage III
The function of Stage II skills in Stage III
Training clients directly in problem-solving skills and methods
Cautions concerning Stage III

Helping Clients Implement Programs: Skills and Strategies

Some clients, once they have a clear idea of just what to do to handle a problem situation, including the steps of the program and a timetable, go ahead and do it. They need little or nothing in terms of further support and challenge from a helper. They either find the resources they need within themselves or they get further support and challenge from the significant others in their lives. Other clients, however, still need support and challenge from a helper at the implementation stage of the problem-solving process. For one reason or another they still feel uncertain about taking action. For instance, they don't trust their own resources or they see the program as extremely demanding. Many clients fall somewhere between these two extremes. For instance, although a client may be able to handle most of the implementation process on her own, she may find that some part of a problem seems so difficult for her to handle that she still needs help.

> Luisa, an unmarried woman in her early fifties, was living in a halfway house after a five-year stay in a mental hospital located in a rural area of the state. At the halfway house she had been trained in various social skills to help her cope with her new urban environment. The aim of the program was to help her develop greater independence with the view, ultimately, of leaving the halfway house and living on her own. One of the programs involved helping her and other residents learn how to use the city transportation system. As part of the program she had already ridden both buses and subways to various locations in the city—for instance, the social security office, the state welfare office, and the park along the lake front— but staff members had up to this point accompanied residents on these journeys. Luisa was now about to "solo" and she was frightened. The counselor helped her understand her fears and encouraged her to take the short and simple trip that was the next part of the program. Luisa wanted to become more independent, but she had learned a great deal of dependence in the hospital and was finding it hard to overcome.

Luisa is one of those clients needing help at the implementation stage. The training programs gave her the basic working knowledge and skills she needed to become more independent, but for her it was a difficult, slow, step-by-step process.

Up to this point in the helping process I have emphasized *strategy*—that is, the overall programs for achieving goals and objectives. In the implementation phase the focus is switched from strategy to *tactics* and *logistics*. Tactics is the art of being able to adapt a plan (program) to the immediate situation. This includes being able to change the plan on the spot in order to handle unforeseen complications. Logistics is the art of being able to provide the *resources* needed for the implementation of any given program. For instance, if money is needed to pay for an evening course, a good logistician will have the money available when it is needed.

> *During the summer Rebecca wanted to take an evening course in statistics so that the first semester of the following school year would be lighter. Having more time would enable her to act in one of the school plays, a high priority for her. Her goal and program were adequate, but she didn't have the money to pay for the course when it was needed. At this university, prepayment for summer courses was the rule. Rebecca had counted on paying for the course from her summer earnings, but this meant that she would not have the money until later. However, she did some quick shopping around and found that the same course was being offered by a community college not too far from where she had intended to go. Her tuition there was minimal because she was a resident of the area the college served. She switched schools.*

In this example, Rebecca keeps to her overall program (strategy). However, she adapts it to an unforeseen circumstance (tactics) by finding another resource (logistics).

All of us have common problems involved in trying to implement programs. We make plans and they seem realistic. We start the initial steps of a program with a good deal of enthusiasm. However, we soon run into tedium, obstacles, and complications. What seemed so easy in the planning stage now seems difficult. We become discouraged, flounder, recover, flounder again, and finally give up, offering ourselves rationalizations as to why we did not want to accomplish those goals anyway.

> *Tina launched herself on a long-needed diet. She found that the novelty of the program carried her along for the first two weeks. However, during the third week the program lost its novelty; her ultimate goal seemed as distant as ever; and she kept telling herself that she was extremely hungry all the time. She became discouraged and depressed. During the middle of the fourth week, she quit the program. She talked about her probably*

> *incurable "glandular imbalance" and the stupid way our culture views "heavier" people.*

Tina did not know the principles of effective implementation and lacked the skills of putting them into practice.

The following strategies will enable you to help clients stick to programs. However, this does not mean that all strategies are to be applied to every client's program or subprogram. Overburdening clients with too much "technology" is obviously self-defeating. Helpers who have the following strategies in their repertoire of helping methods can use them when they judge they will be useful.

Force-Field Analysis

Force-field analysis (Lewin, 1969; Spier, 1973), despite its rather sophisticated name, is, conceptually at least, relatively simple and can be a rather useful tool in helping clients cope with obstacles and develop resources during program or subprogram implementation. Once clients see what their goals are and choose programs to achieve them, they can be helped to discover what forces will keep them from implementing their programs (restraining forces) and what forces will help them implement these programs (facilitating forces). The first step, then, is the *identification* of both restraining and facilitating forces.

RESTRAINING FORCES

Restraining forces are the obstacles that might be encountered during the implementation process; facilitating forces are the resources at hand for moving toward a goal. This process is illustrated in Figure 9–1.

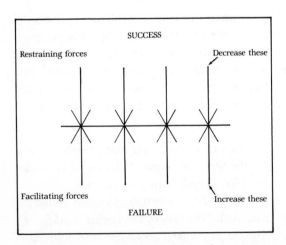

Figure 9–1. Force-field analysis

The identification of possible obstacles to the implementation of a program helps "forewarn" clients.

> *Raul and Maria are a childless couple living in a large midwestern city.*
> *They have been married for about five years and have not been able to have*
> *children. They finally decide that they would like to adopt a child; so they*
> *consult a counselor familiar with adoptions. The counselor helps them*
> *examine their motivation and lifestyle in order to determine whether they*
> *would provide a good home for a child. She then tells them what she*
> *believes their chances are for being accepted as adoptive parents. Their*
> *goal is to adopt a child, and she helps them work out a program, which*
> *includes contacting an agency and preparing themselves for a family-*
> *oriented lifestyle. After the program has been worked out, Raul and Maria,*
> *with the help of the counselor, identify two restraining forces: the negative*
> *feelings that often arise on the part of prospective parents when they are*
> *being scrutinized by an adoption agency and the feelings of helplessness*
> *and frustration caused by the length of time and uncertainty involved in*
> *the process.*

The assumption here is that if clients are aware of some of the "wrinkles" that can accompany any given program, they will be less disoriented when they encounter them. This part of the force-field analysis process is, at its best, a straightforward census of probable pitfalls rather than a self-defeating search for every possible thing that could go wrong.

Once a restraining force is identified, ways of coping with it can be discussed. Sometimes simply being aware of a pitfall is enough to help clients mobilize their resources to handle it. At other times a more explicit coping strategy is needed. For instance, the counselor arranged a couple of role-playing sessions with Raul and Maria in which she played the examiner at the adoption agency and took a "hard line" in her questioning. These rehearsals helped them stay calm during actual questioning periods. The counselor also helped them locate a mutual-help group of parents working their way through the adoption process. The members of the group shared their hopes and frustrations and provided support for one another. Raul and Maria were trained to *cope* with the restraining forces they might encounter on the road toward their goal.

Restraining forces can come from within the clients themselves, from others, and from the social systems of their lives. Sometimes programs go awry because people fail to consider larger environmental factors.

> *Horace had counted heavily on getting a loan to see him through his third*
> *year of college, but he put off applying for it. When he finally applied, it*
> *was a few months after national elections and a predicted sharp upturn in*
> *the rate of inflation had arrived on schedule. He had failed to consider*

> *what happens to federally funded loan programs when elections have been held and when credit is tightened as a means of controlling inflation. By the time he applied for the loan, not only were there no funds available but he was told that it might be a year or more before new applications would be taken. He had to leave school and get a job.*

Both clients and counselors can easily overlook environmental realities unless they are trained to assess them.

FACILITATING FORCES

In a more positive vein, force-field analysis can help clients identify important *resources* to be used in implementing programs. These are the facilitating forces.

> *Shirley was going to stop smoking as part of a physical fitness program. She listed her mother as a facilitating force because she had also decided to quit. Shirley knew that their friendly vying with each other and the mutual encouragement that they got from talking to each other would provide much of the challenge and support they would need.*

Facilitating forces can be persons, as in the previous example, places, as in the next example, or things.

> *Les had let his social life get the best of his academic life. He knew that the coming semester exams would be crucial. If he did not do well, he would be forced to leave school. He listed the smaller study rooms in the library among the facilitating forces in his study program. He found it easier to study when everyone around him was also studying. In the dorm he could always find someone to talk to, and in the library's large study hall there were too many temptations to get together with others. The people who went to the smaller rooms usually meant business.*

Facilitating forces can also be covert or internal.

> *Nora found it extremely depressing to go to her weekly dialysis sessions. She knew that without them she would die but wondered whether it was worth living if she had to depend on a machine. The counselor helped her see how she was making life more difficult for herself by letting herself think such discouraging thoughts. He helped her learn how to think thoughts that would broaden her vision of the world instead of narrowing it to herself and her pain and discomfort. She was a religious person and found in the Bible a rich source of positive thinking. The day before she visited the clinic she began to prepare herself psychologically by reading*

the Bible. Then, as she traveled to the clinic and underwent treatment, she meditated slowly on what she had read.

In this case the client substituted a facilitating force for a restraining one.

CHOOSING COST-EFFICIENT RESTRAINING AND FACILITATING FORCES

Although it is useful to identify the principal facilitating and restraining forces associated with the implementation of any given program, this does not mean that subprograms need to be established to handle each one or that major restraining forces need to be met head on. Sometimes reducing restraining forces that are relatively easy to handle is sufficient.

The principal restraining force facing Shirley and her mother in their attempt to stop smoking was the actual pleasure they received from smoking. They liked to smoke; they liked the taste of cigarettes; they liked to have cigarettes at any kind of break time during the day. They had been using special filters to cut down on the pleasure of smoking. Another restraining force was their being offered cigarettes by their friends. This they could handle more directly. They let their friends know that they had decided to stop smoking and asked them not to offer them cigarettes and, if possible, not to smoke in enclosed rooms when they were together.

The point is that it is useful to determine whether it is cost efficient to try to lessen any given restraining force or bolster any given facilitating force. Good counselors help clients put their resources where the payoff is the greatest.

SYSTEMATIC STEPS IN THE USE OF FORCE-FIELD ANALYSIS

The following four steps may be used. The principal caution, again, is not to overburden any client with too much "technology."

First, *help clients list all the restraining forces that might keep them from participating in the program.* Brainstorming is used in this step.

Deryl was about to join a fraternity as a way of helping himself develop a fuller social life. He identified the restraining forces that he thought might stand in the way of a successful fraternity experience, but he made no attempt to rank them in order of importance. Deryl's list included the following:

- *I'm afraid to meet new people. I feel shy and inadequate, and I end up by running away or making myself as unobtrusive as possible.*
- *I feel that I'm physically unattractive. I fear that I alienate people just by my looks.*

- *I keep thinking of my past social failures—the friends I have alienated—and I fear that the same thing is going to happen in the fraternity.*
- *I don't have anything interesting to say to others. My conversation is dull.*
- *I'm awkward in my manner of presenting myself to others. For instance, because of my shyness and self-consciousness, I end up not listening to what people are saying. Then I can't respond to them, and I feel stupid.*
- *When I'm with people, in my anxiety I talk too much about myself. So others see me as self-centered and boring.*
- *I want others to love me, but few even like me. My needs for attention are great and I'm looking for too much.*

Deryl continues to list any further restraining forces, in whatever order they come tumbling from his mind. When he has finished, he sets this list aside and proceeds to the next step.

This process could be self-defeating if it merely depresses a client and makes him or her think that the program will not work.

The second step is to *help clients list all the facilitating forces at work helping them participate in a program.* This step deals with resources. It forces clients to look at what they have going for themselves.

Deryl asks himself, "What do I have going for me?" He lists everything he can think of that might help him become a good member of the fraternity. His list includes the following:

- *I'm a caring person. I care about others and would like to be helpful when I can.*
- *I'm an intelligent human being. I'm smart enough to know what's called for in social situations, even though I'm awkward in responding.*
- *Tom and Bill are members of the fraternity and they seem to see me as an ordinary guy.*
- *I'm pretty lonely right now, and my motivation to do something about it is high.*
- *I have a number of skills. I'm a good carpenter. I know how to manage finances. I've got something to contribute to the fraternity.*

And Deryl continues to list any other facilitating forces that come to mind.

The client can take the construction of these lists as a homework assignment and then finish filling them out with the counselor's help. Once these lists are reasonably complete, the client is ready for the next step.

The third step is to *have clients underline the forces in each list (facilitating and restraining) that seem most critical with respect to participating in the pro-*

gram. This helps simplify the process. Clients cannot deal with every facilitating and every restraining force. Some are more important than others.

> *Deryl now asks himself, "Which restraining forces are most critical as I join the fraternity? Which facilitating forces can help me the most?" As he reads the list of restraining forces, he notices a most important theme: He keeps telling himself in a variety of ways that he is not the kind of person others will like. He does himself in even before he meets other people. In reading the facilitating forces, he is struck by the fact that two of the members of the fraternity relate to him as they would to anyone else. That is, he begins to see that others are not saying to themselves or to one another all the negative things he's saying to himself.*

Note that the client does not try to juggle all the items on his list all at once. He immediately identifies a self-defeating theme.

Fourth, *help clients identify ways of reducing significant restraining forces and of strengthening significant facilitating forces.* Simple techniques are preferred. Otherwise the whole process gets too complex.

> *Deryl, with the help of the counselor, hits on a simple way of decreasing restraining forces and increasing facilitating forces at the same time. Whenever he finds himself saying self-defeating things to himself about his ability to relate to others, he says to himself internally "Stop!" Then he immediately says to himself something about some positive quality he has that contributes to his ability to relate. He wants to stop apologizing for himself, whether these apologies are directed to himself or others. For instance, when he catches himself saying to himself, "You're not very physically attractive," he says "Stop!" He then says something like, "Listen, you're not ugly or repulsive and even what you look like physically is seen by others in terms of your human qualities, like your ability to care for others. The total package is attractive to others." This technique helps Deryl get rid of a lot of the "static" or "noise" that has long surrounded his relationships to others.*

A WIDER USE OF FORCE-FIELD ANALYSIS

Force-field analysis need not be restricted to the implementation stage of the problem-solving process. It can also be used to establish realistic goals and to choose major programs. For instance, if one of Sissy's career goals is to get a doctorate in psychology, she can examine it in terms of facilitating and restraining forces. An undergraduate grade-point average of 2.3 (on a 4.0 scale) would be a major restraining force, large enough to make her reconsider this goal because few, if any, graduate schools would accept her.

"Check" or "Think" Steps

A practical concept that helps clients bridge between planning and implementing programs is what Carkhuff and Anthony (1979) and Anthony, Pierce, and Cohen (1979) call "check" or "think" steps.

> Check steps are actually "question steps." That is, they indicate to clients what they should be asking themselves during the implementation stage. Check steps are used to guide clients' . . . performance. There are three types of check steps: "before" check steps; "during" check steps; and "after" check steps. As the names suggest, "before" check steps indicate what clients should think about before performing a certain behavior; "during" check steps indicate what clients should think about while performing the step; "after" check steps indicate what clients should think about after performing the step [Anthony, Pierce, & Cohen, 1979, p. 53].

These authors suggest that the last step before program or subprogram implementation is to draw up a list of practical check steps.

The following example deals with Luisa, the person who went to a halfway house after five years in a mental hospital.

> *Luisa has spent a year in the halfway house. She has gotten a good part-time job and is now considering moving out of the halfway house as the next step toward becoming more independent. She does not yet feel ready to live on her own. She would like to live with a family or a friend for a while. The staff of the halfway house acts as an intermediary between its residents and families or individuals who are open to have residents come live with them for a while. Luisa has a couple of friends and knows one family she might ask.*
>
> *With the help of the counselor she decides to talk with a couple of families and a couple of single people. However, it is made clear to both parties that these chats are exploratory. No final decision is being made by either party on the basis of this one talk. This makes Luisa feel free, but she still wants to put her best foot forward in these meetings. The counselor helps her deal with her misgivings by the use of check steps. Luisa thinks it might be important to ask herself the following questions:*
>
> *"Before" check steps:*
> 1. *Is it clear in my mind what I want to say about myself?*
> 2. *Am I going to these meetings with an open mind—that is, without already feeling rejected?*
>
> *"During" check steps:*
> 1. *Am I trying to be myself instead of some person I think these people would like me to be?*

2. *Am I listening to these people, trying to understand their point of view?*
3. *Am I ready to see some negative signs without getting down on myself or thinking ill of these people?*
4. *What do I do if people seem to be putting me down or making a case of me—that is, what do I do with my feelings?*

"After" check steps:
1. *Am I avoiding letting myself get depressed because everything did not go perfectly?*
2. *Is there anything I'd like to add to what I said to them?*
3. *Do I have any further questions of the people I talked to?*

Obviously, check steps should be added to the program if it seems that they will be helpful. Cluttering up the program-development process with unneeded check steps can make clients overly self-conscious. A force-field analysis of the facilitating and restraining factors in program implementation can help pinpoint needed check steps.

Assertiveness in Implementation

The implementation phase, by definition, places demands on clients to be assertive to a greater or lesser degree. If change is to take place, clients must cease being "patients" and become "agents" on their own behalf. Lange and Jakubowski (1976) suggest that there are a number of basic causes for a lack of assertiveness on the part of clients. First, *clients may not know what they want.* If clients' preferences, desires, and feelings are unclear, then they will either not act or will act aimlessly. This highlights the need for both clear goals and clear programs. Without these, action on the part of clients is a random process.

Second, *clients may hold irrational beliefs that stand in the way of assertive behavior.* Often clients are not even aware of the beliefs that keep them from implementing programs or slow them down. They include such sentiments as the following:

- My rights are not important; at least they are not as important as the rights of others.
- I am a fragile person. If I act, I will hurt myself.
- Others are fragile. If I act, I will hurt them.
- I am not entitled to express my own opinions either verbally or in action.
- If I act assertively, I will lose the affection and approval of others.
- If I act assertively, others will see me as "out of role" and consider me stupid or foolish.
- If I act, I might fail and failure is always disgraceful.

If it is clear to you that a client is plagued by irrational beliefs that tend to thwart action, then "cognitive restructuring" procedures may be useful both before and during program implementation (see Bard, 1980; Ellis & Harper, 1975; Goldfried & Goldfried, 1980; Lange & Jakubowski, 1976; Meichenbaum & Genest, 1980).

Third, *clients may lack skills and practice in assertiveness.* There is always some kind of "leap" between planning and action. For some clients this leap seems too much, especially if they have a history of nonassertiveness. Techniques such as rehearsal and role-playing (see Lange & Jakubowski, 1976, Chaps. 6 and 7) can help clients bridge the gap. Counselors who take a training-as-treatment approach to helping first make sure that clients have the skills they need to be assertive and then help clients make assertiveness demands on themselves throughout the helping process. In this case moving from planning to action is less of a leap for clients than it is in approaches to helping in which clients take a much more passive role.

Fourth, *clients may stumble over their feelings and emotions.* They often feel overwhelmed by their feelings and emotions. When action stimulates emotions they are not used to handling well, they retreat. Feelings interfere with their ability to act assertively. According to Lange and Jakubowski (1976, p. 275), this can be seen as a skills deficit: "People may lack strategies for coping with their own excessive anxiety, anger, and guilt—feelings which interfere with their ability to act assertively." Clients may fail to implement programs because they have not developed strategies to cope with normal, but action-inhibiting, feelings.

> *Luisa, the middle-aged woman trying to make her way back into society, begins having her meetings. In a meeting with a single person slightly older than herself, she feels as if she's being treated like a child. She gets angry but manages to keep it to herself. She sees no use in sabotaging the whole program just because this woman lacks social intelligence.*

Because Luisa had formulated the "during" check step —"What do I do if people seem to be putting me down during the meeting?"—she knew how to handle her anger. Instead of indulging in self-defeating angry remarks, she kept telling herself that she was glad that she found out what kind of person this was before it was too late.

Clients can tend to see themselves as the victims of their emotions. They develop an irrational belief, one that all of us fall prey to at one time or another, that "I can't control my feelings." They say "I can't" instead of "I don't." Failure to take responsibility for one's feelings and emotions is ultimately self-defeating (see Passons, 1975, pp. 186–192).

First, he [that is, the person who does not see himself or herself as responsible for and in some way able to control his or her feelings] is "at the mercy" of his feelings rather than being the creator or master of them. As such, an unpleasant degree of powerlessness and, in some cases, hopelessness is experienced. Second, the person will be unable to dismiss or substitute an alternate feeling for one which is inappropriate or destructive for him. These both involve choices which the person is not aware of having. Third, the person will not know how he brought about his pleasant feelings and thereby does not have ready access to them [Passons, 1975, p. 186].

Some clients are so used to seeing their problems as being caused by others that they resist the idea of responsibility for their own feelings. Passons outlines some exercises that can help clients experience some kind of power over their emotional lives. These exercises can be used as preparation for program implementation.

Although it is true that feelings and emotions arise spontaneously, it is also true that people can exercise some degree of control over the stimuli that elicit emotions and over the intensity of feelings and emotions once they do arise. For many clients this is a novel idea, and their first reaction might be one of skepticism. But research and practice have shown that they can learn simple "environmental planning" (Thoresen & Mahoney, 1974) or "stimulus control" (Goldiamond, 1965) methods to decrease the intensity of the emotion-arousing event. For instance, one client found that whenever she talked to her ex-husband alone, she would let her anger get the better of her. However, when she talked to him with at least one other person present, she took a more relaxed approach to their discussions. On the occasions when she would be alone with him, she found that "thought-stopping" methods (Cautela & Wisocki, 1977; Hackman & McLean, 1975; Rimm & Masters, 1974) helped quite a bit. That is, internally she would yell "Stop!" to herself when she began to dwell on the aspects of his behavior that were stimulating her anger. In this case, she could not control the stimuli, but she could control the amount of attention she paid to them.

Fifth, *clients may lack the ability to discriminate between assertiveness and compliance and between assertiveness and aggression.* As I pointed out earlier, clients often have difficulty seeing themselves as others see them. That is one of the reasons why the "new perspectives" step in the helping process is so important. But even when clients come to see that what they consider assertive in their behavior is actually a form of compliance or aggression, they find it difficult to translate these insights into behavior. If this is the case, then it is important for them to attempt to translate their insights into action *during the counseling sessions* so that they are prepared to make accurate discriminations during the implementation phase. In addition to this, it is important for them to get ongoing feedback from others as they attempt to implement programs.

Helping clients become more assertive is another way of saying helping them take reasonable risks. Clients are usually not big risk takers. If they are to take reasonable risks, they may need some kind of structure to help them do so.

Behavior Principles

Counselors can help clients make the principles of behavior, such as reinforcement, punishment, extinction, avoidance, and shaping (all these were considered briefly in Chapter 1) work for instead of against them as they put efforts into implementing programs.

REINFORCEMENT

Clients are more likely to embark on any given step of a program if they have a clear idea of the reward associated with it. It is often not enough that some distant goal appear rewarding. It is often necessary to help clients identify both the intrinsic and the extrinsic reinforcements or rewards available at each step of any given program. Perhaps one of the best things a helper can do is to join with a client in celebrating the successful completion of a step or in savoring what can be learned from even unsuccessful or partially successful attempts to implement a program.

> Randall is seeing a counselor associated with the county probation office. He has been given a suspended sentence for petty larceny and possession of drugs. One of his goals is to get a job, and the program leading to this goal includes identifying job possibilities, ranking them according to desirability, and checking them out one by one either through telephone calls or face-to-face interviews. He goes to his first interview with a relatively high degree of enthusiasm but comes back somewhat dejected because they didn't think he was qualified for the job. He discusses his principal learning with his counselor—that is, finding a job is a full-time job in itself. Because he is going to be repeating the interview process, perhaps a number of times, the following question arises: What reinforcement or reward will help him sustain his search? At this point, the reward of actually getting a job is too distant. He and the counselor explore the possibilities. Some intrinsic reward may come from knowing that he has put in a good day's work searching for a job. There will also be the support and encouragement he receives from the counselor for sticking to a task that can be discouraging. They also discuss the possibility of his participation in a weekly mutual-

support group of people like himself looking for employment. Randall also thinks it important to reward himself for putting in a good day's search or even after each job interview in which he feels he does a reasonable job presenting himself as an applicant. He thinks of such things as watching television, going to movies, spending time with friends, eating favorite foods, reading magazines, having a few beers, and other pleasurable activities that might serve as extrinsic rewards. He then sets about choosing what rewards he thinks will work best and making them contingent on successfully completing substeps in his job search.

You might say that an example like this is unrealistic in that it assumes a great deal of cooperation from the kind of client not known for his or her cooperativeness, and you are probably right. The example is used to illustrate the principle that in the implementation of programs, rewards are important. Reluctant and resistant clients, too, do things because they get something out of it. If they do not cooperate, they obviously find not cooperating more rewarding (or less punishing) than cooperating. The issue of resistance to helping will be discussed in the final chapter.

Even though everybody works for rewards, there are great differences in what appeals to people as rewards. Rewards may be simple things, but if the client sees them as phony, they will soon prove to be meaningless. On the other hand, Premack (1965) showed that there are more rewards in the natural environment than we might first suspect. He demonstrated that clients can use any high-frequency behavior that they would select in a free-choice situation as a reinforcer for desirable but low-frequency behavior. For instance, if taking a shower is a relatively high-frequency behavior, it can be used as a reinforcer for cleaning up the kitchen, a relatively low-frequency behavior. If reading the paper is a relatively high-frequency behavior, it can be used as a reinforcer for telephoning friends, a relatively low-frequency behavior for a shy but lonely person. Counselors do well to help clients appreciate the power of the "Premack principle" and its usefulness in identifying extrinsic rewards that fit into the natural patterns of their lives.

Ideally, once self-enhancing behaviors are learned and developed, they become self-sustaining—that is, they generate their own positive consequences so that there is no longer any need for programmed reinforcement. If Kelly, who is fearful of dating, embarks on a realistic program to foster relationships with men, the rewards found in relating to men may sustain her behavior. There are, of course, certain disagreeable tasks in life that may always demand some kind of programmed reinforcement. The person who must submit to dialysis if she is to stay alive may have to engage in an ongoing search for reinforcers.

Principle. Don't immediately blame clients who do not participate in programs. It may well be that they do not see strong enough short-term or even long-term incentives for doing so. Do work at helping clients find the kinds of intrinsic and extrinsic incentives that will help them stick to programs.

PUNISHMENT OR SANCTIONS

As we have seen, the use of punishment is ordinarily a relatively poor way of changing behavior. There are, of course, exceptions to this. "Many of us have been brought up in the school of 'sin and suffer.' Consequently, self-punishment in the wake of symptomatic behavior may seem like a just reward and, paradoxically, *increase* the future likelihood of the behavior" (Rudestam, 1980, p. 128). In this case, the grief and frustration associated with searching for a job would actually increase the likelihood that the client would continue his or her search. However, it is best not to count heavily on the "sin and suffer" school in clients, even when they seem to be good students of that school.

There is, however, some evidence that self-punishment or sanctions, especially when used in conjunction with rewards, can be effective in changing behavior (see Axelrod, Hall, Weis, & Rohrer, 1971; Bayer, 1972; Cautela, 1967; Mahoney, 1972; Mastellone, 1974; Wisocki, 1970, for examples). Rudestam (1980, p. 131) gives an example of useful self-punishment through the withdrawal of a reinforcer and the use of an aversive consequence: "To discourage smoking, a notoriously difficult target behavior, you might reduce the positive consequences of smoking by going to the basement to smoke and increase the negative consequences by donating some money to charity each time you finish a pack of cigarettes." In a similar way, Randall's contract with himself might include denying himself television in the evening if he fails to go to a job interview during the day.

Rudestam (1980) offers the following suggestions in the use of self-punishment:

1. "To use self-punishment directly, choose an aversive consequence that is easily administered, that is sufficiently potent to terminate the behavior it follows, and that does not have an enduring effect. Ask yourself what negative consequence is apt to discourage or reduce your problem behavior" (p. 129).

   Moira was avoiding a complete physical checkup even though certain physical symptoms were persisting. She planned taking a weekend trip to see a very good friend. She contracted with herself to put off the trip until she had had the checkup.

2. "The punishment must follow the target behavior each and every time. Invoke the negative consequence as early in the behavioral chain as possible. . . . After you have settled on a specific aversive consequence, use it immediately and consistently" (p. 130).

Alvin manipulated others into doing what he wanted to do. While this produced short-term gains, in the long run it was self-defeating. People began to avoid him or to be very cautious when they were with him. He was a staunch Democrat. Whenever it was brought to his attention that he was being manipulative, he sent a check for five dollars to some Republican campaign fund. He kept envelopes addressed to Republican headquarters to remind him of his tendency to manipulate others. Keeping addressed envelopes also enabled him to use this form of self-punishment immediately.

3. "Be sure that the penalty you pay for undesirable behavior is something you can afford to lose" (p. 130).

Beatrice was both gregarious and a heavy eater. She decided that whenever she even opened the door of the refrigerator after supper, she would call a friend and cancel some upcoming social event. She soon discovered that she was punishing not just herself but others. Also, on the days that this self-punishment technique made people disappear from her life, she was more tempted than ever to eat. She soon discovered that this form of self-punishment was something she could ill afford.

4. "It is not sufficient to punish negative behavior. You also need to encourage alternative, more desirable behaviors by reinforcing them" (p. 131).

Constance, an elderly widow, would put off her flexibility exercises when her arthritis flared up even a bit. She contracted with herself not to turn on music until she had done them. The times she did her exercise even though she was feeling pains in her joints she rewarded herself with a brief long-distance call to a close friend who had moved to a neighboring state. It was a luxury, but one she could still afford.

If a client is a self-punishing person, then self-punishment might well be a potent tool for staying on track in implementing programs, but this could merely reinforce a behavior pattern that is ultimately self-defeating. It might be a much more useful tool for a person whose tendency is to be self-indulgent. Still, the use of punishment as a means of changing behavior is a tricky business. If you are to help clients use this form of behavioral control in implementing programs, have a thorough understanding of it both in theory and in practice. This includes estimating its value in your own life. (See Johnston, 1972, on the positive uses of punishment.)

Principle. Although punishment is usually a poor way of changing behavior, in some cases clients can be helped to stick to programs by the reasonable use of self-punishment. However, because punishment is related to decreasing and eliminating self-defeating behavior, make sure clients couple this approach with rewards for carrying out program steps.

AVOIDANCE

Avoidance mechanisms are potent restraining forces in the implementation of programs. Avoidance will take place if the rewards for *not* doing something are stronger than the rewards for doing it. In your dealings with clients at the implementation stage, it can be a mistake to confuse avoidance with ill will. All of us have a tendency to put off the difficult or distasteful and we break out of that pattern only under certain conditions. If clients are not implementing some step of a program, if they are putting it off, or if they are implementing it in only a desultory way, use the following checklist:

- What punishing consequences are involved with implementing any given step of a program and what is being done to minimize them?
- What rewards are there for *not* implementing a step and how can these be neutralized?
- Is there a reasonable but firm time line for completing the step?
- Are there rewards for completing the step and are these clear to the client and suited to his or her needs and wants?

Principle. Never underestimate the power of rewards associated with not doing things. If clients are avoiding participating in programs, or in subparts of them, help them increase the rewarding consequences and decrease the punishing consequences of participating.

EXTINCTION

If the client sees any given step as neither rewarding *nor* punishing, then it is likely that the client's behavior will *extinguish*—that is, grind to a halt. If this is the case, clients will often express ignorance of why they have stopped implementing a program.

Counselor: Tell me how your diet has been going.

Client: Well, I think I've sort of fallen off the wagon.

Counselor: You found it too difficult.

Client: No, it was reasonable. I wasn't starving myself. In fact, when I was busy, I didn't even notice I was on it.

Counselor: Then it's not clear why you let it go.

Client: I don't know. It wasn't really a decision. I just trailed off.

This client felt neither any punishing effects from dropping the diet *nor* any particular reward in sticking to it. Dieting behavior extinguished.

SHAPING

As we have seen, shaping can refer both to rewarding successive approximations to a desired behavior or goal and to the proper sequencing of behaviors toward a goal together with seeing to it that each step in the sequence is properly reinforced. Consider the following interchanges:

Counselor A: Perhaps we could review how your diet is going.

Client (sheepishly): Well, I've been eating over 2500 calories a day and it seemed reasonable to drop down to 1500 for a few weeks. But to be honest, this past week, I've averaged about 1900 a day.

Counselor A: You probably feel bad about violating the contract you made with yourself. Let's review the contract once more and find out what's going wrong.

Counselor B: What do you think would be best to focus on today?

Client (sheepishly): I think I should talk about my diet. I had contracted to move down from 2500 to 1500 calories a day. And I haven't done it. I've managed to drop only to around 1900 a day.

Counselor B: You sound a bit down on yourself.

Client: Well, I think I should be. I did fail.

Counselor B: You talk as if you had failed totally.

Client: Well, I did *something*, but not everything I wanted to do.

Counselor B: Well, you *didn't* do something, but you also *did* something. Do you think it might be best to celebrate what you did, those 600 calories a day you didn't consume? And then we can look at ways you might tighten up your contract.

Counselor B chooses to reinforce an approximation to a goal rather than dwell on a contractual failure. The difference between the two counselors is not that the latter is soft and the former is hard-nosed. The important thing is the actual implementation of programs that achieve goals. In this example, shaping in the sense of rewarding an approximation to a goal seems to make more sense than some kind of rigid pursuit of a contract.

Principle. Help clients who are having difficulty involving themselves in programs move through small steps toward their goals. Help them emphasize what they are doing right.

Self-Contracts

As we have seen, a contract, whether implicit or explicit, gives direction to (or is the cause of the lack of direction in) the helping process. Contracts are also useful in specific ways at the implementation stage. Clients can keep themselves on track in implementing programs by setting up contracts with themselves that specify precisely what they are to do and indicate rewards for success and sanctions for failures (see Cormier & Cormier, 1979, pp. 506–512; Kanfer, 1980; Rudestam, 1980, pp. 122–127). Many clients find it rewarding to make contracts with themselves and keep them. They see it as a sign of their personal integrity. Such contracts are especially helpful for more difficult aspects of a program; they help focus clients' energies. If a self-contract, directly or indirectly, involves things that others must do, then these others need to be aware of and agree to its stipulations. Cormier and Cormier (1979, pp. 507, 509) outline the basic features of a contract:

- The contract terms should be negotiated, not proclaimed, by all involved parties (client, counselor, significant others).
- The contract terms should be clear to all involved parties. The behavior to be achieved and an acceptable criterion level should be specified.
- The contract should include a balance of rewards and sanctions appropriate to the desired behavior.
- Oral and written commitment to the contract should be obtained.
- The client (and any other person involved) should carry out the contractual procedures systematically and regularly.
- The contract should include a recording system (a progress log) that specifies the desired behavior, the amount (frequency or duration) of the

behavior, and the rewards and sanctions administered. If possible, the recording system should be verified by one other person.
- The contract should be reviewed at a later time and revised if necessary.
- The counselor should provide reinforcement to the client as the client implements the contractual procedures.

These provisions apply both to the helping contract and to self-contracts. The focus now, however, is on the latter.

> *Eunice and Edgar are involved in a deteriorating marriage. The assessment stage indicates that the problems are multiple. One aim they both agree to is that the present chaos in the home needs to be reduced. For instance, Eunice does very little housework (neither does Edgar) and Edgar comes and goes as he pleases, missing meals (however poorly prepared) without notice. They seem to be deeply committed to punishing each other by this chaotic behavior. An initial contract to which both agree includes Eunice's keeping the house clean and orderly for a week and Edgar's sticking to a schedule that allows him to take care of work commitments but still leaves him time at home. Actually, both are committing themselves to self-contracts, because each agrees to carry out his or her program despite what the other does.*

In this example the counselor and couple could use Cormier and Cormier's self-contract checklist to draw up and implement their agreement. When a contract is drawn up, it should be stipulated when it is to be reviewed.

In this case the contract proves most useful in introducing a degree of order into their home life. Neither counselor nor clients assume that fulfilling these contracts will handle all the problems of the relationship. What they are trying to do is to create the kind of *climate* that will enable them to begin to work together in sorting out issues that are critical to their marriage.

Feedback on Performance

Gilbert (1978, p. 175), in his book on human competence, claims that "improved information has more potential than anything else I can think of for creating more competence in the day-to-day management of performance." If clients are to be successful in implementing programs, they need adequate information about how well they are performing. The purpose of feedback is not to pass judgment on the client's performance but rather to provide guidance and support. Feedback can be

- *Confirmatory*, when it lets clients know when they are on course—that is, moving successfully through the steps of a program toward a goal

- *Corrective*, when it provides clients with information they need to get back on course if they have strayed
- *Motivating*, when it points out the *consequences* of both adequate and inadequate program implementation

According to Gilbert (1978, p. 179; emphasis added), good feedback does not take away the client's responsibility. He urges those who give feedback to "supply as much backup information as needed to help people troubleshoot *their own* performance." Furthermore, when people give corrective feedback, it should be *concrete*—that is, it should "relate various aspects of poor performance to specific remedial actions."

Client: I can't seem to control myself. I want to stay on the diet, but sometimes almost without knowing what I'm doing I find myself eating. I followed it only a few times earlier in the week.

Counselor A: You don't seem to be motivated enough to stop overeating. I think the diet plan we worked out together was a good one.

Client: I think it was a good one, too. I seem to be lying to myself when I say that I want to lose weight.

Client: I can't seem to control myself. I want to stay on the diet, but sometimes almost without knowing what I'm doing I find myself eating.

Counselor B: Tell me as concretely as possible what happened.

Client: (She describes what she did and didn't do the previous week with respect to dieting.)

Counselor B: Tell me what you think went wrong.

Client: Well, I just blew it. I bought too much food, for one thing.

Counselor B: The times you followed your diet were early in the week, when your enthusiasm was still high. It seems that you showed yourself you can do it when the incentives are there. As for the rest of the week, I see two things. First of all, you forgot to set up immediate rewards for keeping to your diet schedule and perhaps mild "punishments" for not doing so. Second, you probably are right in thinking that you can do something about stimulus control. You could not have eaten what you did if it had not been in the refrigerator! But that seems fairly clear to you now.

Counselor A's "feedback" is vague and at least mildly judgmental. Counselor B offers some confirmatory and some corrective feedback without taking a judgmental tone.

Don't wait for perfect performance before giving encouraging or confirmatory feedback. Counselor B, in her last response, follows Krumboltz and Thoresen's (1976) suggestion to use Homme's "sandwiching" technique for feedback. The first "slice of bread" is some kind of encouragement or reinforcement for what was done right. The "filling" is some description of what was done wrong or some suggestion for improving performance. Finally, the second "slice of bread" is some kind of reinforcement.

According to McKeachie (1976, p. 824), feedback will be helpful if three conditions are met:

1. *Client motivation.* The person receiving the feedback is motivated to improve. But as Gilbert (1978) and Watson and Tharp (1981) suggest, lack of client motivation should not immediately be suspected if the implementation process is running into difficulty. Motivation has two aspects: the client's internal "motives" or values and the *incentives* that bring these motives to life. If motivation seems to be a problem, look first at issues related to incentives, reinforcement, punishment, avoidance, extinction, and shaping before concluding that the client is not motivated.

2. *Moderate dosages.* Feedback should provide an adequate, but not an excessive, dose of information. Again, shaping here is important. If clients need a great deal of feedback, give it to them in doses they can handle. Information overload is a punishment rather than an incentive. In counselor training groups, I consistently see novice trainees' tendency to give one another vague and long-winded feedback.

3. *Suggestions.* Good feedback helps clients identify and implement alternative approaches to carrying out a program. This does not necessarily mean that the helper always comes up with alternatives. Effective helpers leave as much of the responsibility for change as possible with the client. In feedback sessions, clients need not be given alternatives but can be helped to explore alternatives.

There are at least three sources of feedback available to clients. One is the *clients themselves.* Effective helping is an enabling process. It teaches clients how to monitor their own behavior as they implement programs. Seeing themselves become more and more responsible for their own behavior can be rewarding. They can be trained to give themselves all three kinds of feedback—confirmatory, corrective, and motivating. However, if they are to do this, they must first be working toward clear and concrete goals and have a firm grasp of the step-by-step programs leading to these goals. If goals and programs are general and vague, then feedback from whatever source will necessarily be general and vague. Second, as we have seen before, clients can learn to say the "right" sentences to themselves instead of self-defeating ones. Sentences such as "You're on track" or "You really did that well" can be an important source of reinforcement.

The counselor is a second source. Counselors are important sources of all three kinds of feedback. Counselors who fail to give feedback often lack the skills reviewed earlier: primary-level accurate empathy, information giving, advanced accurate empathy, confrontation, and immediacy. Sometimes counselors, falling prey to the MUM effect (described in an earlier chapter), fail to give direct, unequivocal feedback because they are afraid of clients' reactions. And yet clients usually find feedback, even corrective feedback, rewarding rather than punishing because, if done right, it is most useful in helping them achieve their goals.

Ideally, clients find one or more *persons in their everyday lives* on whom they can count for supportive and challenging feedback. I suggested earlier that a standard part of the counseling process is to help clients get "into community." Getting into community includes developing feedback resources.

> *Lamar had developed a drinking problem. He was not an alcoholic, but when he drank, he became a different person. Ordinarily, he was personable and thoughtful. When he drank heavily, he became harsh, loud, sarcastic, and manipulative. It became embarrassing to dine out with him. Finally, his wife and a couple of friends talked to him about the problem. They told him that although ordinarily he was a person of great interpersonal power (first "slice of bread"), once he began drinking heavily, he lost it all; and they went on to describe his annoying behavior and how they felt about being with him at such times (the "filling"). They finished by telling him that when he drank moderately, he was great fun to be with and that everyone had a better time because of his pleasant rather than mordant wit. At his request, they agreed to give him preventive feedback in drinking situations. For instance, in a social situation when he had been drinking moderately but had had enough to drink, his wife or a friend would say something like "It's fun being with you right now." This served as a cue to him that he was nearing his limit. He gradually learned to make that discrimination himself. All this was done without making Lamar the "identified patient" in his group of friends.*

Direct, unequivocal feedback in day-to-day living is not a common commodity. Counselors can help clients develop such resources.

Helping Clients Evaluate the Helping Process

There are at least seven reasons for evaluating any kind of human endeavor, including the helping endeavor. First is *routine*. One reason evaluation is done is that it is expected as part of the complete planning or problem-solving process. This is the assumption of the helping process described in this book. Helpers who fail to evaluate their own performance and who fail to help clients evaluate their participation in the helping process are leaving the helping process unfinished. Without evaluation, clients may persist in the performance of an inadequate course of action instead of trying to find out what the trouble is and correcting it.

Second is *failure*. If any given program seems to be failing, then evaluation addresses the question: What's going wrong and what can be done to correct it?

> *Donna had been convicted of child abuse and was seeing a probation counselor. After a number of sessions, her child was returned to her custody. A few weeks later neighbors called the police because of the noise they heard coming from her apartment. When they arrived, they found the child battered once more.*

The sooner any trouble with a program is discovered, the better.

Partial success is a third reason. If there is some success, but it is not as complete, efficient, or quick as expected, then the evaluation process asks such questions as the following: What can be done to improve the program? What further goals and programs are needed to handle the initial problem situation?

> *Carl came to the counselor lonely and depressed. Together they worked out goals and program steps related to the mission of getting Carl "into community." The program was successful in that Carl no longer felt lonely, but his chronic depression did not lift. It had been assumed that his loneliness was the cause of his depression. Now the helping process focused on his depression. After a new program was in operation for a while, Carl was still depressed, but not as intensely as before. He and the counselor searched for ways of handling his depression.*

Note here two different kinds of partial success, one related to goals, the other related to a program.

Fourth is *complete success*. If the program has met all expectations, then evaluation can be addressed to this rather pleasant question: Where else in life can the models, strategies, skills, and techniques that produced such success be used?

> *Elsa had become a burden to herself and others by constantly complaining about her painful arthritis. A counselor taught her some basic principles of self-control that enabled her to reduce her complaining behavior drastically. This led to an immediate improvement in her relationships with others, which she found most rewarding. Because these self-control strategies worked so well, she and the counselor during the evaluation process decided to see whether the techniques could be used to control not only the complaining behavior but the pain itself. She discovered that people were actually using the principles of behavior in pain-management programs (Fordyce, 1976; Shealy, 1976; Wang, 1977).*

Complete success in a smaller project can suggest approaches to a larger project.

New technologies are another reason for evaluation. If new models, strategies, skills, and techniques have been used in a program, then evaluation can answer the question: Which set of technologies is the most useful?

> *Nelson was extremely shy. He wanted to involve himself with women but was so anxious that he felt he could not. Talking about his problem and setting goals seemed to help a little, but his progress was very slow and he quickly lost ground any week he failed to see the counselor. The counselor, who had been schooled in the nondirective-counseling tradition, felt frustrated enough to try a modest "multimodal" (Lazarus, 1976) approach to helping. She helped Nelson learn general relaxation techniques; she helped him state in very specific ways the fears he had with respect to women and used some desensitization techniques to help him manage these fears; she taught him self-reinforcement procedures. Their evaluation sessions included evaluating the "new" technologies.*

In this case the counselor was evaluating her approach to the helping process.

Sixth is *outside demand.* Some agency may require evaluation. More frequently than ever demands are being placed on helpers to demonstrate that what they are doing with clients is actually helpful. Insurance companies and government agencies are reluctant to provide funds for procedures that cannot be validated. Global statements about a client's "progress" are not acceptable.

Accountability is a seventh reason. One of the most important, it is an ethical issue. Knapper (1978, p. 27) defines accountability as "the delineation and specification of program outcomes in terms of their concomitant cost factors." Because, as noted in Chapter 1, there are grave misgivings concerning the efficacy of helping processes, helpers need to discover whether they are in fact helping—that is, whether helping is "for better or for worse" (Carkhuff & Anthony, 1979; Carkhuff & Berenson, 1976).

An Evaluation Method

Counselors and clients need an evaluation method that proceeds organically from the helping process rather than one that is "stuck on" from outside. This method should be simple enough to be used by the client and yet thorough enough to meet the demands of the helping process.

The following four questions relating to evaluation proceed organically from a problem-solving approach to helping:

1. *Program participation.* Is the client participating in the program? To what degree?

Physical fitness is part of Ivan's overall program and running is one component of physical fitness. He has a schedule of gradually increasing the distance he runs and shortening the time. Ivan is running every day and he is sticking to the schedule. It is clear that he is participating fully in the program.

2. *Program effectiveness.* Is the goal being accomplished through participation in *this* program? To what degree? This kind of evaluation measures progress *toward* a goal.

Ivan's goal is to run three miles per day in under thirty minutes at least five days per week. He uses a step-by-step program to achieve his goal (Collingwood & Carkhuff, 1976) and sees himself making progress week by week. It is clear to Ivan that his present program is a good one—that is, it is helping him make steady progress toward his goal.

3. *Goal achievement.* To what extent has the goal been achieved through participation in the program? This kind of question measures the quality of goal *achievement.*

Obtaining a satisfactory job is one of Randall's goals. By sticking with a job-search program, he finally gets a job and works at it for several weeks. He then evaluates the job according to the criteria he used to make the term satisfactory as concrete as possible. He sees that the job is satisfactory in most respects. However, it violates one criterion. The job demands a great deal of overtime, and Randall preferred a job that demanded no more than 45 hours per week. His job-search program led to the achievement of his goal, but he is not fully satisfied with the goal.

Because here the goal has not been fully achieved, the client must determine whether it is worth the effort to seek a reduction in overtime work.

4. *Problem resolution or need fulfillment.* Is the original problem situation being handled or is the original need being met through the achievement of the goal(s) that had been established? To what degree? This is the ultimate question, for it deals with the reason for starting the helping process in the first place.

Ivan came to the counselor because he felt socially marginal. It seems that his friends and associates could not tolerate his self-centeredness. An assessment of the problem situation showed that Ivan exercised little self-control over his impulses. He ate too much and got little exercise. The physical fitness program was geared not just to his health but to the broader accomplishment of helping him increase his self-control in

> *interpersonal transactions. Ivan finds that making demands on himself
> in the area of physical fitness and living up to them has a generalization
> effect: he is more in control of himself in other areas of life. For
> instance, he is much less impulsive in pushing his needs and wants
> unilaterally in social situations. The physical fitness program contributes
> to the goal of increased self-control. The accomplishment of this goal
> contributes to handling his original complaint. Becoming less pushy
> makes him much more acceptable to others, and he no longer feels
> marginal.*

In all four kinds of evaluation, clients need two skills: (1) the ability to identify the consequences of their actions (results, products, outcomes, accomplishments) and (2) the ability to compare these results to a standard (Heppner, 1978). Evaluation is related to the issue of *feedback*, discussed earlier in this chapter. Clients need accurate feedback on the consequences of their actions if they are to evaluate their participation in the helping process effectively. The following *standards* can be used in evaluating the outcomes of helping:

1. The clearly and behaviorally stated steps of programs and subprograms. If these steps are not clear, then it is impossible to determine whether the client is engaging in them.
2. The clearly stated goal or goals to which programs are leading. If the goals are not clear, it is impossible to determine whether they are being accomplished or not and to what degree.
3. The clearly defined need or problem situation with which the problem-solving process began. If the problem situation has not been clearly defined, then it is impossible to determine whether the achievement of goals contributes to the solution or management of the problem. Clients and helpers need not only a clear conception of these standards but also the ability to compare behavior and accomplishments to these standards.

Recycling

If clients see that they are not participating effectively in a program, that the program is not leading to the goal, that the goal is not satisfactorily achieved through the completion of the program, or that an achieved goal does not lead to fulfillment of the original need or contribute satisfactorily to the management of the original problem situation, then some kind of recycling of the problem-solving process is in order. I have frequently suggested that problem solving is not a magic linear process that works automatically, but then there are few such magical processes in life. Just as researchers recycle their experimental processes (with an occasional dramatic breakthrough) until they achieve their experimental goals, so people recycle problem-solving procedures (with an occasional dramatic breakthrough) until they are satisfied with the way they are meeting their needs and handling their problem situations.

In order to clarify the stages, skills, and techniques of this model, I have used oversimplified examples, often with highly successful outcomes. In real life, solutions work moderately well; there are usually neither spectacular successes nor spectacular failures. For instance, a marriage relationship will improve in a number of ways but still be far from perfect. When expectations are not met in the helping process, decisions need to be made with respect to recycling the entire process or any part of it. The decision to recycle should be based on some realistic expectation that more work will produce proportionate gains. Counselors have to decide whether it is worth their time and effort to continue to help their clients. Clients must decide whether more work is worth the expense in terms of time, energy, and money. A challenging question is: What will happen if I fail to face this problem situation? What is the worst thing that can happen?

The need to recycle, then, is not a sign of failure; it is part of the human condition. Recycling is part of its human messiness. To say this, however, is not the same as encouraging sloppiness in the use of this helping model and its methods. Recycling that comes from ineptness is not the same as recycling that comes from the fact that it is impossible to take into consideration everything that is to happen in a person's life, especially because that life is affected by others and by all the person's social settings and systems.

Use of Stage I and Stage II Skills in Stage III

Stage I Skills in Stage III

Stage I skills remain important in Stage III. As the client begins to act, problems associated with program implementation arise. Clients experience change as both growthful and painful. They meet with both success and failure: for instance, Carlita, who is trying to do without alcohol, makes headway in her struggle with drink but fails on occasion or sometimes sees the world as a very empty place without alcohol. Another client works to change his negative attitude toward his wife but experiences no significant change in his wife's hostile attitude.

The very fact that a client acts to manage some problem can uncover new problems or further dimensions of problems that have already been explored. For instance, a man improves his relationship with his wife but begins to have trouble with his son. As the one relationship improves, the other seems to deteriorate.

Stage I skills are essential here because the problems that arise from the execution of action programs must be listened to and understood. Sometimes action programs fail because helpers abandon clients once the action program is initiated. This is strange because at this time many clients need a great deal of support. Although it would be ideal if this support were to come naturally from the client's inner resources and his or her environment, this is frequently not the case. Stage I skills, then, are important instruments of reinforcement and support. The client's successes, too, must be listened to and affirmed.

Stage II Skills in Stage III

This developmental model is, as we have seen, cumulative: The skills at each stage are necessary in each subsequent stage. In my discussion of Stage II skills, I used the word *tentative* to describe the initial use of such challenging skills as advanced accurate empathy, helper self-sharing, confrontation, and immediacy. I stated that pains should be taken not to overwhelm the client, for Stage II interactions can be "strong medicine." Stage II is geared to helping clients get a more objective view of themselves and their world—that is, to help them understand themselves in a way that lets them see the need for change. When counselors use these skills, they are aware that they are putting clients under pressure to get at the behavioral roots of their problems. Indeed, the entire problem-management model puts clients under a great deal of pressure to change. But there is a certain progression in the application of this pressure. Stage I, skillfully executed, pressures clients to explore the problematic in their lives freely. As the relationship between the counselor and the client grows in trust and caring, it can support stronger and stronger interactions. Therefore, in Stage III, the counselor uses the Stage II skills of advanced accurate empathy, counselor self-sharing, immediacy, and confrontation more fully *to the degree that they help the client formulate and implement action programs.* The work of Stage III is summarized in Box 9–1.

Training Clients Directly in Problem-Solving Methodologies

I have already suggested a number of times that the helper can be, to a greater or lesser extent, a trainer—that is, one who teaches clients the kind of skills that will enable them to grapple with their problems more effectively. This same principle also applies to the skills of Stage III. If counselors can help clients manage their problems in living more effectively by "walking them through" the problem-management process outlined in these pages, then, at least in many cases, they can further help their clients by training them in problem-solving and behavior-change techniques directly. Such training can increase the probability that clients will become more autonomous problem solvers in their own lives and, conversely, decrease the probability that they will become overly dependent on officially designated helpers when the inevitable problems of living arise.

As Thoresen and Mahoney (1974) and others note (see Kanfer, 1980), we are constantly learning more and more about the principles and the technology of self-control, and training clients in these principles and procedures is highly practical.

BOX 9–1:   A SUMMARY OF THE WORK OF STAGE III

Once clients set problem-managing goals (*what* they want to do), help them establish programs that will enable them to achieve these goals (*how* they are to do what they want to do).

Use techniques such as brainstorming to help clients discover a number of different ways of achieving a goal. Help them engage in divergent thinking in order to take a census of program possibilities.

Once a number of different ways of achieving a goal have been discovered, help clients use such techniques as the balance sheet to evaluate and choose a program or a combination of elements from different programs that best fits their resources, values, and preferences and the constraints of the environment.

Before they implement a program, use techniques such as force-field analysis to help them identify the major obstacles they will encounter and the major resources that will be available.

As clients implement programs, provide the kinds of support and challenge they need to give themselves as fully as possible to the work of constructive behavioral change. Use this same problem-solving process to help them cope with the kinds of problems that arise in trying to implement a program.

Help them evaluate the quality of their participation in the program, the degree to which the program is helping them move toward their goal, and the degree to which the achievement of the goal is helping them manage the original problem situation.

Finally, help them make a decision to recycle any or all of the problem-management process, to focus on some other problem, or to terminate the helping relationship.

If a person can be helped to manage his own behavior, less professional time may be required for the desired behavior change. Moreover, the person might be the best possible agent to change his own behavior—he certainly has much more frequent access to it than anyone else, particularly when the behavior is covert. Self-control strategies may also avoid some of the general- ization and maintenance problems that often plague therapist-centered strategies. . . . Finally, training in self-control may provide an individual with technical and analytic talents that will facilitate subsequent attempts at self- control with different behaviors [Thoresen & Mahoney, 1974, p. 7].

Indeed, if self-responsibility is a paramount value in helping, as I suggested it is in Chapter 1, then training clients in self-management skills and strategies can be seen as neither novelty nor luxury. From a broader perspective, it is in the interest of a society as a whole to have its members become skilled in self- management (see Egan & Cowan, 1979). Although such skills are now offered in college courses (Watson & Tharp, 1981; Williams & Long, 1979), it seems to make both developmental and social sense to train people in these principles and strategies much earlier in life (see Shure & Spivack, 1978; Spivack, Platt, & Shure, 1976; Spivack & Shure, 1974).

Cautions Concerning Stage III

Balking at the Mechanistic Flavor of Systematic Behavior-Change Programs

A friend of mine, after reading a short book dealing with a comprehensive problem-solving methodology even more extensive and complicated than the one outlined here, exclaimed, "Who would go through all that?" There is a problem inherent in any comprehensive problem-solving methodology: it can be overly analytical, and the unskilled person can get lost in detail. The unskilled person can be used by methodology instead of using it. The caution I've already mentioned a number of times bears repeating here: this methodology is not an end in itself and should be expanded or abridged or laid aside in keeping with the client's needs. The process should be only as detailed as is necessary to stimulate effective action. Weick (1969, p. 103; 1979) counsels against over- planning:

The point is simply that planning can insulate members from the very envi- ronment which they are trying to cope with. Planning in the absence of action is basically unconstrained; the only actions available for reflective attention are the planning acts themselves. The members can learn more and more about how to plan and how they are planning, but they can lose sight of what they were originally planning for.

Obviously, problem-solving procedures that become ends in themselves are counterproductive and "lose the name of action." There should be a balance between planning and action. Planning is putting order and reason into what is. Problem solving that is not based on a review of "what is" of clients' ineffective behavior and of their resources, both inner and environmental, is doomed from the outset. Neither is problem solving an all-at-once process. Action produces reaction. When the client acts differently toward his or her environment in the execution of an action program, the environment reacts, often in unexpected ways. When the client's environment reacts, it is time to put order and reason into this reaction—that is, to modify previously planned action programs. It can be wasteful to spend too much time trying to anticipate all future contingencies. Stage III demands a productive dialogue between planning and action.

Another possible answer to my friend's question, "Who would go through all that?" is anyone who is interested in the work of living more effectively. At the minimum, problem-solving technologies provide clients with cognitive maps—that is, ways of looking at constructive action. Although they might not follow each step, they do approach action more methodically. Counselor trainees should experiment with problem-solving methodologies in their own lives. These methodologies are not useless merely because most people avoid them. If, in counseling, problem-solving methodologies seem overly logical and rational, it is up to the counselor to construct processes in which the client's feelings and aspirations are dealt with humanly.

The Client Who Chooses Not to Change

There is a kind of inertia and passivity in the makeup of many people that makes change difficult and distressing for them. Therefore, some clients who seem to do well in Stage I and II of the counseling program end up saying, in effect if not directly:

> *Client:* Even though I've explored my problems and understand why things are going wrong—that is, I understand myself and my behavior better and I realize the behavioral demands I should be making on myself—right now I don't want to pay the price called for by action. The price of more effective living is too high.

There are at least two kinds of client dropouts: the ones who are being helped by unskilled counselors and who realize they are going nowhere and the ones with skilled counselors who realize that the price for change is too high. The question of human motivation seems almost as enigmatic now as it must have at the dawning of human history. So often we seem to choose our own misery. Worse, we choose to stew in it rather than endure the relatively short-lived pain of behavioral change.

Never Getting to Stage III

Some low-level counselors stay in the safe waters of Stage I, exploring the client's problems in a rather circular way and hoping that the exploratory phase will suffice. The point is that such helpers are ineffective even in what they think they are doing well; accurate empathy along with concreteness, when communicated genuinely and respectfully to the client, has a way of putting pressure on the client to move to deeper self-exploration—the kind of self-exploration that produces the kind of self-understanding that verges on action. The logic of the social-influence process is embedded in the interactions of the developmental model itself.

The high-level helper is a doer, an agent in his or her own life, and therefore at home with action programs. Some counselors are unable to help in the action phase of the counseling process because they are basically passive people—nondoers. Therefore, in this respect, they are not living more effectively than their clients and cannot be expected to help.

Starting with Stage III

Some counselors move to advice giving almost immediately. They fail to see that in most cases action for the sake of action is rootless. Stages I and II ordinarily provide the roots for action. Moving too quickly into action programs satisfies the helper's needs rather than the client's, violating one of the primary principles of counseling: helping is for the client.

Conclusion

To borrow a phrase from T. S. Eliot's *Murder in the Cathedral*, most people are "living and partly living"—that is, people live relatively fully in one or more developmental areas of life and less fully or even in impoverished ways in others. Do our clients want to live more fully than they are in this or that area of life? Do they find within themselves, in the smaller social settings of their lives such as family and friends, and in society itself the incentives to do so? Questions such as these lurk constantly at the edges of the helping process and lead to such ultimate ones as "How is life to be defined and its success measured?" Each helper and each client has to work out the answers to such ultimate questions. The way they are answered can profoundly affect how we give ourselves to the helping process.

Chapter 10

Epilogue

This chapter deals with the following topics:

Dealing with reluctant and resistant clients
Moving upstream: Prevention and development

293

Reluctant and Resistant Clients

As noted earlier, in most of the examples used up to this point clients have been at least minimally cooperative. However, all helpers encounter reluctant or resistant clients—that is, clients who do not seem to know what they want, who present themselves as not needing help, who, though unwilling, are forced to see a helper or come only at the urging of a third party, who feel abused, who are resentful, who talk about only safe or low-priority issues, who sabotage the helping process by being overly cooperative, who are directly or indirectly uncooperative, who set unrealistic goals and then use them as an excuse for not working, who unwarrantedly blame others or the social settings and systems of their lives for their troubles, who show no willingness to establish a relationship with the helper, who do not work very hard at changing their behavior, who play games with helpers, who are slow to take responsibility for themselves, or who are either testy or actually abusive and belligerent. Resistance to helping is, of course, a matter of degree and not all these behaviors in their most virulent forms are seen in all resistant clients. Moreover, resistance is hardly an uncommon phenomenon. Although it may or may not be that "involuntary clients may well account for the majority of caseloads throughout the land" (Dyer & Vriend, 1975, p. 102), there is probably some degree of resistance in every client: "Resistance is an unavoidable process in every effective treatment, for that part of the personality that has an interest in the survival of the pathology actively protests each time therapy comes close to inducing a successful change" (Redl, 1966, p. 216). Clients come "armored" against change to a greater or lesser degree. Resistance can even be seen as something positive, a sign of life and struggle, rather than just another form of pathology. Here, then, are some considerations that will help you deal with reluctant clients or the resistance found to one degree or another in all clients. These considerations are based on the relatively little that has been written about client reluctance (for instance, Dyer & Vriend, 1975; Paradise & Wilder, 1979; Riordan, Matheny, & Harris, 1978; Smaby & Tamminen, 1979) and on my experience.

Reluctance versus Resistance

It is possible to make a distinction between reluctance and resistance, although the principles for handling both are basically the same.

294

RELUCTANT CLIENTS

Reluctant clients do not want to come in the first place; they are not self-referred. They come because they are more or less forced to come. For instance, in marriage counseling one of the clients might be there willingly while the other is there because he or she feels pressured by the helper, the spouse, or both to be there.

Helpers can expect to find a large proportion of such clients in settings where clients are forced to see a counselor (for instance, the case of the high school student in trouble with his or her teacher—going to a helper is a form of punishment) or in settings where some reward can be achieved only on the condition of being involved in some kind of counseling process (for instance, being counseled as part of getting a job—going to a counselor is the price that must be paid). Clients like these are found in schools, especially schools below college level, correctional settings, marriage counseling (especially if court mandated), employment agencies, welfare agencies, court-related settings, and other social agencies. Also children sent to helpers by their parents are likely to be reluctant.

The fact that a client is self-referred does not automatically mean that he or she is ready to participate in the helping process wholeheartedly. Paradise and Wilder (1979) studied a group of self-referred clients and found varying degrees of reluctance among even these. They also found that reluctant clients, perhaps as a kind of self-fulfilling prophecy ("What am I doing here; they're not going to help me anyway"), found the helping process less satisfactory and improved less than those who were not reluctant, saw the agency as not geared to handle their kinds of problems, and tended to terminate the counseling process prematurely. On the other hand, the fact that a client is not self-referred does not automatically mean that he or she is reluctant, even though the evidence seems to indicate that most are. Furthermore, even if initial reluctance is overcome, it can be expected that, as in the case of self-referred clients, some greater or lesser degree of resistance will be found. If counseling is seen as a cooperative venture, then Smaby and Tamminen (1979) wonder whether it makes sense to talk about counseling reluctant clients. Perhaps it does not until the problem of their reluctance is faced and resolved.

RESISTANT CLIENTS

Resistant clients are those who, insofar as it can be judged, come more or less willingly or who, though initially reluctant, overcome their reluctance, but who still fail to give themselves adequately to the helping process at one or more points along the way. For instance, a client might willingly explore some problem situation, set some goals, cooperate with the helper in devising a program, and then balk at the implementation of the program or begin to implement it, but only halfheartedly.

Causes of Reluctance and Resistance

In order to deal with reluctance and resistance, it is helpful first to understand some of their common causes. The following kinds of clients are likely to be reluctant and/or resistant:

- Clients who see no reason for going to the helper in the first place.
- Clients who resent third-party referrers (parents, teachers, agencies) and whose resentment carries over to the helper.
- Clients who fear the unfamiliar. (They do not know what counseling is or they have misconceptions about it.)
- Clients who do not know how to participate effectively—that is, how to be "good" clients.
- Clients who have a history of being rebels against systems. (They rock the boat, and boat rockers are more likely to get referred.)
- Clients who see the goals of the helper or the helping system as different from their own. (For instance, the goal of counseling in a welfare setting may be to help the clients become financially independent, whereas some clients might be satisfied with the present arrangement. The goal of helping in a mental hospital may be to help the clients get out, whereas some clients might feel quite comfortable in the hospital.)
- Clients who have developed negative attitudes about helping and helping agencies and who harbor suspicions about helping and helpers. (Helpers are referred to in derogatory and inexact terms—"shrinks.")
- Clients who have discovered that the helper or the agency has a reputation for being inept or experience ineptness during counseling.
- Clients who believe that going to a helper is the same as admitting weakness, failure, and inadequacy. (They feel they will lose face by going. By resisting the process, they preserve their self-esteem.)
- Clients who feel that counseling is something that is being done to them. (They feel that their rights are not being respected.)
- Clients who feel they have not been invited by helpers to be participants in the decisions that are to affect their lives. (This includes expectations for change and decisions about procedures to be used in the helping process.)
- Clients who feel a need for personal power and find it through resisting a "powerful" figure or agency. ("I may be relatively powerless, but I still have the power to resist." Riordan, Matheny, and Harris [1978, p. 8] suggest that this can be a healthy sign in that "clients are grasping for a share in the control of their destiny.")
- Clients who are testing the helper's level of support and competence.
- Clients who dislike their helpers but do not discuss this with them.
- Clients who see no payoffs for changing.

- Clients who, during the helping process, discover that the price of behavioral change is higher than they had expected.
- Clients who remain ambiguous about change.
- Clients who have a conception of the degree of change desired that differs from the helper's conception.

Many sociopsychological variables such as sex, prejudice, race, religion, social class, upbringing, and cultural and subcultural blueprints can play a part in resistance. For instance, a man might instinctively resist being helped by a woman. A black person might instinctively resist being helped by a white. A person with no religious affiliation might instinctively think that help coming from a minister will be "pious" or will automatically include some form of proselytizing.

Unhelpful Responses to Reluctance and Resistance

Helpers, especially beginning helpers who are unaware of the pervasiveness of resistance, are disconcerted by it and find themselves facing unexpected feelings and emotions in themselves when they encounter it. For instance, they feel confused, panicked, irritated, hostile, guilty, hurt, rejected, meek, submissive, or depressed. Distracted by these unexpected feelings, they can react in ways that are not helpful, such as the following:

- They accept the guilt and try to placate the client.
- They become impatient and hostile and manifest this either verbally or nonverbally.
- They do nothing and hope the resistance will disappear.
- They lower their expectations of themselves and proceed with the helping process, but in a halfhearted way.
- They try to become warmer and more accepting, hoping to win the client over by love.
- They blame the client and end up in a power struggle with him or her.
- They allow themselves to be abused by clients, playing the role of a scapegoat.
- They lower their expectations of what can be achieved by counseling.
- They hand the direction of the helping process over to the client.
- They give up and terminate counseling.

When helpers meet resistance, they experience stress, and some give in to dysfunctional "fight or flight" approaches to handling it.

The source of this stress is not just the client's behavior; it also comes from the helper's self-defeating attitudes and beliefs about the helping process, some of which are the following:

- All clients should be self-referred and adequately committed to change before appearing at my door.
- Every client must like me and trust me.
- I am a consultant and not a social influencer; it should not be necessary to place demands on clients.
- Every unwilling client can be helped.
- No unwilling client can be helped.
- I alone am responsible for what happens to this client.
- I have to succeed completely with every client.

Confronting and coming to terms with these disabling beliefs is not the same as giving up or settling for less. Effective helpers neither court resistance nor are surprised by it.

More Productive Approaches to Dealing with Reluctance and Resistance

First, because reluctance and resistance are forms of avoiding, helpers need to understand the principles and mechanisms underlying avoidance behavior (see the discussion of the principles of behavior in Chapter 1). If clients are avoiding counseling because they see it as either punishing or at least as lacking in suitable rewards, then helpers have to demonstrate to them in concrete and specific ways that engaging in the helping process can be rewarding rather than punishing and that change can be more rewarding than maintaining the status quo. Effective helpers realize that motivation usually has more to do with *incentives* than "motives" locked away in the hearts of clients (Gilbert, 1978). Some of the ways these principles can be translated into specific behaviors follow.

EXPLORING YOUR OWN RESISTANCE

Examine resistance in your own life. Intensive training in the models, methodologies, and skills of helping provides you an opportunity to examine more or less at your leisure the ways in which you resist growth and development. If you are in touch with the various forms of resistance in yourself and are finding ways of overcoming them, you are more likely to help clients deal with theirs.

EXAMINING THE QUALITY OF YOUR INTERVENTIONS

Without giving in to unwarranted guilt, examine your helping behavior. See if you are doing anything to elicit resistance in the client. For instance, you may have become too directive without realizing it. Take stock of the emotions welling up in you because of the client's resistance and the ways you're communicating them to the client. Do not deny these feelings; own them and find ways of coming to terms with them. For instance, do not *overpersonalize* the client's resistance. If you are allowing a hostile client to get under your skin, you are probably reducing your effectiveness.

ACCEPTING AND WORKING WITH THE CLIENT'S RESISTANCE

Start with the client's frame of reference. Accept both the client and his or her resistance. Do not ignore it or be intimidated by it. Let clients know how you experience it and then explore it with them. Model openness to challenge. Be willing to explore your own negative feelings. The skill of immediacy is extremely important here. Help clients work through the emotions associated with resistance. Avoid moralizing.

SEEING SOME RESISTANCE AS NORMATIVE

Help clients see that they are not odd because they are reluctant or resistant. Beyond that, help them see the positive side of resistance. It may well be a sign of their affirmation of self.

EXPLORING THE ROOTS OF THE RESISTANCE

Try to determine the causes of the resistance. Help clients see and appreciate the roots and even the legitimacy of their resistance. If they discover the payoff that is associated with and helps maintain their resistance, they may be open to finding other ways of getting the same kinds of payoff. Use challenging skills to help clients develop new perspectives on their resistance.

PRIZING CLIENT SELF-RESPONSIBILITY

Even though a client's resistance has some legitimacy, he or she is still ultimately responsible for coping with it. Do not take responsibility for the client's resistance except insofar as you see yourself contributing to it. Teach clients how to involve themselves effectively in the helping process and show them how this can serve their self-interest.

ESTABLISHING A "JUST SOCIETY"

Very often reluctant and resistant clients feel like victims. Therefore, in the helping relationship, provide what Smaby and Tamminen (1979, p. 509) call a "two-person just society." Establish as much mutuality as is consonant with helping goals. A just society is based on mutual respect and shared planning.

INVITING PARTICIPATION

Invite resistant clients to participate in every step of the helping process and in all the decision making. Share expectations. Discuss and get reactions to helping procedures. Have the client help design a minicontract related only to the first couple of sessions.

SEARCHING FOR INCENTIVES

Help clients find incentives for participating in the helping process. Use client self-interest as a way of identifying these. Use brainstorming as a way of discovering possible incentives. For instance, the realization that they are going to remain in charge of their own lives may be an important incentive for clients.

BEGINNING WITH SMALL GOALS

Begin with moderate, realizable goals that you and the client have cooperatively set. Do not let the client use perfectionism in the form of unrealistic short-term or long-term goals as a cop-out. Help the client experience some kind of real success in the helping process as soon as possible. For instance, one goal may be that within one or two sessions both of you will have explored how each is resisting the helping process. Help clients choose goals that will improve their life.

SHAPING

Reinforce successive approximations to the kind of behavior that makes helping work.

> *Client* (after complaining at length about being forced to come): Of course this doesn't mean that you're a lousy dude. You probably don't like this any more than I do. Who would?
> *Counselor:* I'm glad you can look at it from my side of the fence too.

TAPPING SIGNIFICANT OTHERS AS RESOURCES

Do not see yourself as the only helper in your client's life. Engage significant others, such as peers and family members, in helping clients face their resistance. For instance, lawyers who belong to Alcoholics Anonymous might be able to deal with a lawyer's resistance to joining a treatment program more effectively than you can.

EMPLOYING CLIENTS AS HELPERS

If possible, find ways to get resistant clients into situations where they are actually helping others. The change of perspective involved can help them come to terms with their own resistance. One person who did a great deal of work for Alcoholics Anonymous had a resistant alcoholic go with him on his city rounds, which included visiting hospitals, nursing homes for alcoholics, jails, flophouses, and down-and-out people on the streets. The alcoholic saw through all the lame excuses other alcoholics offered for their plight. After a week, he joined AA himself. Another, more immediately usable form of this approach to resistance is role reversal. In the interview, take the client's role and manifest the same kind of resistance he or she is. Have the client take the counselor role and help you overcome your resistance. Group counseling, too, is a forum in which clients become helpers. Helping others can be hard work. Dealing with resistance can be one of the hardest parts of it.

Moving Upstream: Prevention and Development

There is a story that encapsulates the message of this section. A person walking alongside a river sees someone drowning. This person jumps in, pulls the victim out, and begins artificial respiration. While the reviving process is taking place, another person in the river calls for help. The rescuer jumps into the water again, pulls the second victim out, and begins artificial respiration. This process repeats itself until the rescuer, on hearing from the river the voice of yet another victim, gets up and begins walking away. By now the rescuer has drawn a small crowd. The bystanders ask in surprise where the rescuer is going; a state of emergency still exists. The rescuer replies, "You save that one and whoever else comes floating down the river. I'm going *upstream* to find out who's pushing all these people in and see if I can do something to stop it."

Helper "Burn-Out"

Helpers spend most of their time "downstream" dealing with people who are already in trouble. I have stated several times that this is hard work. As time goes by, it can also become discouraging work. More and more people in the helping professions are becoming concerned about what can be called helper "burn-out" (Edelwich, 1980). Newman and Newman (1979, p. 430) give a brief description of this syndrome.

In daily work interactions, human service professionals often encounter situations that are emotionally arousing, frustrating, and perhaps personally threatening. In response to these intense experiences some people begin to take a very cynical, derogatory view of the people they are hired to help. They become callous, claiming that the clients deserve their fate. They begin to experience physical symptoms, increased use of drugs, marital conflict, and needs for solitude or detachment from all social contacts. They come to see themselves as bad people and their clients as deserving of bad treatment. In this and other examples of stagnation, the person loses sight of the potential for nurturing, educating, or guiding others and becomes trapped in the struggle to protect or maintain the self.

Edelwich (1980) probes the causes of burn-out, describes four stages of disillusionment—enthusiasm, stagnation, frustration, and apathy—and suggests remedies for both individuals and institutions.

If you are just preparing yourself to become a helper, talk about burn-out might seem quite foreign to you. However, you have been in school long enough to experience burn-out in one or more of your teachers. Few of us have not run into a teacher who seems to be merely putting his or her time in until something better comes along or until retirement. Learning from such a person, if indeed any learning takes place, is usually a boring and otherwise unpleasant experience. The fact that the burn-out syndrome afflicts helpers to a greater or lesser degree need not discourage you from becoming a helper. Once you know that such a phenomenon exists, and it obviously does, you are in a better position to do something about it.

Education and Training for Human Development

Once people get into trouble, they are in need of some form of treatment, and this, although necessary, is still "downstream" work. One way to prevent the burn-out syndrome from taking hold of you in your downstream work is to adopt creative "upstream" approaches to helping—for instance, group and training-as-treatment approaches. Although in a sense you are still in the work of rescuing, you are now helping people learn the skills and strategies of prevention. This is usually more exciting than just helping them cope with their current problem situations.

A second way to avoid burn-out is to spend at least some of your time upstream—that is, in human-resource-development programs that help people avoid getting into trouble in the first place. For instance, training people who are about to get married in communication and problem-solving skills can increase the probability that they will be able to cope with the natural ups and downs of marriage without professional help.

Dr. R. was a psychologist in a large VA hospital. She spent most of her time seeing patients, many of whom would never get out of the hospital. Once she began to experience the first symptoms of burn-out, she felt that she had to do something about it or get out. The hospital had over a thousand employees. Most were not professional staff and yet spent more of their time with the patients than did the professional staff. Patients were in contact with nonprofessional or paraprofessional staff all the time. Dr. R. began training programs with them, teaching them communication skills and helping strategies to increase their effectiveness with patients. This became her way of moving upstream in a downstream system that she was letting discourage her.

Institutions, like individuals, suffer from the psychopathology of the average. Dr. R. attempted to deal with her own problem at an institutional level.

Prevention (Albee & Joffe, 1977; Murphy & Frank, 1979) is perhaps not the best word to describe upstream approaches. If prevention programs are successful, *nothing* happens. For instance, if accident prevention programs are successful, accidents don't happen. People usually receive little reinforcement from things that don't happen, especially if they don't even know that they *might* happen. However, prevention programs that give people working knowledge and skills that enable them to *do* something are likely to be more effective than programs that merely keep people out of trouble. A people-in-systems model urges that education and training for social-emotional fitness begin as early as possible in life (see White, 1980; White, Kaban, & Attanucci, 1979; White, Kaban, Attanucci, & Shapiro, 1978). These issues are discussed more thoroughly in *People in Systems* (Egan & Cowan, 1979).

A Final Note

Technology is only as human as its user. The technology of helping becomes human when it is placed at the service of clients, when they are allowed to make their own as much of it as they want or can, and when these processes are facilitated by a helper-consultant who knows how to use technology rather than being used by it. The problem-solving model of helping presented here presents a *framework* for helping, not a rigid process that is to be imposed on clients at all costs. Its eight steps are eight basic *tasks* that are to be accomplished in any kind of helping, including self-help, but they can be accomplished in a wide variety of ways. Skilled helpers, while not pursuing novelty for its own sake, are constantly open to new methods that make the execution of these tasks both more efficient and more human.

It is impossible to write a book on almost any subject without inadvertently at least implying that the subject being written about, in this case a model of helping others, is just about the most important subject in life. Helping others and learning the models, skills, and methods that enable you to do so are important; but important as they are, they need to be seen in the context of the rest of life. Life also involves household tasks, poetry, the larger institutions of society, music, international conflict, friends, sickness, books, fun, the poor, learning, work, politics, romance, religion, vacations, pain, career, leisure, failures, hobbies, successes, and dying. What you learn in this book and through the training it implies can help you invest yourself more creatively in the rest of life.

References

Albee, G. W., & Joffe, J. M. (Eds.). *Primary prevention of psychopathy. Vol. 1: The issues.* Hanover, N.H.: University Press of New England, 1977.

Anthony, W. A. Psychological rehabilitation: A concept in need of a model. *American Psychologist,* 1977, *32,* 658–662.

Anthony, W. A. A human technology for human resource development. *Counseling Psychologist,* 1978, *7*(3), 58–65.

Anthony, W. A. *The principles of psychiatric rehabilitation.* Amherst, Mass.: Human Resource Development Press, 1979.

Anthony, W. A., Pierce, R. M., & Cohen, M. R. *The skills of rehabilitation programming.* Amherst, Mass.: Carkhuff Institute of Human Technology, 1979.

Axelrod, S., Hall, R. V., Weis, L., & Rohrer, S. *Use of self-imposed contingencies to reduce the frequency of smoking behavior.* Paper presented at the fifth annual meeting of the Association for the Advancement of Behavior Therapy, Washington, D.C., September 1971.

Bandura, A. *Principles of behavior modification.* New York: Holt, Rinehart & Winston, 1969.

Bandura, A. Self-efficacy: Toward a unifying theory of behavioral change. *Psychological Review,* 1977, *84,* 191–215. (a)

Bandura, A. *Social learning theory.* Englewood Cliffs, N. J.: Prentice-Hall, 1977. (b)

Bard, J. A. *Rational-emotive therapy in practice.* Champaign, Ill.: Research Press, 1980.

Bargo, M., Jr. *Choices and decisions: A guidebook for constructing values.* San Diego: University Associates Press, 1980. (a)

Bargo, M., Jr. *A facilitator's manual for choices and decisions: A guidebook for constructing values.* San Diego: University Associates Press, 1980. (b)

Bayer, C. A. Self-monitoring and mild aversion treatment of trichotillomania. *Journal of Behavior Therapy and Experimental Psychiatry,* 1972, *3,* 139–141.

Bayless, O. L. An alternative pattern for problem-solving discussion. *Journal of Communication,* 1967, *17,* 188–197.

Begelman, D. A. Ethical and legal issues of behavior modification. In M. Hersen, R. M. Eisler, & P. M. Miller (Eds.), *Progress in behavior modification* (Vol. 1). New York: Academic Press, 1975.

Beier, E. G. *The silent language of psychotherapy.* Chicago: Aldine, 1966.

Bellingham, R. L. On researching the researchers. *Counseling Psychologist,* 1978, *7*(3), 55–58.

Benjamin, A. *The helping interview* (3rd ed.). Boston: Houghton Mifflin, 1981.

Berenson, B. G., & Mitchell, K. M. *Confrontation: For better or worse.* Amherst, Mass.: Human Resource Development Press, 1974.

Bergin, A. E. The evaluation of therapeutic outcomes. In A. E. Bergin & S. L. Garfield (Eds.), *Handbook of psychotherapy and behavior change*. New York: Wiley, 1971.

Bergin, A. E. Negative effects revisited: A reply. *Professional Psychology*, 1980, *11*, 93–100.

Bergin, A. E., & Lambert, M. J. The evaluation of therapeutic outcomes. In S. L. Garfield & A. E. Bergin (Eds.), *Handbook of psychotherapy and behavior change: An empirical analysis* (2nd ed.). New York: Wiley, 1978.

Berne, E. *Games people play*. New York: Grove Press, 1964.

Bernstein, B. L., & Lecompte, C. Self-critique technique training in a competency-based practicum. *Counselor Education and Supervision*, 1979, *19*, 69–76.

Binder, V., Binder, A., & Rimland, B. (Eds.). *Modern therapies*. Englewood Cliffs, N. J.: Prentice-Hall, 1976.

Brammer, L. *The helping relationship: Process and skills*. Englewood Cliffs, N. J.: Prentice-Hall, 1973.

Brammer, L., & Shostrom, E. *Therapeutic psychology: Fundamentals of actualization counseling and psychotherapy* (3rd ed.). Englewood Cliffs, N. J.: Prentice-Hall, 1977.

Braun, S. H. Ethical issues in behavior modification. *Behavior Therapy*, 1975, *6*, 51–62.

Brilhart, J. K., & Jochem, L. M. Effects of different patterns on outcome of problem-solving discussion. *Journal of Applied Psychology*, 1964, *48*, 175–179.

Buber, M. *I and thou*. New York: Scribner's, 1970. (Originally published, 1937.)

Bucker, L. Joint effect of feedback and goal setting on performance: A field study of residential energy conservation. *Journal of Applied Psychology*, 1978, *63*, 428–433.

Bullmer, K. *The art of empathy: A manual for improving accuracy of interpersonal perception*. New York: Human Sciences Press, 1975.

Carkhuff, R. R. *Helping and human relations*. Vol. 1: *Selection and training*. New York: Holt, Rinehart & Winston, 1969. (a)

Carkhuff, R. R. *Helping and human relations*. Vol. 2: *Practice and research*. New York: Holt, Rinehart & Winston, 1969. (b)

Carkhuff, R. R. *The development of human resources*. New York: Holt, Rinehart & Winston, 1971. (a)

Carkhuff, R. R. Training as a preferred mode of treatment. *Journal of Counseling Psychology*, 1971, *18*, 123–131. (b)

Carkhuff, R. R., & Anthony, W. A. *The skills of helping: An introduction to counseling*. Amherst, Mass.: Human Resource Development Press, 1979.

Carkhuff, R. R., & Berenson, B. G. *Teaching as treatment*. Amherst, Mass.: Human Resource Development Press, 1976.

Cautela, J. R. Covert sensitization. *Psychological Reports*, 1967, *20*, 245–250.

Cautela, J. R., & Wisocki, P. A. The thought stopping procedure: Description, application, and learning theory interpretations. *Psychological Record*, 1977, *27*, 255–264.

Chelune, G. J. (Ed.). *Self-disclosure: Origins, patterns, and implications of openness in interpersonal relationships*. San Francisco: Jossey-Bass, 1979.

Chinsky, J. M., & Rappaport, J. Brief critique of the meaning and reliability of "accurate empathy" ratings. *Psychological Bulletin*, 1970, *73*, 379–382.

Claiborn, C. D. Counselor verbal intervention, nonverbal behavior, and social power. *Journal of Counseling Psychology*, 1979, *26*, 378–383.

Clark, K. B. Empathy: A neglected topic in psychological research. *American Psychologist*, 1980, *35*, 187–190.

Collingwood, T., & Carkhuff, R. R. *Get fit for living*. Amherst, Mass.: Human Resource Development Press, 1976.

Corey, G. *Theory and practice of counseling and psychotherapy*. Monterey, Calif.: Brooks/Cole, 1977.

Cormier, W. H., & Cormier, L. S. *Interviewing strategies for helpers: A guide to assessment, treatment, and evaluation*. Monterey, Calif.: Brooks/Cole, 1979.

Corrigan, J. D., Dell, D. M., Lewis, K. N., & Schmidt, L. D. Counseling as a social influence process: A review. *Journal of Counseling Psychology Monograph*, 1980, *27*, 395–431.

Corsini, R. J. (Ed.). *Current psychotherapies* (2nd ed.). Itasca, Ill.: Peacock, 1979.

Coyne, J. C., & Widiger, T. A. Toward a participatory model of psychotherapy. *Professional Psychology*, 1978, *9*, 700–710.

Cozby, P. C. Self-disclosure: A literature review. *Psychological Bulletin*, 1973, *79*, 73–91.

Crutchfield, R. S. Nurturing the cognitive skills of productive thinking. In *Life skills in school and society*. Washington, D.C.: Association for Supervision and Curriculum Development, 1969.

Dalton, R. F., & Sundblad, L. M. Using principles of social learning in training for communication of empathy. *Journal of Counseling Psychology*, 1976, *23*, 454–457.

Davis, G. A. Current status of research and theory in human problem solving. *Psychological Bulletin*, 1966, *66*, 36–54.

Davis, G. A., & Manske, M. E. An instructional method of increasing originality. *Psychonomic Science*, 1966, *6*, 73–74.

DeForest, C., & Stone, G. L. Effects of sex and intimacy on self-disclosure. *Journal of Counseling Psychology*, 1980, *27*, 93–96.

Derlega, V. J., & Grzelak, J. Appropriateness of self-disclosure. In G. J. Chelune (Ed.), *Self-disclosure: Origins, patterns, and implications of openness in interpersonal relationships*. San Francisco: Jossey-Bass, 1979.

Derlega, V. J., Lovell, R., & Chaikin, A. L. Effects of therapist self-disclosure and its perceived appropriateness on client self-disclosure. *Journal of Consulting and Clinical Psychology*, 1976, *44*, 866.

Deutsch, M. Field theory in social psychology. In G. Lindzey (Ed.), *The handbook of social psychology* (Vol. 1). Cambridge, Mass.: Addison-Wesley, 1954.

Dimond, R. E., Havens, R. A., & Jones, A. C. A conceptual framework for the practice of prescriptive eclecticism in psychotherapy. *American Psychologist*, 1978, *33*, 239–248.

Dixon, D. N., Heppner, P. P., Petersen, C. H., & Ronning, R. R. Problem-solving workshop training. *Journal of Counseling Psychology*, 1979, *26*, 133–139.

Doster, J. A., & Nesbitt, J. G. Psychotherapy and self-disclosure. In G. J. Chelune (Ed.), *Self-disclosure: Origins, patterns, and implications of openness in interpersonal relationships*. San Francisco: Jossey-Bass, 1979.

Dreikurs, R. Goals of psychotherapy. In A. Maher (Ed.), *The goals of psychotherapy*. New York: Appleton-Century-Crofts, 1967.

Dyer, W. W., & Vriend, J. *Counseling techniques that work: Applications to individual and group counseling*. Washington, D.C.: APGA Press, 1975.

D'Zurilla, T. J., & Goldfried, M. R. Problem solving and behavior modification. *Journal of Abnormal Psychology*, 1971, *78*, 107–126.

Edelwich, J. *Burn-out: Stages of disillusionment in the helping professions*. New York: Human Sciences Press, 1980.

Egan, G. *Encounter: Group processes for interpersonal growth*. Monterey, Calif.: Brooks/Cole, 1970.

Egan, G. *Interpersonal living: A skills-contract approach to human-relations training in groups*. Monterey, Calif.: Brooks/Cole, 1976.

Egan, G. *You and me: The skills of communicating and relating to others*. Monterey, Calif.: Brooks/Cole, 1977.

Egan, G. *Exercises in helping skills* (Rev. ed.). Monterey, Calif.: Brooks/Cole, 1981.

Egan, G., & Cowan, M. A. *People in systems: A model for development in the human-service professions and education*. Monterey, Calif.: Brooks/Cole, 1979.

Ekman, P., & Friesen, W. V. The repertoire of nonverbal behavior: Categories, origins, usage, and coding. *Semiotica*, 1969, *1*, 49–98.

Ellis, A. *Reason and emotion in psychotherapy*. New York: Lyle Stuart, 1962.

Ellis, A. Should some people be labeled mentally ill? *Journal of Consulting Psychology*, 1967, *31*, 435–446.

Ellis, A. *Growth through reason*. Palo Alto, Calif.: Science and Behavior Books, 1971.

Ellis, A. *Humanistic psychotherapy: The rational-emotive approach*. New York: Julian Press, 1973. (New York: McGraw-Hill Paperbacks, 1974.)

Ellis, A. *Disputing irrational beliefs (DIBS)*. New York: Institute for Rational Living, 1974.

Ellis, A., & Harper, R. A. *A new guide to rational living*. Englewood Cliffs, N. J.: Prentice-Hall, 1975.

Erez, M. Feedback: A necessary condition for the goal-setting performance relationship. *Journal of Applied Psychology*, 1977, *62*, 624–627.

Erikson, E. H. *Insight and responsibility*. New York: Norton, 1964.

Eysenck, H. J. The effects of psychotherapy: An evaluation. *Journal of Counseling Psychology*, 1952, *16*, 319–324.

Eysenck, H. J. The effects of psychotherapy. In H. J. Eysenck (Ed.), *Handbook of abnormal psychology*. New York: Basic Books, 1960.

Eysenck, H. J. The effects of psychotherapy. *International Journal of Psychiatry*, 1965, *1*, 97–178.

Eysenck, H. J. An exercise in mega-silliness. *American Psychologist*, 1978, *33*, 517.

Festinger, L. *A theory of cognitive dissonance.* New York: Harper & Row, 1957.

Flowers, J. Goal clarity as a component of assertive behavior and a result of assertion training. *Journal of Clinical Psychology,* 1978, *34,* 744–747.

Fordyce, W. E. *Behavioral methods for control of chronic pain and illness.* St. Louis: Mosby, 1976.

Frank, J. D. *Persuasion and healing* (2nd ed.). Baltimore: Johns Hopkins University Press, 1973.

Franks, C. M., & Mays, D. T. Negative effects revisited: A rejoinder. *Professional Psychology,* 1980, *11,* 101–105.

Fretz, B. R., Corn, R., Tuemmler, J. M., & Bellet, W. Counselor nonverbal behaviors and client evaluations. *Journal of Counseling Psychology,* 1979, *26,* 304–311.

Fridman, M. S., & Stone, S. C. Effect of training, stimulus context, and mode of stimulus presentation on empathy ratings. *Journal of Counseling Psychology,* 1978, *25,* 131–136.

Gallo, P. S., Jr. Meta-analysis—A mixed meta-phor? *American Psychologist,* 1978, *33,* 515–517.

Garfield, S. L., & Bergin, A. E. (Eds.). *Handbook of psychotherapy and behavior change: An empirical analysis* (2nd ed.). New York: Wiley, 1978.

Garfield, S. L., & Kurtz, R. A survey of clinical psychologists: Characteristics, activities, and orientations. *The Clinical Psychologist,* 1974, *28,* 7–10.

Garfield, S. L., & Kurtz, R. A study of eclectic views. *Journal of Consulting and Clinical Psychology,* 1977, *45,* 78–83.

Gartner, A., & Riessman, F. *Self-help in the human services.* San Francisco: Jossey-Bass, 1977.

Gazda, G. M. *Human relations development: A manual for educators.* Boston: Allyn & Bacon, 1973.

Gelatt, H. B., Varenhorst, B., & Carey, R. *Deciding: A leader's guide.* Princeton, N. J.: College Entrance Examination Board, 1972.

Genther, R. W., & Moughan, J. Introverts' and extraverts' responses to nonverbal attending behavior. *Journal of Counseling Psychology,* 1977, *24,* 144–146.

Gibb, J. R. The counselor as a role-free person. In C. A. Parker (Ed.), *Counseling theories and counselor education.* Boston: Houghton Mifflin, 1968.

Gibb, J. R. *Trust: A new view of personal and organizational development.* Los Angeles: The Guild of Tutors Press, 1978.

Gilbert, T. F. *Human competence: Engineering worthy performance.* New York: McGraw-Hill, 1978.

Gladstein, G. Nonverbal communication and counseling/psychotherapy. *Counseling Psychologist,* 1974, *4,* 34–57.

Gladstein, G. Empathy and counseling outcome: An empirical and conceptual review. *Counseling Psychologist,* 1977, *6*(4), 70–79.

Glaser, R. (Ed.). *The nature of reinforcement.* New York: Academic Press, 1971.

Glass, G. V., & Smith, M. L. Reply to Eysenck. *American Psychologist,* 1978, *33,* 517–519.

Goldfried, M. R., & Davison, G. C. *Clinical behavior therapy.* New York: Holt, Rinehart & Winston, 1976.

Goldfried, M. R., & D'Zurilla, T. J. A behavioral-analytic model for assessing competence. In C. D. Spielberger (Ed.), *Current topics in clinical and community psychology* (Vol. 1). New York: Academic Press, 1969.

Goldfried, M. R., & Goldfried, A. P. Cognitive change methods. In F. H. Kanfer & A. P. Goldstein (Eds.), *Helping people change: A textbook of methods* (2nd ed.). New York: Pergamon, 1980.

Goldiamond, I. Self-control procedures in personal behavior problems. *Psychological Reports,* 1965, *17,* 851–868.

Goldstein, A. P. Psychotherapy research by extrapolation from social psychology. *Journal of Counseling Psychology,* 1966, *13,* 38–45.

Goldstein, A. P. *Psychotherapeutic attraction.* New York: Pergamon, 1971.

Goldstein, A. P. Relationship-enhancement methods. In F. H. Kanfer & A. P. Goldstein (Eds.), *Helping people change: A textbook of methods* (2nd ed.). New York: Pergamon, 1980.

Goldstein, A. P., Heller, K., & Sechrest, L. B. *Psychotherapy and the psychology of behavior change.* New York: Wiley, 1966.

Goodyear, R. K., & Bradley, F. O. The helping process as contractual. *Personnel and Guidance Journal,* 1980, *58,* 512–515.

Gordon, T. *Parent effectiveness training.* New York: Wyden, 1970.

Greenberg, L. S., & Higgins, H. M. Effects of two-chair dialogue and focusing on conflict resolution. *Journal of Counseling Psychology,* 1980, *27,* 221–224.

Greenberg, L. S., & Kahn, S. E. The stimulation phase in counseling. *Counselor Education and Supervision,* 1979, *19,* 137–145.

Greenwald, H. *Direct decision therapy*. San Diego: Edits, 1975.

Gross, S. J. The myth of professional licensing. *American Psychologist*, 1978, *33*, 1009–1016.

Guilford, J. P. Factors that aid and hinder creativity. *Teachers College Record*, 1962, *63*, 380–392.

Guzzetta, R. A. Acquisition and transfer of empathy by the parents of early adolescents through structured learning training. *Journal of Counseling Psychology*, 1976, *23*, 449–453.

Haase, R. F., & Tepper, D. Nonverbal components of empathic communication. *Journal of Counseling Psychology*, 1972, *19*, 417–424.

Hackman, A., & McLean, C. A comparison of flooding and thought-stopping in the treatment of obsessional neurosis. *Behavior Theory and Research*, 1975, *13*, 263–269.

Hackman, J. R. *The nature of the task as a determiner of job behavior*. Paper presented at the meeting of the American Psychological Association, Washington, D.C., September 1967.

Hackney, H. The evolution of empathy. *Personnel and Guidance Journal*, 1978, *57*, 35–38.

Hackney, H., & Cormier, L. S. *Counseling strategies and objectives* (2nd ed.). Englewood Cliffs, N. J.: Prentice-Hall, 1979.

Hall, E. T. *Beyond culture*. Garden City, N.Y.: Anchor Press, 1977.

Hare-Mustin, R. T., Marecek, J., Kaplan, A. G., & Liss-Levinson, N. Rights of clients, responsibilities of therapists. *American Psychologist*, 1979, *34*, 3–16.

Harper, R. A. *The new psychotherapies*. Englewood Cliffs, N. J.: Prentice-Hall, 1975.

Harré, R. *Social being*. Totowa, N.J.: Adams, Littlefield, 1980.

Harris, T. *I'm OK—You're OK: A practical guide to transactional analysis*. New York: Harper & Row, 1969.

Hatcher, C., Brooks, B., & Associates. *Innovations in counseling psychology*. San Francisco: Jossey-Bass, 1977.

Heath, D. H. The maturing person. In G. Walsh & D. Shapiro (Eds.), *Beyond health and normality*. New York: Van Nostrand Reinhold, 1980. (a)

Heath, D. H. Wanted: A comprehensive model of healthy development. *Personnel and Guidance Journal*, 1980, *58*, 391–399. (b)

Heppner, P. A review of problem-solving literature and its relationship to counseling process. *Journal of Counseling Psychology*, 1978, *25*, 366–375.

Higgins, W., Ivey, A., & Uhlemann, M. Media therapy: A programmed approach to teaching behavioral skills. *Journal of Counseling Psychology*, 1970, *17*, 20–26.

Hill, C. A process approach for establishing counseling goals and outcomes. *Personnel and Guidance Journal*, 1975, *53*, 571–576.

Hill, P. C., Bedau, H. A., Chechile, R. A., Crochetiere, W. J., Kellerman, B. L., Ounjian, D., Pauker, S. G., Pauker, S. P., & Rubin, J. Z. *Making decisions: A multidisciplinary approach*. Reading, Mass.: Addison-Wesley, 1979.

Hodge, E. A., Payne, P. A., & Wheeler, D. D. Approaches to empathy training: Programmed methods versus individual supervision and professional versus peer supervisors. *Journal of Counseling Psychology*, 1978, *25*, 449–453.

Holland, J. L. Creative and academic performance among talented adolescents. *Journal of Educational Psychology*, 1961, *52*, 136–147.

Hosford, R., & De Visser, L. *Behavioral approaches to counseling: An introduction*. Washington, D.C.: APGA Press, 1976.

Hovland, C. T., Janis, I. L., & Kelley, H. H. *Communication and persuasion: Psychological studies of opinion change*. New Haven, Conn.: Yale University Press, 1953.

Hurvitz, N. Peer self-help psychotherapy groups and their implication for psychotherapy. *Psychotherapy: Theory, Research, and Practice*, 1970, *7*, 41–49.

Hurvitz, N. Similarities and differences between conventional psychotherapy and peer self-help psychotherapy groups. In P. S. Roman & H. M. Trice (Eds.), *The sociology of psychotherapy*. New York: Aronson, 1974.

Hurvitz, N. The origins of the peer self-help psychotherapy group movement. *Journal of Applied Behavioral Science*, 1976, *12*, 283–294.

Huxley, A. *The doors of perception*. New York: Harper & Row (Colophon), 1963. (Originally published, 1954.)

Ivey, A. E. *Microcounseling: Innovations in interviewing training*. Springfield, Ill.: Charles C Thomas, 1971.

Ivey, A. E. *Counseling and psychotherapy: Skills, theories, and practice*. Englewood Cliffs, N. J.: Prentice-Hall, 1980.

Ivey, A. E., & Authier, J. *Microcounseling.* (2nd ed.). Springfield, Ill.: Charles C Thomas, 1978.

Ivey, A. E., & Hinkle, J. *The transactional classroom.* Unpublished paper, University of Massachusetts, 1970.

Jacobson, N. S. Problem solving and contingency contracting in the treatment of marital discord. *Journal of Consulting and Clinical Psychology,* 1977, *45,* 92–100.

James, M., & Jongeward, D. *Born to win: Transactional analysis with Gestalt experiments.* Reading, Mass.: Addison-Wesley, 1971.

Janis, I. L., & Mann, L. *Decision making: A psychological analysis of conflict, choice, and commitment.* New York: Free Press, 1977.

Johnson, D. M., Parrott, G. R., & Stratton, R. P. Production and judgment of solutions to five problems. *Journal of Educational Psychology Monograph Supplement,* 1968, *59,* No. 6, Pt. 2.

Johnston, J. M. Punishment of human behavior. *American Psychologist,* 1972, *27,* 1033–1054.

Jones, G. B. Evaluation of problem-solving competence. In J. D. Krumboltz & C. E. Thoresen (Eds.), *Counseling methods.* New York: Holt, Rinehart & Winston, 1976.

Jourard, S. M. *Disclosing man to himself.* New York: Van Nostrand Reinhold, 1968.

Jourard, S. M. *Self-disclosure: An experimental analysis of the transparent self.* London: Wiley-Interscience, 1971. (a)

Jourard, S. M. *The transparent self* (Rev. ed.). New York: Van Nostrand Reinhold, 1971. (b)

Journal of Abnormal Psychology. Learned helplessness as a model of depression. *87* (1), 1978.

Jurjevich, R-R. M. (Ed.). *Direct psychotherapy: Twenty-eight American originals* (Vols. 1, 2). Coral Gables, Fla.: University of Miami Press, 1973.

Kagan, N. Can technology help us toward reliability in influencing human interaction? *Educational Technology,* 1973, *13,* 44–51.

Kagan, N. *Influencing human interaction.* Washington, D.C.: American Personnel and Guidance Association, 1975.

Kanfer, F. H. Self-management methods. In F. H. Kanfer & A. P. Goldstein (Eds.), *Helping people change: A textbook of methods* (2nd ed.). New York: Pergamon, 1980.

Kanfer, F. H., & Goldstein, A. P. (Eds.). *Helping people change: A textbook of methods* (2nd ed.). New York: Pergamon, 1980.

Kazdin, A. E. Self-monitoring and behavior change. In M. J. Mahoney & C. E. Thoresen (Eds.), *Self-control: Power to the person.* Monterey, Calif.: Brooks/Cole, 1974.

Kazdin, A. E. The application of operant techniques in treatment, rehabilitation, and education. In S. L. Garfield & A. E. Bergin (Eds.), *Handbook of psychotherapy and behavior change: An empirical analysis.* New York: Wiley, 1978.

Kelley, C. Assertion: The literature since 1970. In J. E. Jones & J. W. Pfeiffer (Eds.), *The 1977 annual handbook for group facilitators.* San Diego, Calif.: University Associates, 1977.

Knapp, M. L. *Nonverbal communication in human interaction* (2nd ed.). New York: Holt, Rinehart & Winston, 1978.

Knapper, E. Q. Counselor accountability. *Personnel and Guidance Journal,* 1978, *57,* 27–30.

Koocher, G. P. Credentialing in psychology: Close encounters with competence? *American Psychologist,* 1979, *34,* 696–702.

Krasner, L. Behavior modification: Ethical issues and future trends. In H. Leitenberg (Ed.), *Handbook of behavior modification and behavior therapy.* Englewood Cliffs, N. J.: Prentice-Hall, 1976.

Krumboltz, J. D. (Ed.). *Revolution in counseling: Implications of behavioral science.* Boston: Houghton Mifflin, 1966.

Krumboltz, J. D. A second look at the revolution in counseling. *Personnel and Guidance Journal,* 1980, *58,* 463–466.

Krumboltz, J. D., Becker-Haven, J. F., & Burnett, K. F. Counseling psychology. *Annual Review of Psychology,* 1979, *30,* 555–602.

Krumboltz, J. D., & Thoresen, C. E. (Eds.). *Counseling methods.* New York: Holt, Rinehart & Winston, 1976.

LaCrosse, M. B. Nonverbal behavior and perceived counselor attractiveness and persuasiveness. *Journal of Counseling Psychology,* 1975, *22,* 563–566.

LaForge, R. Interpersonal check list (ICL). In J. E. Jones & J. W. Pfeiffer (Eds.), *The 1977 annual handbook for group facilitators.* San Diego: University Associates Press, 1977.

Lambert, M. J., Bergin, A. E., & Collins, J. L. Therapist-induced deterioration in psychotherapy. In A. S. Gurman & A. M. Razin (Eds.), *Effective psychotherapy: A handbook of research.* New York: Pergamon, 1977.

Lange, A. J., & Jakubowski, P. *Responsible assertive behavior: Cognitive/behavioral procedures for trainers*. Champaign, Ill.: Research Press, 1976.

Latham, G., & Rinne, S. Improving job performance through training in goal setting. *Journal of Applied Psychology*, 1974, *59*, 187–191.

Lazarus, A. A. *Multimodal behavior therapy*. New York: Springer, 1976.

Leitenberg, H. (Ed.). *Handbook of behavior modification and behavior therapy*. Englewood Cliffs, N. J.: Prentice-Hall, 1976.

Levy, L. H. *Psychological interpretation*. New York: Holt, Rinehart & Winston, 1963.

Levy, L. H. Fact and choice in counseling and counselor education: A cognitive viewpoint. In C. A. Parker (Ed.), *Counseling theories and counselor education*. Boston: Houghton Mifflin, 1968.

Lewin, K. Quasi-stationary social equilibria and the problem of permanent change. In W. G. Bennis, K. D. Benne, & R. Chin (Eds.), *The planning of change*. New York: Holt, Rinehart & Winston, 1969.

Lichtenstein, E. *Psychotherapy: Approaches and applications*. Monterey, Calif.: Brooks/Cole, 1980.

Lieberman, M. A., Yalom, I. D., & Miles, M. B. *Encounter groups: First facts*. New York: Basic Books, 1973.

London, P. *Behavior control*. New York: Harper & Row, 1969.

London, P. The end of ideology in behavior modification. *American Psychologist*, 1972, *27*, 913–920.

Luborsky, L., & Spence, D. P. Quantitative research on psychoanalytic therapy. In S. L. Garfield & A. E. Bergin (Eds.), *Handbook of psychotherapy and behavior change: An empirical analysis*. New York: Wiley, 1978.

Lynd, H. M. *On shame and the search for identity*. New York: Science Editions, 1958.

Mahoney, M. J. Research issues in self-management. *Behavior Therapy*, 1972, *3*, 45–63.

Mahoney, M. J. Reflections on the cognitive-learning trend in psychotherapy. *American Psychologist*, 1977, *32*, 5–13.

Mahoney, M. J., & Arnkoff, D. B. Cognitive and self-control therapies. In S. L. Garfield & A. E. Bergin (Eds.), *Handbook of psychotherapy and behavior change*. New York: Wiley, 1978.

Maier, N. R. F. Screening solutions to upgrade quality: A new approach to problem solving under conditions of uncertainty. *Journal of Psychology*, 1960, *49*, 217–231.

Maier, N. R. F. *Problem solving and creativity in individuals and groups*. Monterey, Calif.: Brooks/Cole, 1970.

Maier, N. R. F., & Hoffman, L. R. Financial incentives and group decision in motivating change. *Journal of Social Psychology*, 1964, *64*, 369–378.

Malott, R., Tillema, M., & Glenn, S. *Behavior analysis and behavior modification: An introduction*. Kalamazoo, Mich.: Behaviordelia, 1978.

Maltzman, I. On the training of originality. *Psychological Review*, 1960, *67*, 229–242.

Mansfield, R. S., & Busse, T. V. Meta-analysis of research: A rejoinder to Glass. *Educational Researcher*, 1977, *6*, 3.

Marks, I. Behavioral psychotherapy of adult neurosis. In S. L. Garfield & A. E. Bergin (Eds.), *Handbook of psychotherapy and behavior change: An empirical analysis*. New York: Wiley, 1978.

Martin, G., & Pear, J. *Behavior modification: What it is and how to do it*. Englewood Cliffs, N. J.: Prentice-Hall, 1978.

Maslow, A. H. Synanon and Eupsychia. *Journal of Humanistic Psychology*, 1967, *7*, 28–35.

Maslow, A. H. *Toward a psychology of being* (2nd ed.). New York: Van Nostrand Reinhold, 1968.

Maslow, A. H. *The farther reaches of human nature*. New York: Viking, 1971.

Mastellone, M. Aversion therapy: A new use of the old rubberband. *Journal of Behavior Therapy and Experimental Psychiatry*, 1974, *5*, 311–312.

Mayeroff, M. *On caring*. New York: Perennial Library (Harper & Row), 1971.

Mays, D. T., & Franks, C. M. Getting worse: Psychotherapy or no treatment—the jury should still be out. *Professional Psychology*, 1980, *11*, 78–92.

McCarthy, P. R. Differential effects of self-disclosing versus self-involving counselor statements across counselor-client gender pairings. *Journal of Counseling Psychology*, 1979, *26*, 538–541.

McClelland, D. C. Managing motivation to expand human freedom. *American Psychologist*, 1978, *33*, 201–210.

McGuire, W. J. The nature of attitudes and attitude change. In G. Lindzey & E. Aronson (Eds.), *The handbook of social psychology* (Vol. 3) (2nd ed.). Reading, Mass.: Addison-Wesley, 1969.

McKeachie, W. J. Psychology in America's bicentennial year. *American Psychologist*, 1976, *31*, 819–833.

Meadow, A., Parnes, S. J., & Reese, H. Influence of instructions and problem sequence on a creative problem-solving test. *Journal of Applied Psychology*, 1959, *43*, 413–416.

Mehrabian, A. *Tactics of social influence.* Englewood Cliffs, N. J.: Prentice-Hall, 1970.

Mehrabian, A. *Silent messages.* Belmont, Calif.: Wadsworth, 1971.

Mehrabian, A., & Reed, H. Factors influencing judgments of psychopathology. *Psychological Reports,* 1969, *24,* 323–330.

Meichenbaum, D. H. *Cognitive behavior modification.* Morristown, N. J.: General Learning Press, 1974.

Meichenbaum, D. *Cognitive-behavior modification: An integrative approach.* New York: Plenum, 1977.

Meichenbaum, D., & Genest, M. Cognitive behavioral modification: An integration of cognitive and behavioral methods. In F. H. Kanfer & A. P. Goldstein (Eds.), *Helping people change: A textbook of methods* (2nd ed.). New York: Pergamon, 1980.

Mezz, S., & Calia, V. F. Counseling the culturally different child: A black-white collaborative view. *Counseling and Values,* 1972, *16,* 263–272.

Miller, G. A. Psychology as a means of promoting human welfare. *American Psychologist,* 1969, *24,* 1063–1075.

Miller, G. A. Giving away psychology in the 80's: George A. Miller interviewed by Elizabeth Hall. *Psychology Today,* 1980, *13*(8), 38–50, 97–98.

Miller, G. A., Galanter, E., & Pribram, K. H. *Plans and the structure of behavior.* New York: Holt, Rinehart & Winston, 1960.

Mowrer, O. H. Loss and recovery of community: A guide to the theory and practice of integrity therapy. In G. M. Gazda (Ed.), *Innovations in group psychotherapy.* Springfield, Ill.: Charles C Thomas, 1968. (a)

Mowrer, O. H. New evidence concerning the nature of psychopathology. *University of Buffalo Studies,* 1968, *4,* 113–193. (b)

Mowrer, O. H. Integrity groups today. In R-R. M. Jurjevich (Ed.), *Direct psychotherapy: Twenty-eight American originals* (Vol. 2). Coral Gables, Fla.: University of Miami Press, 1973. (a)

Mowrer, O. H. My philosophy of psychotherapy. *Journal of Contemporary Psychotherapy,* 1973, *6*(1), 35–42. (b)

Mowrer, O. H., & Vattano, A. J. Integrity groups: A context for growth in honesty, responsibility, and involvement. *Journal of Applied Behavioral Science,* 1976, *12,* 419–431.

Murphy, K. C , & Strong, S. R. Some effects of similarity self-disclosure. *Journal of Counseling Psychology,* 1972, *19,* 121–124.

Murphy, L. B., & Frank, C. Prevention: The clinical psychologist. *American Review of Psychology,* 1979, *30,* 173–207.

Newman, B. M., & Newman, P. R. *Development through life: A psychosocial approach* (Rev. ed.). Homewood, Ill.: Dorsey Press, 1979.

Nilsson, D. E., Strassberg, D. S., & Bannon, J. Perceptions of counselor self-disclosure: An analogue study. *Journal of Counseling Psychology,* 1979, *26,* 399–404.

Osborn, A. F. *Applied imagination: Principles and procedures of creative problem solving* (3rd ed.). New York: Scribner's, 1963.

Paradise, L. V., & Wilder, D. H. The relationship between client reluctance and counseling effectiveness. *Counselor Education and Supervision,* 1979, *19,* 35–41.

Parloff, M. B., & Handlon, J. H. The influence of criticalness on creative problem-solving in dyads. *Psychiatry,* 1964, *27,* 17–27.

Parnes, S. J. *Creative behavior guidebook.* New York: Scribner's, 1967.

Passons, W. R. *Gestalt approaches in counseling.* New York: Holt, Rinehart & Winston, 1975.

Patterson, C. H. *Theories of counseling and psychotherapy* (3rd ed.). New York: Harper & Row, 1980.

Piaget, J. *Construction of reality in the child.* New York: Basic Books, 1954.

Premack, D. Reinforcement theory. In D. Levine (Ed.), *Nebraska symposium on motivation.* Lincoln: University of Nebraska Press, 1965.

Presby, S. Overly broad categories obscure important differences between therapies. *American Psychologist,* 1978, *33,* 514–515.

Rappaport, J., & Chinsky, J. M. Accurate empathy: Confusion of a construct. *Psychological Bulletin,* 1972, *77,* 400–404.

Raths, L., Harmin, M., & Simon S. B. *Values and teaching.* Columbus, Ohio: Merrill, 1960.

Redl, F. *When we deal with children.* New York: Free Press, 1966.

Remer, P., & O'Neill, C. Clients as change agents: What color should my parachute be? *Personnel and Guidance Journal,* 1980, *58,* 425–429.

Rimland, B. Psychological treatment vs. megavitamin therapy. In V. Binder, A. Binder, & B. Rimland (Eds.), *Modern therapies.* Englewood Cliffs, N. J.: Prentice-Hall, 1976.

Rimland, B. Death knell for psychotherapy? *American Psychologist*, 1979, *34*, 192.

Rimm, D. C., & Masters, J. C. *Behavior therapy*. New York: Academic Press, 1974.

Riordan, R. J., Matheny, K. B., & Harris, C. W. Helping counselors minimize reluctance. *Counselor Education and Supervision*, 1978, *18*, 6–13.

Robertshaw, J. E., Mecca, S. J., & Rerick, M. N. *Problem-solving: A systems approach*. New York: Petrocelli Books, 1978.

Rogers, C. R. *Client-centered therapy*. Boston: Houghton Mifflin, 1951.

Rogers, C. R. The necessary and sufficient conditions of therapeutic personality change. *Journal of Consulting Psychology*, 1957, *21*, 95–103.

Rogers, C. R. *On becoming a person*. Boston: Houghton Mifflin, 1961.

Rogers, C. R. (Ed.). *The therapeutic relationship and its impact*. Madison: University of Wisconsin Press, 1967.

Rogers, C. R., Perls, F., & Ellis, A. *Three approaches to psychotherapy I: Parts 1, 2, and 3*. Orange, Calif.: Psychological Films, Inc., 1965. (Film)

Rogers, C. R., Shostrom, E., & Lazarus, A. *Three approaches to psychotherapy II: Parts 1, 2, and 3*. Orange, Calif.: Psychological Films, Inc., 1977. (Film)

Rogers, C. R., & Truax, C. B. The therapeutic conditions antecedent to change: A theoretical view. In C. R. Rogers (Ed.), *The therapeutic relationship and its impact*. Madison: University of Wisconsin Press, 1967.

Rosen, S., & Tesser, A. On the reluctance to communicate undesirable information: The MUM effect. *Sociometry*, 1970, *33*, 253–263.

Rosen, S., & Tesser, A. Fear of negative evaluation and the reluctance to transmit bad news. *Proceedings of the 79th Annual Convention of the American Psychological Association*, 1971, *6*, 301–302.

Rosenthal, T. L., Hung, J. H., & Kelley, J. E. Therapist social influence: Sternly strike while the iron is hot. *Behavior Research and Therapy*, 1977, *15*, 253–259.

Rotter, J. B. Generalized expectancies for interpersonal trust. *American Psychologist*, 1971, *26*, 443–452.

Rubenstein, E. A., & Parloff, M. B. (Eds.). *Research in psychotherapy*. Washington, D.C.: American Psychological Association, 1959.

Rudestam, K. E. *Methods of self-change: An ABC primer*. Monterey, Calif.: Brooks/Cole, 1980.

Schofield, W. *Psychotherapy: The purchase of friendship*. Englewood Cliffs, N. J.: Prentice-Hall, 1964.

Schuster, R. Empathy and mindfulness. *Journal of Humanistic Psychology*, 1979, *19*(1), 71–77.

Scott, N. A. Beyond assertiveness training: A problem-solving approach. *Personnel and Guidance Journal*, 1979, *57*, 450–452.

Selby, J. W., & Calhoun, L. G. Psychodidactics: An undervalued and underdeveloped treatment tool of psychological intervention. *Professional Psychology*, 1980, *11*, 236–241.

Seligman, M. E. P. *Helplessness: On depression, development, and death*. San Francisco: Freeman, 1975.

Selye, H. *Stress without distress*. Philadelphia: Lippincott, 1974.

Selye, H. *The stress of life* (Rev. ed.). New York: McGraw-Hill, 1976.

Shaffer, H. Psychological rehabilitation, skills-building, and self-efficacy. *American Psychologist*, 1978, *33*, 394–396.

Shaffer, J. B. P., & Galinsky, M. D. *Models of group therapy and sensitivity training*. Englewood Cliffs, N. J.: Prentice-Hall, 1974.

Shaffer, W. F., & Hummel, T. J. Three experiments using an algorithm for empathic responses. *Journal of Counseling Psychology*, 1979, *26*, 279–284.

Shapiro, S. B. Some aspects of a theory of interpersonal contracts. *Psychological Reports*, 1968, *22*, 171–183.

Shealy, C. W. *The pain game*. Millbrae, Calif.: Celestial Arts, 1976.

Sherman, A. R. *Behavior modification: Theory and practice*. Monterey, Calif.: Brooks/Cole, 1973.

Shure, M. B., & Spivack, G. *Problem-solving techniques in childrearing*. San Francisco: Jossey-Bass, 1978.

Simon, S. B. *Meeting yourself halfway: Thirty-one value clarification strategies for daily living*. Niles, Ill.: Argus, 1974.

Simon, S. B., Howe, L. W., & Kirschenbaum, H. *Values clarification: A handbook of practical strategies for teachers and students*. New York: Hart, 1972.

Simons, H., Berkowitz, N., & Moyer, R. Similarity, credibility, and attitude change: A review and theory. *Psychological Bulletin*, 1970, *73*, 1–16.

Skinner, B. F. *Science and human behavior*. New York: Free Press, 1953.

Sloane, R. B., Staples, F. R., Cristol, A. H., Yorkston, N. J., & Whipple, K. *Psychotherapy versus behavior therapy.* Cambridge, Mass.: Harvard University Press, 1975.

Smaby, M., & Tamminen, A. W. Can we help belligerent counselees? *Personnel and Guidance Journal,* 1979, *57,* 506–512.

Smith, D. L. Goal attainment scaling as an adjunct to counseling. *Journal of Counseling Psychology,* 1976, *23,* 22–27.

Smith, M. *A practical guide to value clarification.* San Diego: University Associates Press, 1977.

Smith, M. L., & Glass, G. V. Meta-analysis of psychotherapy outcome studies. *American Psychologist,* 1977, *32,* 752–760.

Smith-Hanen, S. Effects of nonverbal behaviors on judged levels of counselor empathy and warmth. *Journal of Counseling Psychology,* 1977, *24,* 87–91.

Spier, M. S. Kurt Lewin's "force-field analysis." In J. W. Pfeiffer & J. E. Jones (Eds.), *The 1973 annual handbook for group facilitators.* San Diego: University Associates, 1973.

Spivack, G., Platt, J. J., & Shure, M. B. *The problem-solving approach to adjustment: A guide to research and intervention.* San Francisco: Jossey-Bass, 1976.

Spivack, G., & Shure, M. B. *Social adjustment of young children: A cognitive approach to solving real-life problems.* San Francisco: Jossey-Bass, 1974.

Standal, S. *The need for positive regard: A contribution to client-centered theory.* Unpublished doctoral dissertation, University of Chicago, 1954.

Stone, G. L., & Morden, C. J. Effect of distance on verbal productivity. *Journal of Counseling Psychology,* 1976, *23,* 486–488.

Strong, S. R. Counseling: An interpersonal influence process. *Journal of Counseling Psychology,* 1968, *15,* 215–224.

Strong, S. R. Social psychological approach to psychotherapy research. In S. L. Garfield & A. E. Bergin (Eds.), *Handbook of psychotherapy and behavior change: An empirical analysis.* New York: Wiley, 1978.

Strupp, H. H., Hadley, S. W., & Gomes-Schwartz, B. *Psychotherapy for better or worse: The problem of negative effects.* New York: Jason Aronson, 1977.

Sue, D. W., & Sue, D. Barriers to effective cross-cultural counseling. *Journal of Counseling Psychology,* 1977, *24,* 420–429.

Swan, G. E. On the structure of eclecticism: Cluster analysis of eclectic behavior therapists. *Professional Psychology,* 1979, *10,* 732–739.

Talland, G. A., & Clark, D. H. Evaluation of topics in therapy group discussion. *Journal of Clinical Psychology,* 1954, *10,* 131–137.

Tennov, D. *Psychotherapy: The hazardous cure.* New York: Abelard-Schuman, 1975.

Tepper, D., & Haase, R. Verbal and nonverbal communication and facilitative conditions. *Journal of Counseling Psychology,* 1978, *25,* 35–44.

Tesser, A., & Rosen, S. Similarity of objective fate as a determinant of the reluctance to transmit unpleasant information: The MUM effect. *Journal of Personality and Social Psychology,* 1972, *23,* 46–53.

Tesser, A., Rosen, S., & Batchelor, T. On the reluctance to communicate bad news (the MUM effect): A role play extension. *Journal of Personality,* 1972, *40,* 88–103.

Tesser, A., Rosen, S., & Tesser, M. On the reluctance to communicate undesirable messages (the MUM effect): A field study. *Psychological Reports,* 1971, *29,* 651–654.

Thoresen, C. E., & Mahoney, M. J. *Behavioral self-control.* New York: Holt, Rinehart & Winston, 1974.

Thorne, F. C. An eclectic evaluation of psychotherapeutic methods. In R-R. M. Jurjevich (Ed.), *Direct psychotherapy: Twenty-eight American originals* (Vol. 2). Coral Gables, Fla.: University of Miami Press, 1973. (a)

Thorne, F. C. Eclectic psychotherapy. In R. Corsini (Ed.), *Current psychotherapies.* Itasca, Ill.: Peacock, 1973. (b)

Truax, C. B. The meaning and reliability of accurate empathy: A rejoinder. *Psychological Bulletin,* 1972, *77,* 397–399.

Truax, C. B., & Carkhuff, R. R. Client and therapist transparency in the psychotherapeutic encounter. *Journal of Counseling Psychology,* 1965, *12,* 3–9.

Tryon, W. W. A system of behavioral diagnosis. *Professional Psychology,* 1976, *7,* 495–506.

Wagman, M. Systematic dilemma counseling: Theory, method, research. *Psychological Reports,* 1979, *44,* 55–72.

Wagman, M. PLATO DCS: An interactive computer system for personal counseling. *Journal of Counseling Psychology*, 1980, *27*, 16–30. (a)

Wagman, M. Systematic dilemma counseling: Transition from counselor mode to autonomous mode. *Journal of Counseling Psychology*, 1980, *27*, 171–178. (b)

Wagman, M., & Kerber, K. W. PLATO DCS: An interactive computer system for personal counseling: Further development and evaluation. *Journal of Counseling Psychology*, 1980, *27*, 31–39.

Wallen, J. L. Developing effective interpersonal communication. In R. W. Pace, B. D. Peterson, & T. R. Radcliffe (Eds.), *Communicating interpersonally.* Columbus, Ohio: Merrill, 1973.

Wang, J. Breaking out of the pain trap. *Psychology Today*, 1977, *11*(2), 78–86.

Watson, D., & Tharp, R. *Self-directed behavior* (3rd ed.). Monterey, Calif.: Brooks/Cole, 1981.

Weick, K. E. *The social psychology of organizing.* Reading, Mass.: Addison-Wesley, 1969.

Weick, K. E. *The social psychology of organizing* (2nd ed.). Reading, Mass.: Addison-Wesley, 1979.

Weigel, R. G., Dinges, N., Dyer, R., & Straumfjorn, A. A. Perceived self-disclosure, mental health, and who is liked in group treatment. *Journal of Counseling Psychology*, 1972, *19*, 47–52.

Weisskopf-Joelson, E., & Eliseo, S. An experimental study of the effectiveness of brainstorming. *Journal of Applied Psychology*, 1961, *45*, 45–49.

Weitz, S. Attitude, voice, and behavior: A repressed affect model of interracial interaction. *Journal of Personality and Social Psychology*, 1972, *24*, 14–21.

Wheeler, D. D., & Janis, I. L. *A practical guide for making decisions.* New York: Free Press, 1980.

White, B. L. Primary prevention: Beginning at the beginning. *Personnel and Guidance Journal*, 1980, *58*, 338–343.

White, B. L., Kaban, B., & Attanucci, J. *The origins of human competence: The final report of the Harvard preschool project.* Lexington, Mass.: Lexington Books, 1979.

White, B. L., Kaban, B., Attanucci, J., & Shapiro, B. *Experience and environment: Major influences on the development of the young child* (Vol. 2). Englewood Cliffs, N. J.: Prentice-Hall, 1978.

Williams, R. L., & Long, J. D. *Toward a self-managed life style* (2nd ed.). Boston: Houghton Mifflin, 1979.

Wisocki, P. A. Treatment of obsessive-compulsive behavior by covert sensitization and covert reinforcement: A case report. *Journal of Behavior Therapy and Experimental Psychiatry*, 1970, *1*, 233–239.

Author Index

Adler, A., 192
Albee, G. W., 303
Anthony, W. A., 5, 7, 11, 58, 99, 200, 209, 266, 282
Arnkoff, D. B., 7, 8
Attanucci, J., 303
Authier, J., 59, 170, 200
Axelrod, S., 272

Bandura, A., 14, 16, 104
Bannon, J., 200
Bard, J. A., 268
Bargo, M., Jr., 107
Batchelor, T., 179
Bayer, C. A., 272
Bayless, O. L., 232
Becker-Haven, J. F., 134
Bedau, H. A., 7
Begelman, D. A., 23
Beier, E. G., 172, 191
Bellet, W., 59
Bellingham, R. L., 99
Benjamin, A., 101
Berenson, B. G., 5, 11, 163, 175, 177, 186, 194, 282
Bergin, A. E., 5
Berkowitz, N., 134
Berne, E., 191, 202
Bernstein, B. L., 175
Binder, A., 6
Binder, V., 6
Bradley, F. O., 24
Brammer, L., 9, 97, 159, 162
Braun, S. H., 23
Brilhart, J. K., 234
Brooks, B., 10
Buber, M., 146–147
Bucker, L., 209
Bullmer, K., 98
Burnett, K. F., 134
Busse, T. V., 5

Calhoun, L. G., 163
Calia, V. F., 95
Carey, R., 245
Carkhuff, R. R., 5, 7, 11, 28, 58, 111, 128, 141, 146, 200, 209, 266, 282, 283
Cautela, J. R., 269, 272
Chaikin, A. L., 199
Chechile, R. A., 7

Chelune, G. J., 140
Chinsky, J. M., 99
Claiborn, C. D., 59
Clark, D. H., 112
Clark, K. B., 98
Cohen, M. R., 266
Collingwood, T., 283
Collins, J. L., 5
Corey, G., 6
Cormier, L. S., 24, 66, 91, 102, 103, 125, 276
Cormier, W. H., 24, 66, 125, 276
Corn, R., 59
Corrigan, J. D., 15, 133
Corsini, R. J., 7
Cowan, M. A., 11, 73, 288, 303
Coyne, J. C., 24
Cozby, P. C., 140
Cristol, A. H., 6
Crochetiere, W. J., 7

Dalton, R. F., 99
Davis, G. A., 8, 232
Davison, G. C., 7, 16
DeForest, C., 200
Dell, D. M., 15
Derlega, V. J., 140, 199
Deutsch, M., 110
DeVisser, L., 16
Dimond, R. E., 8
Dinges, N., 198
Dixon, D. N., 7
Doster, J. A., 140, 198, 199
Dreikurs, R., 192
Dyer, R., 198
Dyer, W. W., 294
D'Zurilla, T. J., 7, 10, 32, 227, 232, 234

Edelwich, J., 301, 302
Egan, G., 11, 13, 14, 73, 111, 140, 200, 288, 303
Einstein, A., 230
Ekman, P., 64
Eliot, T. S., 290
Eliseo, S., 234
Ellis, A., 13, 103, 189, 190, 191, 268
Erez, M., 209
Erikson, E. H., 13, 58
Eysenck, H. J., 5

Festinger, S., 133, 181
Flowers, J., 209

317

Subject Index

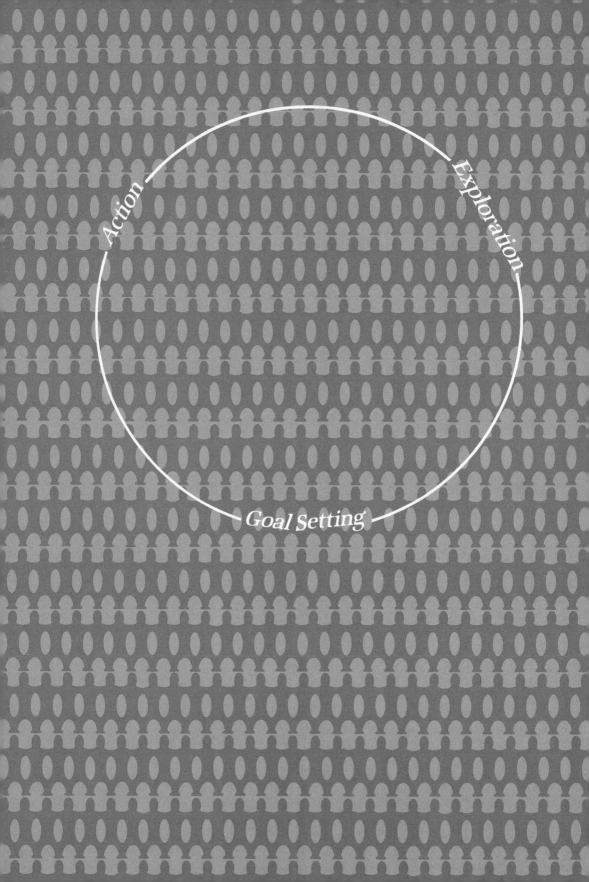